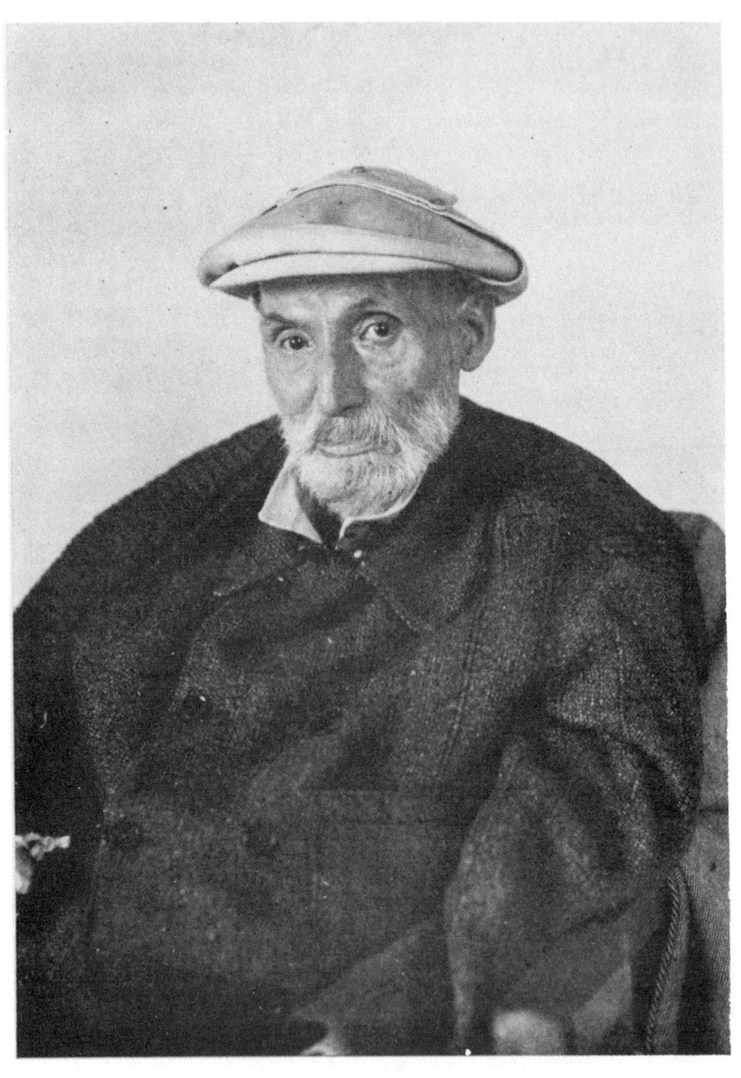

RENOIR IN HIS 78TH YEAR

RENOIR

AN INTIMATE RECORD

by

AMBROISE VOLLARD

Authorized translation by
Harold L. Van Doren and
Randolph T. Weaver

DOVER PUBLICATIONS, INC.
New York

Published in Canada by General Publishing Company, Ltd., 30 Lesmill Road, Don Mills, Toronto, Ontario.
Published in the United Kingdom by Constable and Company, Ltd., 3 The Lanchesters, 162–164 Fulham Palace Road, London W6 9ER.

This Dover edition, first published in 1990, is a republication, with unabridged text, of the work originally published by Alfred A. Knopf, Inc., New York, in 1925. For this edition, several obvious typographical errors have been silently corrected, and the selection of black-and-white plates of Renoir's paintings has been changed. This Dover edition is published by arrangement with Alfred A. Knopf, Inc., 201 East 50th Street, New York, New York 10022.

Manufactured in the United States of America
Dover Publications, Inc., 31 East 2nd Street, Mineola, N.Y. 11501

Library of Congress Cataloging-in-Publication Data

Vollard, Ambroise, 1867–1939.
[Auguste Renoir (1841–1919). English]
Renoir : an intimate record / by Ambroise Vollard ; authorized translation by Harold L. Van Doren and Randolph T. Weaver.
p. cm.
Translation of: Auguste Renoir (1841–1919).
Reprint. Originally published: New York : Knopf, 1925.
ISBN 0-486-26488-2
1. Renoir, Auguste, 1841–1919. 2. Painters—France—Biography. I. Title.
ND553.R45V56 1990
759.4—dc20
[B] 90-44795
CIP

TRANSLATORS' NOTE

Because of the irregular order of the episodes in the ensuing pages, a brief outline chronology of the life of the artist has been given to clarify any confusion which might ensue from the author's arrangement. In addition, there will be found a very condensed list of his principal works. Some of the longer footnotes have likewise been relegated to the appendices, in order to interrupt the narrative as little as possible. Only those which are indispensable to the text have been preserved *in situ*. Titles of pictures have been occasionally left in French where translation was difficult.

The translators wish to express their sincere thanks to Messrs. Jean and Pierre Renoir, sons of the painter, Georges Rivière, author of *Renoir et ses Amis,* and J. Durand-Ruel, for valuable assistance in compiling the appendices.

FOREWORD

The book presented herewith is in no sense a formal biography. It has been composed of a thousand touches: interrupted conversations with Renoir about the events of his life and the tendencies of ancient and modern art; observations of the characteristic gestures of the painter; details of his family and his circle of friends. The author has also endeavoured to present certain figures in the world of art: the collector-speculators, the snobs of painting, the critics, the modern Mæcenases.

The classification of a great number of notes and the co-ordination of many disparate elements have been no easy task. But it is hoped that the reader will find in this intimate record, told almost entirely by the artist himself, something more than a mere biography.

CONTENTS

I	How I Made the Acquaintance of Renoir	1
II	The Beginnings	5
III	The Gleyre Studio	9
IV	"Mother Anthony's Cabaret"	15
V	La Grenouillère	19
VI	During the War of 1870 and under the Commune	22
VII	The Exhibitions of the Impressionists	25
VIII	"Serious" Purchasers	30
IX	The Café Guerbois, the Nouvelle Athènes, the Café Tortoni	36
X	The Salon of Madame Charpentier	40
XI	Early Travels	46
XII	The Impressionist Theories	52
XIII	Renoir's Dry Manner	56
XIV	The Trip to Spain	60
XV	London, Holland, Munich	64
XVI	Renoir at Pont-Aven	67
XVII	The Portrait of Madame Morisot	69
XVIII	The Family	71
XIX	Essoyes, Cagnes	75
XX	The Models and the Maids	78
XXI	Renoir and His Patrons	85
XXII	Portrait of a Great Collector	89
XXIII	Renoir Paints My Portrait	95
XXIV	Luncheon with Rodin	104
XXV	Artists of Former Days	110

XXVI The Last Years 113

Appendix I 116

Appendix II: List of Important Works 121

ILLUSTRATIONS

Renoir in His 78th Year	frontispiece
	facing page
Renoir as a Young Man	14
Mother Anthony's Cabaret (1865)	15
Lise (1866–67)	24
Diana (1867)	25
Pont Neuf, Paris (1872)	38
The Seine at Argenteuil (1873)	39
The Sisley Family (1868)	52
La Loge (1874)	53
Le Moulin de la Galette (1875)	66
The Swing (1875)	67
Portrait of Victor Chocquet (1875)	74
Portrait of Jeanne Samary (1877)	75
Portrait of Richard Wagner (1881)	84
Bathers (1887)	85
Luncheon of the Boatmen at Bougival (1881)	94
The Dance at Bougival (1882–83)	95
The Artist's Family (1896)	102
Portrait of Ambroise Vollard (1908)	103

CHRONOLOGY

1841. Born at Limoges, February 25.
1845. Removal of family to Paris.
1854. Apprenticed to a porcelain-decorator.
1858. Enters the studio of Gleyre.
1863. First picture exhibited at the *Salon: Esmeralda.*
1864. Exhibits at the *Salon des Refusés,* having been rejected at the *Salon.*
1865–8. Frequent sojourns to the environs of the Forest of Fontainebleau: Marlotte, Chailly, Barbizon, etc. Meeting with Diaz.
1870–1. Franco-Prussian War. Enlists in the 10th *chasseurs à cheval.*
1871. Returns to Paris under the Commune.
1873. Meeting with Durand-Ruel, the first dealer to put any faith in his work.
1874. First exhibition of the Society of Painters, Sculptors and Gravers, later called the Impressionists.
1876. Disastrous sale organized by the Impressionists at the suggestion of Renoir at the Hotel Drouot.
1877. Second exhibition of the Impressionists. (The *Moulin de la Galette, The Swing* and several other important canvases figured at this exhibition.)
1879. Trip to Algeria.
1880. Marriage. Trip to the Isle of Guernsey.
1880–1. Voyage to Italy.
1881. Second trip to Algeria.
1884–90. Experiments in fresco colour and painting on cement: called the "dry" manner.
1890–3. Pont Aven.
1892. Retrospective exhibition at Durand-Ruel's, and beginning of the public acceptance of his work.
1895. Trip to Spain.
1899. First attack of rheumatism which was later to deprive him of the use of his limbs.

1900. Decorated with the Cross of the Legion of Honour. (Later made an officer and finally a commander.)
1907. Purchase of *Les Collettes* and final establishment at Cagnes. (Previous to this, one year was spent at Cannet and three at Magagnosc.)
1911. Permanently confined to his wheel-chair.
1919. Died at Cagnes, December 3. Renoir is buried at Essoyes.

Chapter One

HOW I MADE THE ACQUAINTANCE OF RENOIR

I WANTED to know who had posed for a Manet in my possession. It was a canvas representing a man seated on a camp-stool in a pathway of the Bois de Boulogne, wearing a grey hat, a mauve jacket, a yellow vest, white trousers, and varnished pumps—and I nearly forgot to mention a rose in his buttonhole. I had been told that Renoir would know who it was, so I set out to look for him. I found that he was then living in an old house in Montmartre called *The Château in the Mist.* In the garden I found a housemaid, dressed in bohemian fashion; she told me to wait, and pointed to the hallway of the house. Just then a young woman appeared, who was as buxom and amiable as one of those pastels by Perroneau of some good lady of the time of Louis XV. It was Madame Renoir.

"Oh, didn't the maid ask you to come in? . . . Gabrielle!"

The maid was taken aback by her mistress's tone of rebuke.

"But it's all muddy outside! And La Boulangère[1] forgot to put the mat back in front of the door!"

Madame Renoir went to call her husband, leaving me in the dining-room, where I found the finest Renoirs I had yet seen on the walls.

The painter soon came in. It was the first time that I had ever seen him. He was a spare man, sharp-eyed, and very nervous, giving one the impression that he never stood still.

I explained the occasion of my visit.

"Your man is Monsieur Brun, a friend of Manet's," he said. "But we can talk better upstairs. Will you come up to the studio?"

Renoir showed me into the most commonplace sort of room. There were two or three badly matched pieces of furniture, a mass of coloured stuffs, and some straw hats, which the painter was apparently accustomed to crumple in his fingers while posing the models. Canvases everywhere, stacked one against the other. Near the model's chair I observed a pile of copies—their wrappers unbroken—of *La Revue Blanche,* an "advanced" magazine very popular with the public. I remembered having read many a eulogy of Impressionist art in its pages.

[1] "The Bakery Girl," the nickname of one of Renoir's servants.

"That is a very interesting magazine," I observed.

"Yes, indeed," Renoir replied. "My friend Natanson sends it to me; but I must confess that I've never looked at the thing."

And as I reached out to pick up a copy, Renoir exclaimed: "Don't touch them! I put them there for the model to rest her foot on."

Renoir had sat down before his easel and opened his colour-box. I was amazed at the order and cleanliness of it: palette, brushes, tubes flattened and rolled up as they were emptied—all gave an impression of an almost feminine neatness.

I told the painter how delighted I had been with the two nudes in the dining-room.

"They are studies of the maids. Some of our servants have had admirable figures, and have posed like angels. But I must admit I'm not hard to please. I had just as lief paint the first old crock that comes along, just so long as she has a skin that takes the light. I don't see how artists can paint those over-bred females they call society women! Have you ever seen a society woman whose hands were worth painting? A woman's hands are lovely—if they are accustomed to housework. At the Farnesina in Rome there is a *Venus Supplicating Jupiter,* by Raphael. What marvelous hands and arms! She looks like a great, healthy housewife snatched for a moment from her kitchen to pose for Venus! That's why Stendhal thought that Raphael's women were common and gross."

My visit was cut short by the arrival of a model. I said good-bye, and asked if I might come again.

"As often as you like! But come preferably towards evening when I have finished my work."

Renoir's existence was ordered like that of a bank employé. He went to his studio just as punctually as a clerk to his office. In the evening, after a game of chequers or dominoes with Madame Renoir, he went to bed early; he was afraid it would affect his work the next day if he stayed up late. All his life, painting was his only pleasure, his only relaxation.

I remember in 1911 meeting Madame Renoir as she was coming out of a hospital where Renoir was to be operated on.

"How is he getting along?" I asked.

"The operation has been put off until to-morrow," she replied. "I'm afraid you will have to excuse me. I am in a great hurry. . . . My husband has sent me to get his paints. He wants to do the flowers that were brought to him this morning."

Renoir worked at these flowers the entire day and all the next morning until it was time to go on the operating-table.

Another time, in 1916 (Renoir had passed his seventy-fifth birthday), during the course of a visit to his home in Cagnes, I was struck by his sudden look of discouragement. I asked about the canvas he was then working on.

"There's no use, I can't paint," he answered. "I'm no good for anything any more." He closed his eyes dispiritedly, and I went down into the garden for fear I was not wanted. A moment later I heard La Grande Louise[2] calling me.

"Monsieur Renoir wants you in the studio," she said.

I found him at his easel, radiant. He was struggling with some dahlias.

"Look, Vollard, isn't that almost as gorgeous as a Delacroix battle-piece? I think this time I've got the secret of painting! . . . What a pity that every bit of progress one makes is only a step towards the grave! If I could only live long enough to do a masterpiece!"

It is easy to imagine how eager I was to take advantage of Renoir's invitation to come again. The following week I called after dinner. This time he had just gone to bed! "I was all alone this evening," he explained, "so I went to bed earlier than usual. Gabrielle is going to read me *La Dame de Monsoreau.* You're invited to the party."

But *La Dame de Monsoreau* could not be found.

"Well, then, Gabrielle," said Renoir, "see what there is in the library."

Gabrielle opened a little bookcase where twenty or more books were lying in a heap, and began reading the titles aloud: "*Cruelle Enigme, Peints par Eux-Mêmes, Lettres à Françoise, Les Confessions d'un Amant, Deuxième Amour, Les Fleurs du Mal* . . ."

Renoir, interrupting: "I detest that book above all others! I have no idea who brought *that* here. If you had heard Mounet Sully (I think he was the one) recite *La Charogne,* at Madame Charpentier's, as I did, with all those silly asses gushing around about it! . . . It's just as bad as the rest of the stuff Gabrielle was reading over. My friends are always trying to make me read a lot of rubbish."

Gabrielle continued: "*Mon Frère Yves, La Chanson des Gueux, Les Misérables* . . ."

Renoir, who was listening indifferently, waved his hand in a gesture of annoyance on hearing this last title.

"They say that Hugo's poetry is very beautiful," I observed.

"Anyone would be a fool to say that Hugo is not a man of genius," Renoir replied, "but as far as I'm concerned, I don't like him. The chief grievance I have against him is that he has got the French people out of the habit of using simple language. Gabrielle, I want you to get me *La Dame de Monsoreau* to-morrow without fail."

Then, turning to me: "There's a masterpiece for you! . . . The chapter in which Chicot blesses the procession is simply superb!"

"Oh, Monsieur Renoir!" cried Gabrielle suddenly. "I've found a book by Alexandre Dumas."

Renoir's face brightened.

---

[2]An old servant of the Renoirs.

"Good. Let's have a look at it."

But when Gabrielle announced triumphantly *La Dame aux Camélias,* Renoir exclaimed: "Never! I detest everything the younger Dumas wrote, and that book more than all the others. I have always had a horror of sentimental harlotry."

On top of the side-board in the dining-room, I saw a little coffee service and two porcelain candlesticks, decorated by hand. Any industrious young girl might have painted them. I presumed that they were a gift of some kind. Renoir saw me looking at them.

"Those are the only souvenirs I have left of my china-painting days," he said.

And he proceeded to tell me something about his youth. It interested me so profoundly that I adopted the plan of asking the painter, every time I saw him, to tell me something about his life. This, then, is the story of the career of a great painter, told in his own words and set down faithfully from day to day.

CHAPTER TWO

THE BEGINNINGS

RENOIR: I was born at Limoges in 1841. There is a legend about the name Renoir which has been handed down in our family from generation to generation. My grandmother often recounted how my grandfather, a man of noble birth, whose family perished during the Reign of Terror, was picked up as a child and adopted by a shoemaker called Renoir. However that may be, my father, at the time I came into the world, was a poor tailor, and, being hard put to it to make a living in Limoges, went to seek his fortune in Paris. Don't ask me to tell you about Limoges. I was scarcely four years old when I left the place, and I have never been back.

At Paris we lived in a house situated in that part of the Rue d'Argenteuil which, in extension across the Place du Carrousel, was included within the wings of the Louvre.

At the public school to which I was sent, my teachers reprimanded me for spending my time drawing pictures in my copy-books; but my parents, contrary to all traditions, were quite happy over it, for immediately they had hopes of my becoming a china-painter. Inasmuch as my father came from a city famous for its porcelain, it was natural that the profession of china-painting should seem the finest in the world in his eyes, finer even than music, which the music professor at school—who was none other than Gounod, then about thirty years old—urged me to follow.

When it was fully decided that I was to become an "artist," I was apprenticed to a manufacturer of glazed ware. At thirteen I was earning my own living. The work consisted in painting little bouquets on a white background. For this I was paid five cents a dozen. When there were large pieces to decorate, the bouquets were larger. From then on, prices went up—a trifling amount to be sure—for a wise employer mustn't spoil his men with too much gold. . . . The entire output was sent to Oriental countries, and, I may add, the "Sèvres" trademark was stamped on the back of each piece before it was shipped.

When I was a little more sure of myself, I was promoted from bouquets to portraits, always at starvation wages. I remember that the profile of Marie Antoinette brought me eight sous. The shop where I worked was situated in the Rue du Temple. I had to be there by eight o'clock in the morning. At ten I ran to the Louvre to sketch from the antique, for recreation, until noon. As for my meals, I managed to eat a bite wherever my errands took me.

One day I found myself in the Halles quarter and, in hunting for one of those wine-shops where they serve fried food and beef, I stopped spellbound in front of the *Fountain of the Innocents* by Jean Goujon, which I had never even noticed before. I at once decided to forego the wine-shop, and after buying a bit of sausage at a near-by store, I spent my hour of freedom studying the fountain from every angle. Perhaps because of this encounter long ago, I have always had a very special affection for Jean Goujon. He has purity, naïveté, elegance; and at the same time the form itself is amazingly solid. The sculpture of our day looks as if it had been carved out of soap; the old sculptors hacked out the stone themselves with a heavy mallet and a chisel, but they gave you the texture of flesh.

Germain Pilon tried to emulate Goujon, but he made a sorry job of it. For one thing, his draperies are too complicated. And drapery is terribly hard to do well! Goujon knew how to make it cling to the figure. One doesn't realize how much drapery brings out the form.

After the luncheon hour, I used to return to the shop, where I painted my cups and dishes till nightfall. But that was not all. After dinner I would go to the house of an old sculptor, a good old soul who made models of vases for my employer. He was very friendly to me and proved his interest by having me copy his models.

My apprenticeship lasted four years. I was seventeen then and I saw before me the magnificent career of a painter of porcelain at six francs a day. Then a catastrophe occurred which ruined my dreams of the future.

The first experiments in printing on faïences and porcelain had just been made; the infatuation of the public for this new process knew no bounds . . . invariably the case when hand-work is replaced by machinery! Our shops had to close, and I tried to compete with the machine-made product by working for the same prices. But I was soon obliged to give it up. The dealers to whom I showed my cups and saucers all seemed to have conspired against me. "Oh, that's hand-made," they would say. "Our clientele prefers machine-work. It's more even." So I began decorating fans with copies of Watteau, Lancret, and Boucher. I even used Watteau's *Embarkation for Cythera!* I was brought up, you see, on the eighteenth-century French masters.

To be more precise, Boucher's *Diana at the Bath* was the first picture that took my fancy, and I have clung to it all my life as one does to one's first love. I have been told many a time that I ought not to like Boucher, because "he is only a decorator." As if being a decorator made any difference! Why, Boucher is one of the painters who best understood the female body. What fresh, youthful buttocks he painted, with the most enchanting little dimples! It's odd that people are never willing to give a man credit for what he can do. They say: "I like Titian better than Boucher." Good Lord, so do

I! But that has nothing to do with the fact that Boucher painted lovely women superbly. A painter who has the feel for breasts and buttocks is saved!

Here is an anecdote that will amuse you. One day I was admiring a Fragonard—a shepherdess in a captivating little skirt which itself made the entire picture—when I heard someone remark that shepherd girls were probably just as slovenly then as they are now. What do you think of that! Wouldn't you admire an artist the more who can take a filthy model and give you a jewel?

Vollard: And what about Chardin?

Renoir: Chardin makes me sick. He has done some pretty still-lifes, perhaps. . . .

But I was telling you about my fans. They were fortunately not my only source of income. My elder brother, who was an engraver, sometimes obtained coats of arms for me to copy. I remember doing a *Saint George with a Shield.* On the shield I drew another Saint George in the same position, and so on until the last shield and the last St. George could be seen only with the aid of a magnifying-glass. But the fans and the Saint Georges brought in very little, and I hardly knew which way to turn, when one day I saw at the back of a court-yard in the Rue Dauphine a large café, enclosed in glass, with painters at work decorating the walls. As I came nearer, I heard a dispute going on: the employer was cursing and storming at his lazy workmen, because the paintings in his café were not going to be done in time. I immediately offered to do the decorations myself.

"Oh, I need at least three men, and I want regular workmen," said the proprietor contemptuously, for I was small and slightly built.

But without waiting for further objections, I took up a brush and showed him to his delight that I could paint as fast as any three workmen.

When I finished the frescoes in the café, I went back to my fans without much enthusiasm, promising myself to get out of that kind of thing at the first opportunity. The opportunity soon came. As I was passing a shop I saw a little sign pasted on the door:

PAINTER WANTED FOR WINDOW SHADES.

I went in.

"Where have you worked?" asked the proprietor. I was taken by surprise and said "Bordeaux" at a hazard. I had presence of mind enough to name a place far away, for I was afraid he would want to look up my references. But he evidently had some other idea in mind, for all he said was: "Bring me a sample of what you can do. Good-bye, young man."

Before leaving, I had time to talk with one of the employés, who seemed to be a good sort, and I asked him for information about painting shades. "Come and see me at my house next Sunday," he answered.

My first question was to find out if the boss was a good sort.

"Oh, he's a fine man," came the reply. "He's my uncle."

After much hesitation, I confessed that I had never painted window shades. "It's not very hard," he said. "Have you ever done the figure?" I commenced to breathe again. It was reassuring to find that painting shades was not unlike other kinds of painting—about all you had to do was to add a certain quantity of turpentine to the colour.

This particular shade-maker worked for missionaries who carried with them rolls of calico painted with religious subjects in imitation of stained-glass windows. When the missionaries reached their destination, they unrolled the calico around four upright poles, which gave the Negroes the illusion of being in a real church.

Before long I had dashed off a superb *Virgin with Magi and Cherubim.* My instructor could not conceal his admiration. "How would you like to try a *St. Vincent de Paul?*" he asked. I must explain that in the Virgin pictures the background consisted of clouds which were done easily enough by rubbing the canvas with a cloth, but if you didn't know the trick, the colour ran down into your sleeves. Whereas the *St. Vincents* required more skill. This personage was generally represented giving alms at the church-door, which required painting a certain amount of architecture.

I emerged from the second test victoriously, and was engaged on the spot. I took the place of an old employé, the glory of the studio, who was sick and showed no signs of recovery. "If you follow in his footsteps," said my new boss, "you will some day be as fine an artist as he."

Only one thing worried my employer. He liked my work and even went so far as to confess that he had never found such a clever hand; but he knew the value of money and it disturbed him that I should be making it so easily, for we were paid by the piece. My predecessor, who was always held up to new-comers as the perfect example, never painted anything without long preparation and a careful preliminary sketch. When the boss saw me paint in my figures directly on the bare cloth, he was aghast: "What a pity it is that you are so anxious to make money! You'll find that in the long run you will lose your skill."

When he was finally forced to admit that the "squaring" process could be discarded, he wanted to cut down the prices. But his nephew advised me to stick to my guns. "He can't get along without you," he said.

When I had put by a tidy little sum, however, I decided to say good-bye to the shade-maker. You can imagine how upset he was. He even promised me a partnership if I would stay on. The offer was tempting, but I did not allow myself to be persuaded, and, having saved enough to live on for a while (if I were not extravagant), I went to learn "serious painting" at Gleyre's studio, where I could work from a living model.

Chapter Three

THE GLEYRE STUDIO

Renoir: I chose the Gleyre studio because I wanted to be with my friend Laporte, whom I had known as a child. I might have stayed on with the window-shade maker if Laporte had not begged me so often to join him. Our comradeship did not last, however; our interests were too dissimilar. But I am more than grateful to Laporte for having influenced me to turn seriously towards painting, which resulted in my meeting Monet, Sisley and Bazille.

Gleyre was Swiss; he was a very estimable painter[1] but of no help to his pupils; he had the merit, however, of leaving them pretty much to their own devices. Before long I met the three artists whom I just mentioned. Bazille, after giving high promise, was shot down in the first battle of 1870, while still a young man. The public has barely begun to do him justice. The first buyers of "Impressionism" did not take Bazille's work very seriously, doubtless because he was rich.

Vollard: What painters were your group most drawn to?

R.: Monet, being a native of Havre, had known Jongkind there and admired him a great deal; Sisley was influenced chiefly by Corot; my hero was Diaz. His pictures have become very black, but in those days they sparkled like precious stones.

V.: Did you ever work at the Beaux Arts?

R.: The Beaux Arts was far from being what it is to-day. There were only two courses then, one in drawing, from eight o'clock until ten in the evening; the other in anatomy. From time to time the School of Medicine near by would obligingly lend a corpse to the anatomy class. Sometimes I attended these two classes, but I really learned the elementary technique of painting at Gleyre's.

V.: What instructors did you have at the Beaux Arts?

R.: The only one I remember particularly was Signol. One day I was drawing a cast from the antique. When he came to me he exclaimed: "Don't you realize that the big toe of Germanicus ought to have more majesty than the big toe of the coal dealer round the corner?" He walked away muttering solemnly: "The big toe of Germanicus . . ."

---

[1]The painter of *Lost Illusions* in the Louvre.

Just at that moment, somebody at the easel next to me, dissatisfied with his drawing, muttered an oath which Signol thought was intended for him. What is more, he imagined that I was responsible for it. He had me expelled instantly. An oil study that I had brought to his class aroused his antagonism the very first day; he was fairly beside himself on account of an ugly red that I had used in my picture. "Look out you don't become another Delacroix!" he warned me sarcastically.

V.: But people are beginning to get used to your colour now. In fact, they are even beginning to like it. At the Luxembourg one day, I made the acquaintance of a connoisseur who was fairly bursting with enthusiasm. "Renoir is the very God of colour!" he declared. But I must tell you frankly that your drawing did not please him as much. Later he stopped in front of the *Mater Dolorosa* and exclaimed: "Wonderful drawing, you'll have to admit! What a pity that Renoir cannot combine that magical colour of his with Bouguereau's draughtsmanship!"

R.: There is nothing more absurd than a "connoisseur." I once overheard two of your so-called connoisseurs discussing a picture. "No doubt it has excellent qualities," said one, "but is it a genre picture or a historical picture?" And the necktie magnate—I can't remember his name—was even worse; you know, the fellow who used to buy Gustave Moreaus. He took me to his villa in the suburbs of Paris and showed me two wretched little pictures signed Corot, and then, when I suggested some doubt as to their authenticity, he said: "Oh, well, they're good enough for the country!"

I could paint with molasses now, and everybody would praise my brilliant colour; but you should have seen the dirty colour on my palette when people were already beginning to call me revolutionary! I must admit that I floundered about in bitumen without any great enthusiasm. I was encouraged in the bad habit by a picture dealer, the first one to give me any commissions. Much later I found out why my black period was so popular. In the course of a trip to England, I made the acquaintance of a collector who claimed that he owned a Rousseau. He took me to his house, and, having made me tiptoe, by way of respect for the master's work, into the room where the picture was enshrined, he threw back a hanging from a huge frame, and in a hushed voice said: "Behold!"

"It's a bit black, isn't it?" I ventured, recognizing one of my own early products. He repressed a smile at my lack of taste, and launched into such a eulogy of his treasure that I could not refrain from telling him that I was responsible for it. I was really annoyed at the result: the worthy Englishman suddenly changed his tune; he proceeded to let loose a torrent of abuse on the dealer who had sold it. The effrontery of the man, to have foisted a Renoir on him for a Rousseau! (And I had fancied that my name was getting to be known—for all this took place at a time when I had long since abandoned the use of bitumen.)

One of the chief reasons why I stopped painting "black" was my encounter with Diaz. I met him under very curious circumstances, on a day when I was working in the Forest of Fontainebleau, where I used to go in the summer to paint landscapes with Sisley. In those days, even when working out of doors, I wore the blouse which porcelain-decorators usually wear in the shops. On this particular day I got into a quarrel with some loafers who were making fun of my costume. I got mad, and that only made things worse. At this moment a man came up, who, though hampered by a wooden leg, succeeded in putting the rascals to rout with the aid of a heavy cane, which he handled with great skill. When I thanked him, he said: "I am a painter too. My name is Diaz." I told him my admiration for his work and fearfully showed him the canvas I was then doing. "It's not badly drawn," he said. (That was perhaps the only time I have ever heard my draughtsmanship praised!) "But why the devil do you paint so black?"

I immediately began another landscape, and tried to render the light on the trees, in the shadows, and on the ground as it really appeared to me. "You're crazy!" exclaimed Sisley when he saw my picture. "The idea of making trees blue and the ground purple!"

V.: When did you exhibit at the Salon for the first time?

R.: In 1863. A big canvas of mine was accepted in that year. Oddly enough I was championed by Cabanel, who was chairman of the Jury. Not that he cared for my work. On the contrary, he declared that he thoroughly disliked it. "But in spite of that," he hastened to add, "it is an effort which ought to be recognized." The canvas represented *Esmeralda* dancing with her goat around a fire, surrounded by a circle of beggars. I remember the reflections of the flame and the great shadows on the cathedral. After the Salon was over, I destroyed it, partly because it was too cumbersome, and partly because I had conceived a distaste for bitumen, which I had not yet discarded when it was painted. Just my luck! The same day an Englishman, who wanted that very picture, came to see me. I can honestly say that the *Esmeralda* was the last thing I ever painted with bitumen.

My friends at Gleyre's had braved the Salon the same year, but they were less fortunate. Other painters, much better known than I, had also been refused that year, from Manet down. The way they were treated gave rise to such protests in the press that the Emperor Napoleon III consented to a *Salon des Refusés* being held in one of the rooms in the Louvre. But a member of the Academy was given charge of it. It goes without saying that the exhibitors were given the worst rooms in the museum. Yet nowadays there would be small chance either of a Minister of the Beaux Arts authorizing such an exhibition in the Louvre, or a Bonnat agreeing to organize it. They were very liberal under the Empire. But there were not so many painters at that time as now, although even then they were beginning to be a nuisance. The reply that Balzac made when asked to write up a Salon during the reign of Louis Philippe is indicative: "You don't expect a man to look at four hundred pictures, do you?"

It goes without saying that the *Salon des Refusés* was a huge joke from the public's point of view. Manet had sent his *Al Fresco Luncheon*. This canvas had just been refused at the Salon, as much on account of the actual painting, which was considered bad, as the subject, which was thought somewhat indecent. Apparently the members of the jury were unaware not only that Manet had borrowed one of the subjects of the great Venetian school but also that his nude woman was practically a copy from Raphael.

It was that year also (1863) that I met Cézanne. At that time I had a little studio in the Rue de la Condamine in the Batignolles quarter, which I shared with Bazille. Bazille came in one day accompanied by two young men. "I've brought you two fine recruits!" he announced. They were Cézanne and Pissarro.

I came to know them both intimately later on, but it was Cézanne who made the sharpest impression on my mind. I do not believe that a case like Cézanne's is to be found in the whole history of art. Think of his living to the age of sixty-six, and, from the first day he took a brush in his hand, remaining as isolated as if he were on a desert island! And then, along with a passionate love for his art, was that strange indifference to the fate of his pictures, once they were done, even when he was lucky enough to "realize."[2] Can you picture Cézanne having to wait for a purchaser to be sure of his next meal if he had not had an income? Can you imagine him forcing a complacent smile for an "amateur" who dared disparage Delacroix? And with all that, he was "so unpractical in the ways of the world," as he himself used to say.

One day I met him carrying a picture, one end of which was dragging along the ground. "There's not a cent left in the house!" he informed me. "I'm going to try to sell this canvas. It's pretty well realized, don't you think?" (It was the famous *Bathers* of the Caillebotte Collection—a superb thing!) A few days later I met Cézanne again. "My dear Renoir," he said feelingly, "I am so happy! I've had great success with my picture. It has been taken by someone who really likes it!"

"What luck!" I said to myself. "He's found a buyer."

The "buyer" was Cabaner,[3] a poor devil of a musician, who had all he could do to earn four or five francs a day. Cézanne had met him in the street, and Cabaner went into such ecstasies over the canvas that the painter made him a present of it.

I shall never forget the good times I had at Cézanne's home in the Midi, called the *Jas de Bouffan* (Home of the Winds). It was a lovely eighteenth-century place. Those were the days when they built really livable houses. There were great high-ceilinged rooms, and it was delightful to sit in front

---

[2]"Realizing" a picture was Cézanne's picturesque way of saying that he had succeeded in translating satisfactorily the impressions he received from Nature. (Trans. Note.)

[3]For further information about Cabaner, see *Paul Cézanne, His Life and His Art*, by Ambroise Vollard, translated by Harold L. Van Doren. (Nicholas L. Brown, New York, 1923. Reprinted by Dover as *Cézanne*.)

of a huge fire-place with a screen at your back. What fine fennel soups Cézanne's mother used to make for us! It seems only yesterday that I heard her giving her recipe: "Now take a branch of fennel, a teaspoonful of olive oil . . ." and so on. What a fine person she was!

Renoir went on: I have told you about the Salon of 1863. I was not so fortunate the following year, and therefore I had to exhibit at the *Refusés*. This time, the *Refusés* was not much of a success. In 1865, however, I had the good fortune to be again admitted to the Salon of Cabanel, with a picture of a young man walking in the forest of Fontainebleau, accompanied by his dogs; the painter Lecœur posed for it. It was done with the knife, a method which does not suit me very well, and which I rarely use. I remember, however, having painted in the same year a life-size nude, also with the knife. It was intended to be nothing more than a study of the nude. But the picture was thought improper, so I put a bow in the model's hand and a doe at her feet. I added an animal skin to make it less blatantly naked, and the picture became a *Diana!* But even then I did not succeed in selling it. A prospective buyer appeared one day, but we couldn't come to any agreement, for he wanted to buy the doe only, and I did not propose to "retail" my canvas.

This conversation took place during a walk in the woods at Louveciennes. Suddenly Renoir stopped and pointed to a near-by hillock. "I know only three artists who could paint those trees and that sky—Claude Lorrain, Corot, and Cézanne."

By chance one day I met the painter Laporte, the friend of Renoir's youth to whom Renoir attributed his decision to become a painter.

Madame Ellen Andrée, who had posed for some of Renoir's finest studies, asked me to take luncheon with her one day at her house at Ville d'Avray. "We shall dine out of doors under the rose arbour, and we shall talk of Renoir," she said. I accepted with infinite pleasure.

In that delightful garden where everything grows haphazard *Mon Paradou,* as Madame Andrée used to call it—I was presented to a well-preserved, elderly gentleman who had all the traditional glamour of the artist: a soft hat with a wide brim, and a romantic-looking cape. It was Laporte.

At table, one of the guests, Henri Dumont, a painter of delicate flower pictures, began praising Renoir's work.

"You mean Renoir the Impressionist?" the old gentleman demanded. "I knew him well in my youth; in fact we were quite intimate. If you see him, ask him about his friend Laporte; he will surely remember me. In those days I used to paint church windows for my daily bread, and very bitter bread it was, if you realize that I was already a confirmed free-thinker."

"Do you own any of Renoir's pictures?" I asked.

"Yes, I have a *Rose* that he gave me once, and in exchange I made him a present of a *Sheep* painted in bitumen, a study from nature that I was rather pleased with. But I soon got out of touch with Renoir. Life . . . women . . . separated us."

"I thought that Renoir regarded women only as subjects for painting," I said.

"Well, *I* don't feel that way about them," replied Monsieur Laporte sharply. "Indeed, when I started falling in love, I began to neglect my friends a bit." After a pause, he went on: "Renoir's weak point is his drawing, don't you think? Heaven knows I begged him often enough to guard against it! I have always had a great weakness for David. There's a painter who doesn't trifle with line! If Renoir had listened to me and had paid as much attention to drawing as to colour, who knows if he might not have become another David, like my eminent friend Lecomte du Nouy! I once said to Renoir: 'You must *make* yourself draw!' and do you know what he replied? 'I am like a cork thrown into a stream and tossed about on the current. When I paint I just let myself go completely.' "

"In any case, Renoir seems to have succeeded rather well," I observed.

Laporte thought I was speaking of the prices Renoirs were bringing. "Yes, if you count the sales at the *Hotel des Ventes* as cash! But you can't fool an old hand like me! I know only too well how little that means. And do you know what I've just heard? The dealers are encouraging their artists to run into debt in order to keep them well in hand!"

Later I found another acquaintance of Renoir's youth. My housekeeper had said to me: "I see by the paper that the pictures by this Monsieur Renoir who comes here, sell for big prices. There's a gentleman in the house where I work sometimes, used to know Monsieur Renoir . . . he's a janitor on the Grand Boulevards."

I went to the address she gave me. "Renoir?" said the janitor. "I saw his picture in a paper the other day and I recognized him right away. Fifty years ago we used to eat in the same creamery. There were several of us painters at the same table. . . . Renoir was always talking about painting. He took me with him to the Louvre once or twice. At that time I was clerking for a painting and decorating firm which has since . . ."

"But do you remember anything Renoir said?" I interrupted.

"Like it was yesterday, sir. At our table, for instance, we'd agreed that each day a different person was to get the marrowbone, but every day Renoir said it was his turn!"

He became silent; his recollections of the painter ended there.

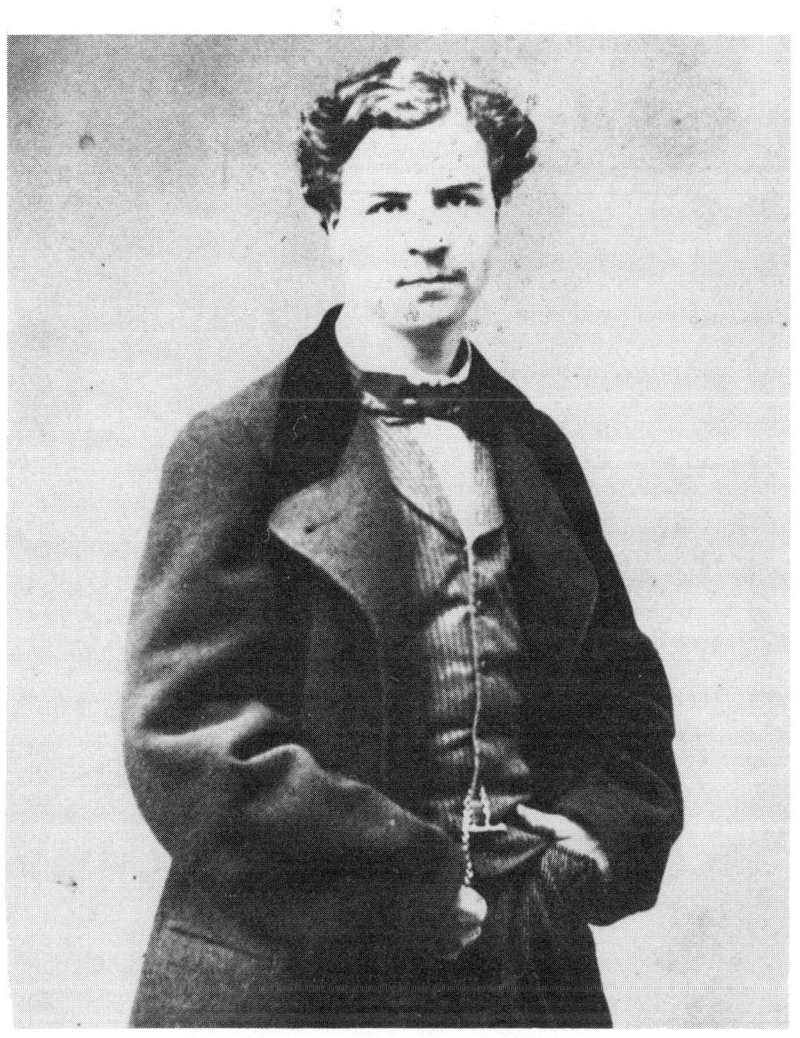

RENOIR AS A YOUNG MAN

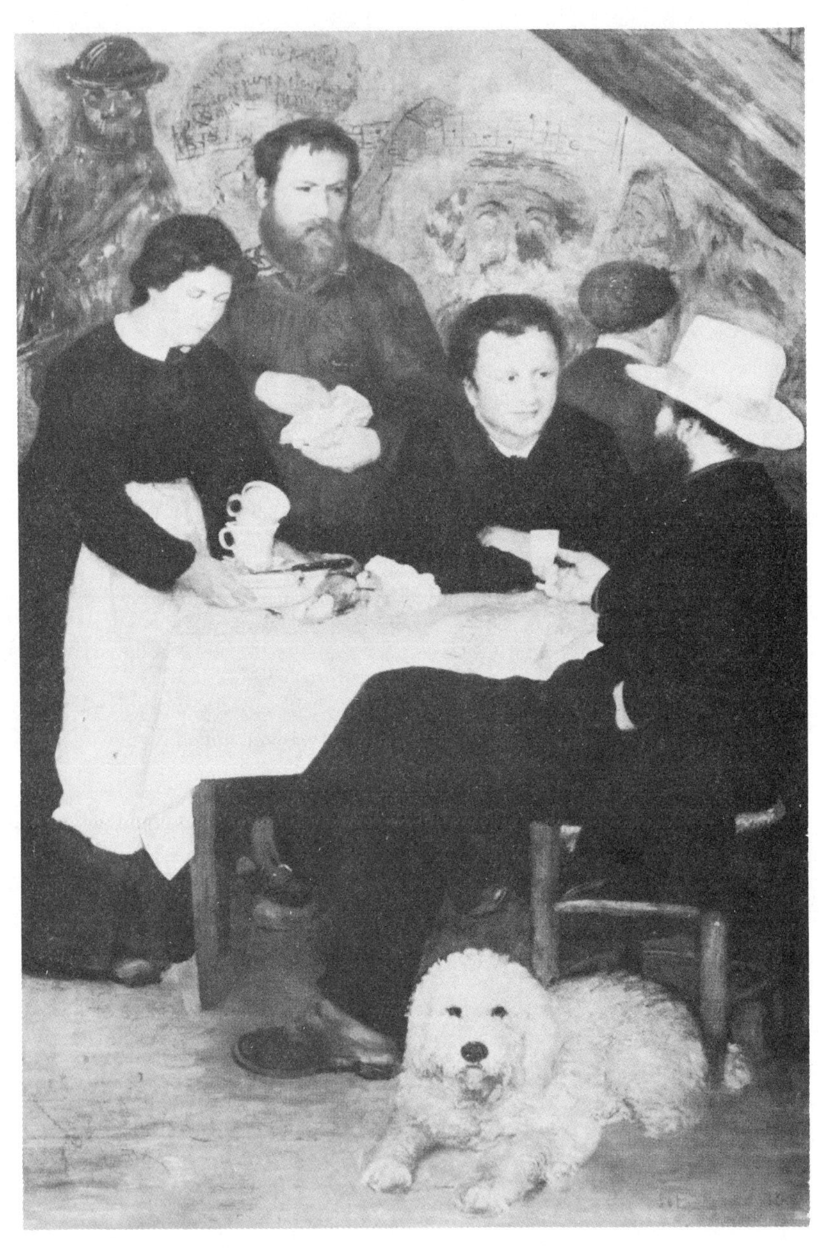

MOTHER ANTHONY'S CABARET (1865)

CHAPTER FOUR

"MOTHER ANTHONY'S CABARET"

RENOIR: A picture of mine called *Mother Anthony's Cabaret* brings back some of the most agreeable memories of my life. Not that I find the canvas particularly exciting in itself, but it reminds me of good old Mother Anthony and her inn at Marlotte, a real village inn. The subject of the picture is the common room, which did double duty as dining-room and lounge. The old lady with the kerchief round her head is Mother Anthony herself. The handsome young girl handing round the drinks is the servant Nana. The frizzly white dog is "Toto"—who had a wooden paw! I got some of my friends to pose around the table, among them Sisley and Lecœur. The *motifs* in the background of the picture were borrowed from sketches actually painted on the wall. These "frescoes," unpretentious but often quite successful, were the work of the artist habitués of the place. I myself painted the profile of Mürger,[1] which appears in *Mother Anthony's Cabaret,* high up at the left. Some of these decorations pleased me infinitely, and I made Mother Anthony promise never to have them scraped away. I thought that I had saved them from destruction by telling her that if the house were one day demolished, she could get a good price for her "frescoes."

The following summer I settled in Chailly, a village near Marlotte, where I painted *Lise* (1866). One day as I was working *sur le motif,* as Cézanne would have said, I overheard one of a group of young men near by talking about me.

"The nerve of this fellow Renoir!" he said. "He's had those funny pictures scraped off, so he could put one of his own big blobs in their place!" I hurried to the inn. It seems that Henri Regnault, who was already celebrated, had stopped for a few days at Mother Anthony's, and was appalled by the vulgarity of the decorations: some art student had taken it upon himself to turn the nude backsides of an old woman into the face of an old soldier, with whiskers and a peaked cap!

"Scrape out those horrible things at once!" Regnault had exclaimed. "I will paint you something really artistic."

Mother Anthony, taking him at his word, had a man come in to clean

[1]The author of *La Bohème* was a familiar figure in Marlotte.

them off; but Regnault departed without giving his promise a second thought. To cover the bareness of the wall, she then decided to use the canvas I had left when I went away the previous summer, and which had been put away in the garret.

Vollard: Was the *Lise,* which you just mentioned, accepted by the Salon?

R.: Yes, in 1867, the year of the World's Fair. That year I also did a picture of a garden at the World's Fair grounds, which was not finished until 1868. This inoffensive picture was considered too daring for the Salon. For many years it remained in a corner at Louveciennes, where my family was living.

The World's Fair was not the only sensation of 1867——the private exhibitions of Courbet and Manet were also held that year!

V.: Did you know Courbet?

R.: Yes, quite well. He was the most astounding man you can possibly imagine. I shall never forget an incident at his exhibition of 1867.[2] He had built a kind of balcony or *soupente,* on which he slept and from which he could watch his exhibition. When the first visitors arrived, he was just getting dressed. In order not to miss any of the public's enthusiasm, he came down in his flannel undershirt, not even taking time to put on the rest of his clothes, which he still carried in his hand. There he stood, in grave contemplation of his own pictures, and exclaimed: "How beautiful! How magnificent! It's incredible! It's enough to take your breath away!"

And he kept repeating: "Incredible! Incredible!"

At some exhibition where his pictures had been hung near the entrance, he is said to have remarked: "How stupid of them! There's such a crowd, you can't even get in!"

This kind of admiration, mind you, he reserved for *his* work only. One day he tried his best to compliment Monet, with whom he was very intimate. "Your Salon picture is pretty bad, you know," said Courbet. "But Lord! how it's going to annoy the Jury!"

V.: Do you like Courbet's work yourself?

R.: His early things, yes. But as soon as he became "Monsieur" Courbet . . .

V.: By the way, what about the picture that is so much talked about, *Good Morning, Monsieur Courbet?*

R.: I always get the impression from it that the painter must have spent months in front of a mirror "finishing off" that beard of his. And poor little Bruyas stands there bent over as if he were out in the rain, doing his best to keep from getting wet. But take the *Demoiselles de la Seine,* on the other hand. There's a magnificent picture for you! It is hard to believe that the

---

[2]The Jury of the World's Fair had refused to admit Courbet's pictures. With characteristic energy he rented a vacant lot just outside the Exposition grounds, had a small wooden building erected, put a large sign over the door reading: "G. Courbet, Painter," and managed his own exhibition. (Trans. Note.)

man who painted the portrait of Prud'hon, and the curates on their donkeys, painted that!

V.: I heard some Courbet admirers say that the donkey picture is inferior to the others only because Courbet did not have real priests pose for it, but dressed up some models in clerical clothes—in short, that the natural quality indispensable to Courbet was lacking.

R.: Another of Courbet's manias—Nature! I wish you could have seen the studio he fixed up to "do Nature," with a calf tied to the model stand!

V.: Have you ever heard the story about the young artist who came to Courbet for an opinion on a *Head of Christ* that he had painted? Courbet took one look at the picture and then turned a severe eye on the unfortunate young man. "Have you ever seen Christ?" he demanded. "Why don't you paint a portrait of your father instead?"

R.: Not bad, if somebody else had said it; but, coming from Courbet, it doesn't impress me very much. When Manet painted his *Christ with the Angels*—what painting, by the way! what a wonderful impasto!—Courbet said to him: "Have you ever seen an angel? How do you know whether an angel has a behind or not?"

V.: Whenever Courbet is mentioned, people always speak of his "power."

R.: Just what Degas was for ever praising in Legros. As far as I am concerned, I had rather have a penny plate done in three pretty colours than miles of your "powerful"—and tedious—painting!

V.: How did things stand between Manet and Courbet?

R.: Manet was attracted to Courbet, but Courbet didn't have much use for Manet's work. It was only natural, when you come to think of it. Courbet was still in the tradition, whereas Manet belonged to a new era in painting. Of course I am not naïve enough to pretend that there are any absolutely new currents in the arts. In art, as in Nature, what we are likely to think new is, at bottom, only a more or less modified continuation of what has gone before. But that does not alter the fact that the Revolution of 1789 began the destruction of all traditions. The disappearance of traditions in painting, as in the other arts, was brought about only by imperceptible degrees, and the masters of the first half of the nineteenth century—Géricault, Ingres, Delacroix, Daumier—were still impregnated with the old traditions. Even Courbet himself, with his rather gross drawing. But Manet and our group came along at a moment when the destructive forces deriving from the Revolution were exhausted. To be sure, certain among the newcomers would have liked to link themselves with tradition, the immense benefits of which they felt, unconsciously; but to do that, they would first of all have had to learn the traditional technique of painting, but when you are left to your own resources, you necessarily begin with the simple before attempting the complex, just as, to be able to read, you must first learn the letters of the alphabet. You realize, then, that for us the great task has been to paint as simply as possible; but you also realize how much the inheritors of tradition—from such men as Abel de Pujol, Gérome, Cabanel, etc., with whom these traditions, which they did not comprehend, were lost in the commonplace and the vulgar, up to painters like Courbet, Delacroix, Ingres—were bewildered by what seemed to them merely the naïve efforts of an *imagier d'Epinal.*[3] Daumier is said to have remarked at a Manet exhibition: "I'm not a very great admirer of Manet's work, but I find it has this important quality: it is helping to bring art back to the simplicity of playing-cards."

The very qualities in Manet that attracted Daumier, repelled Courbet.

"I'm not academic," said Courbet, "but art is not so simple as designing playing-cards!"

V.: If Manet liked Courbet, how could he have conformed to the teachings of such a man as Couture?

R.: It is hardly accurate to say that he conformed to them. He went to Couture's studio as one goes to any place where there are models to work from——even to Robert-Fleury's . . .

V.: Someone said to Manet about Robert-Fleury: "Come, come, Manet; don't be so nasty—the poor man has one foot in the grave . . ." Whereupon Manet retorted: "Yes, but meanwhile his other foot is in burnt sienna mud!"

R.: Couture and Manet could not hit it off for very long. When Manet left, the master said to his pupil: "Good-bye, young Daumier!"

[3]A maker of primitive but expressive woodcuts printed in colours. (Trans. Note.)

CHAPTER FIVE

LA GRENOUILLÈRE

RENOIR: In 1868 I painted a good deal at La Grenouillère. I remember an amusing restaurant there called Fournaise's, where life was a perpetual holiday. The world knew how to laugh in those days! Machinery had not absorbed all of life; you had leisure for enjoyment and no one was the worse for it.

By the way, have you read *La Femme de Paul,* by de Maupassant?

Vollard: You mean the story about a young man who threw himself into the river because his wife deceived him with another woman?

R.: De Maupassant exaggerates a bit, sometimes. At La Grenouillère women sometimes kissed each other on the mouth, but Lord knows they were normal enough! The "old girl" of sixty, dressed up like a twelve-year-old, with a doll under her arm and a hoop in her hand, had not yet come on the scene.

I always stayed at Fournaise's. There were plenty of pretty girls to paint; and you were not reduced, as you are to-day, to chasing after a model for an hour only to be treated finally as if you were a disgusting old man. I brought him a good many customers, so, by way of appreciation, Fournaise ordered a portrait of himself and one of his charming daughter, Madame Papillon. I painted Papa Fournaise in his white café vest, in the act of drinking an absinth. That canvas, which was then considered the last word in vulgarity, has suddenly become very distinguished in its handling, now that my pictures are fetching large prices at the auctions. The people who prattle with such conviction to-day about the "refined" manner of the portrait of Fournaise, would not even have parted with a hundred francs for a portrait, at the time when that amount would have been a godsend to me. All I could get my friends to do for me was to have their mistresses pose . . . sweet little things they were, too.

If by chance I got a paid portrait to do, I had a terrible time of it getting my money! I remember especially the portrait of the cobbler's wife, which I painted in exchange for a pair of shoes. Every time I thought the picture was finished and saw myself wearing the shoes, along came the aunt, the daughter, or even the old servant, to criticize:

"Do you think that my niece" (my mother, Madame, according to the occasion) "has a nose as long as that?"

Finally, in order to get my shoes, I gave the old girl a nose like Madame de Pompadour! Then there was another uproar; the eyes had been all right before, but now it would seem that the left one, etc., etc. So the entire family would gather around the portrait to look for further faults. Those were the good old days, just the same. . . .

The cobbler, however, couldn't hold a candle to Berton, a friend of mine in those days, who asked me how much I would charge for a portrait of his "little friend." I suggested fifty francs. Thirty-five years later he brought a woman around to my studio who would have stopped a clock.

"I've come for the portrait," he said.

"What portrait?"

"Come now, Renoir, you haven't forgotten that back in '68 you said you'd do a lady's portrait for me for fifty francs. Well, here she is. She's the daughter of an army officer, and she has got her normal school diploma," he added, as if, by giving me her pedigree, he hoped to compensate in some measure for her lack of beauty.

I felt I had to keep my word. I'm much too easy, you know. But I got my revenge by making her discard her flowered hat, her muff, and her poodle, so that the picture was bare of all the frills so dear to the heart of the "collector."[1]

V.: We were talking about your first pictures done at La Grenouillère, that is, the canvases painted in 1868–9. Does the large snow picture with figures belong to the same period?

R.: Yes, the *Bois de Boulogne*—the one with skaters and pedestrians in it. I have never been able to stand the cold; it is the only winter landscape I ever did. . . . Oh, no, there were two or three other studies, too. But then, even if you can stand the cold, why paint snow? It is a blight on the face of Nature.

V.: Was *The Harem* also of that period?

R.: The Harem was done in 1872, to be exact. It's a miracle that that canvas still exists. Shortly after painting it, I moved away from the studio I then occupied. I have always hated loading myself up with big things, so I left that picture behind in the studio. The concierge asked me if I was sure I had taken everything out. I nodded, and took to my heels. A long time afterwards, when I had forgotten all about it, I was walking through the same street, and I heard somebody hail me.

It was the concierge of my old studio building.

"Don't you remember me?" she called. "I'm your old concierge. I am keeping a picture for you that you forgot."

"Oh, thanks very much," I replied. "I'll call for it soon."

---

[1]I myself saw Berton coming out of a picture dealer's shop with his "little friend" and the portrait. On catching sight of me, he called out: "That's a fine portrait Renoir painted of my poor Anna! Would you believe it, we can't get more than five thousand francs for it!" (Author's Note.)

But I vowed to myself I'd never go near the place again. The time passed; one day, while walking in a remote quarter, what should I do but run straight into the same woman again.

"You never came for your picture!" she cried. "I've still got it. . . ."

I was convinced by that time that that cursed picture would pursue me all my life, and if I wanted to get rid of it, I would have to pay for a cab and take it away. I finally screwed up the courage to call for it, and finally sold the thing, along with a lot of other canvases, eleven in all, for the sum of five hundred francs.[2] In the lot were *The Arbour,* a *Portrait of Sisley,* the *Woman with a Finger on Her Lips,* and the portrait of the purchaser himself. . . . I can't recall his name, and I know it as well as my own! Do you know whom I mean? He was a caterer who turned painter. I went into his shop one day to buy a cake. He was just putting up the shutters. "It's decided," he said. "I'm going to quit pastry and take up painting. In this rotten business, if a piece of pastry is only a week old, we have to mark down the price. You artists are the lucky ones; your goods keep indefinitely; in fact they even improve with age!"

The Harem I was speaking to you about, makes me think of another picture that I painted the same year, an Oriental scene. It was done in a studio in Paris. The wife of a rug dealer posed for it. By the way, see if you can find that picture, Vollard. With this craze for insisting on my earlier manner, it might be a good bit of business for you.

For years I hunted for that canvas at all the Oriental rug stores in Paris. Finally one day an antique dealer, Madame Y., who had a shop on the Grand Boulevards, almost at my own door, invited me to come and look at a portrait that Benjamin Constant had done of her.

"I have another portrait of myself," she remarked casually, "but it is by a painter who is not so well known. I'd like to get rid of it." After several invitations, I went in to see the Benjamin Constant, but I did not even have the curiosity to ask the name of the painter who was "not so well known."

"We've just had the good luck to get three hundred francs for my other portrait," she told me. "It was painted by someone named Renoir, at the time I was in the Oriental rug business."

[2]The purchaser finally sold them, after twenty years, for over two hundred thousand francs. (Trans. Note.)

Chapter Six

DURING THE WAR OF 1870 AND UNDER THE COMMUNE

Renoir: When war was declared, General Douay, whom I knew slightly, proposed that I should serve as an officer under his command. The offer was tempting; but I have never tried to plan out my life in advance; I have always accepted things as they came along. And therefore I preferred rather to remain in the ranks. It turned out to be the best idea in the end, for in the very first battle General Douay was taken prisoner and sent to Germany. Had I been with him, in my delicate state of health, I would never have lived to tell the tale. Instead, I spent the entire winter in Bordeaux, where my regiment, the 10th cavalry, had been sent.

On account of my rather easy-going nature and, I dare say, my ingenuity (for I could nail up a crate with the best of them), my captain believed that I had a military bent and wanted me to continue my army career. Lord, if I'd gone into half the professions that people wanted me to! I think I told you—didn't I?—that when I was young, Gounod, who was the music teacher at the public school I attended, begged my parents to have me study singing. Just the other day I ran across a friend who remembered the days when I used to sing solos at Saint-Eustache.

On returning from Bordeaux [1871], I tumbled into Paris in the full swing of the Commune. I was obliged to give up my studio in the Rue Visconti immediately. It had become an unhealthy hole, what with shells exploding all around the quarter. And then, because I had a decided weakness for the Left Bank, I moved over into a room at a corner of the Rue du Dragon.

At the outbreak of the war, I was just beginning to get a little recognition; I had done a portrait of Bazille, which luckily attracted the notice of Manet, although Manet didn't like my work on the whole. As each one of my pictures came along, Manet would say: "No, that's not so good as the portrait of Bazille," thereby giving the impression that I had painted at least one thing that wasn't bad.[1]

---

[1]In fact, Manet owned this picture at the time that it was exhibited in 1877. Bazille's father came to the exhibition, and saw the portrait for the first time. He was nearly overcome by the striking likeness to his dead son, and Manet, hearing the story, graciously made him a present of it. (Trans. Note.)

With the war my affairs went to pieces, and under the Commune I found myself wandering penniless back and forth from Paris to Versailles. Finally my luck turned. One day I made the acquaintance of a kind lady from Versailles, who ordered a portrait of herself and daughter for three hundred francs. I will say to her credit that she refrained from all comment on either my painting or my draughtsmanship. It was quite a new experience to find a sitter who never once remarked: "Couldn't you bring out the eye just a little more!"

I don't mind that sort of thing so much when it's a question of people who obviously don't know what they're talking about. But when it comes to a man like Bérard, it's going too far. One day I showed him a study of a nude that I was rather pleased with.

"Now if you'd put two or three more days on that . . ." Bérard began.

I cut him short. "Come now, that's too much! I wish you to understand that I'm the only one qualified to know when a picture I've painted is finished or not!"

Poor Bérard gaped at me, speechless, and I went on: "Listen! When I've painted a woman's behind so that I want to touch it, then it's finished!"

But to come back to the Commune. This shuttling back and forth between Paris and Versailles had its disadvantages, the least of which was being cornered by bands of ruffians who forced you to sign up in the Federal ranks with the charming prospect of having your jaw broken subsequently when the Friends of Order should come back to Paris. Just to give you an idea of the stupidity of those idiots . . . One day I was making a study on the Terrasse des Feuillants in the Tuileries, when a Federal officer accosted me.

"Listen to me," he ordered. "You move on and don't let me catch you around here again. My men are convinced your painting is a dodge, and you're making a map of the country so you can hand us over to the Versailles crowd."

I did not have to be told twice, for I was only too glad to escape with a whole skin.

It was even worse than that, sometimes. One day, for instance, the Communards held up an omnibus I was riding in, and put all the passengers under arrest. I was on the driver's box, and I managed to escape by slipping down between the horses. I can't tell you how much I hated that crowd! But whenever I got a good look at some of the Versaillais, I couldn't help feeling that one side was as ridiculous as the other.

The only reason I did not get into serious trouble during that period was simply because I was so careful. It got so that I went out only at night. One evening my friend Maître and I were looking in a window in the Odéon quarter, when my eye was caught by an engraving representing the principal personages of the Commune. There, in the centre, was a portrait of Raoul Rigault.

"I know that chap!" I exclaimed. "Why, he's the new Prefect of Police!"

"There's your chance," said Maître. "If you have a pull with the police, you can get all the passes you want."

I had made Rigault's acquaintance under rather curious circumstances. Working in the Forest of Fontainebleau one day in the latter years of the Empire, I had observed a man seated not far from me, his clothes covered with dust. There was an air of indecision about him, and when I had finished my sitting, and was preparing to go, he approached me.

"I'm going to put myself in your hands," he said. "I used to be the editor of *La Marseillaise;* the paper has just been shut down, and some of my colleagues arrested; the police are after me too."

"You needn't worry," I told him. "There's nothing but painters around here; I'll introduce you to them as an old friend of mine."

This I did, and Raoul Rigault stayed for some time at Mother Anthony's Inn. One fine day he went away, and I never saw him again.

The day after my discovery I went to the Prefecture. I asked for Monsieur Rigault, thinking that when they heard that name, they would bestir themselves a bit. Imagine my consternation when I was told that they had never heard of such a person. I persisted and at last someone came to my rescue. "What do you mean by 'Monsieur' Rigault? We don't know anyone here but 'Citizen' Rigault!"

But in spite of the fact that the word "Monsieur" had been discarded in favour of "Citizen," the administrative red tape was the same as it had always been. No one was received, it seemed, without a request for an interview submitted beforehand. I wrote on a slip of paper the words, "Do you remember Marlotte?"

A few minutes later Citizen Rigault appeared and, with both hands extended, cried: "Strike up the Marseillaise in honour of Citizen Renoir!" (There was a great deal of band-playing during the Commune!)

I then informed the new prefect that I desired to finish my study on the Terrasse des Feuillants and also to have the liberty to go about Paris and the suburbs unmolested. Needless to say, I came away provided with a safe-conduct which specified that the authorities "were to aid and assist Citizen Renoir" in whatever way was needful. So I was let alone as long as the Commune lasted. I was able to visit my parents at Louveciennes, and, what was more, I loaned my pass to many of my friends whose business took them out of town.

Nor did Rigault stop there. Every time we met, he was at great pains to convert me to the beauties of the communal system.

"But, my good friend," I said to him one day, "you don't know what you're talking about. You ought to pray for the Commune to fall, instead. Don't you realize that if the Commune is victorious, your satiated Communards will become worse bourgeois than the others? But if the Commune is defeated, just watch the tricks the Versaillais will use to keep themselves in power . . . free bread, cake in place of bread . . . the People King!"

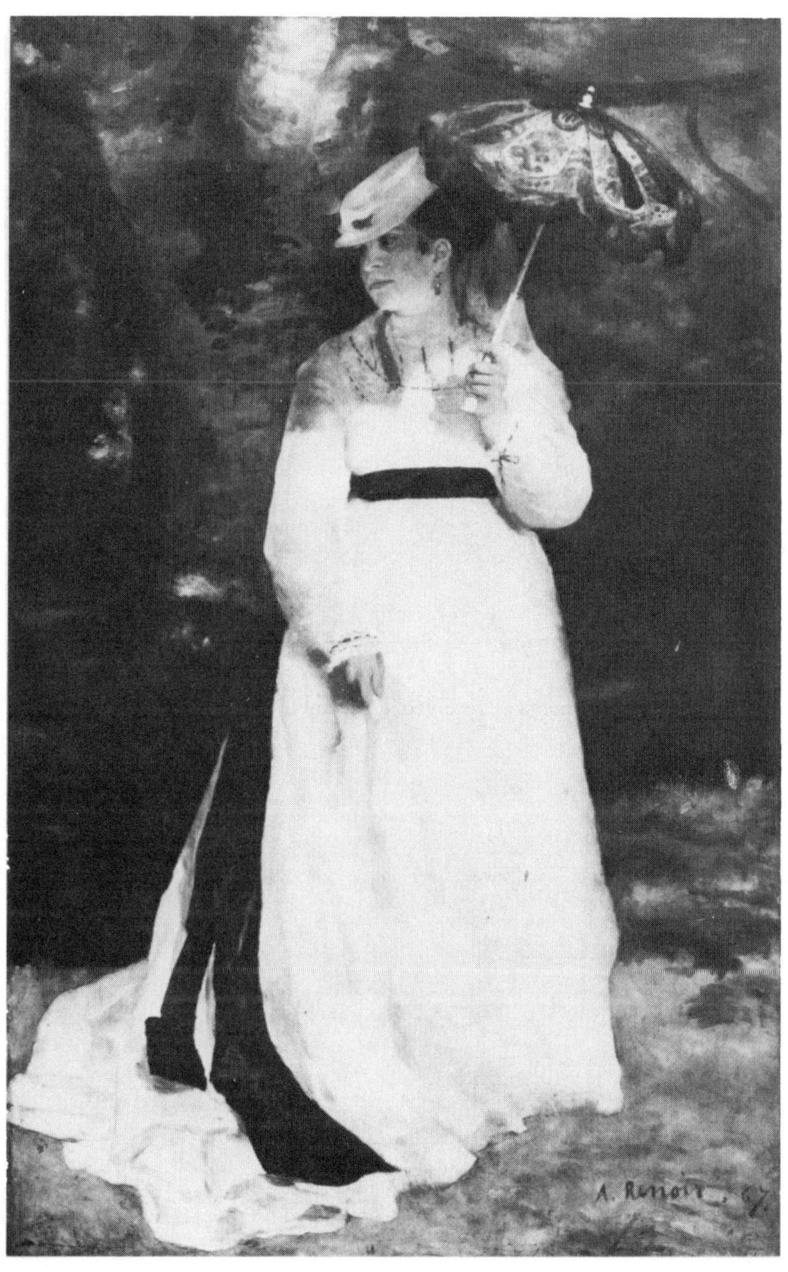

LISE (1866–67)

See pp. 15–16.

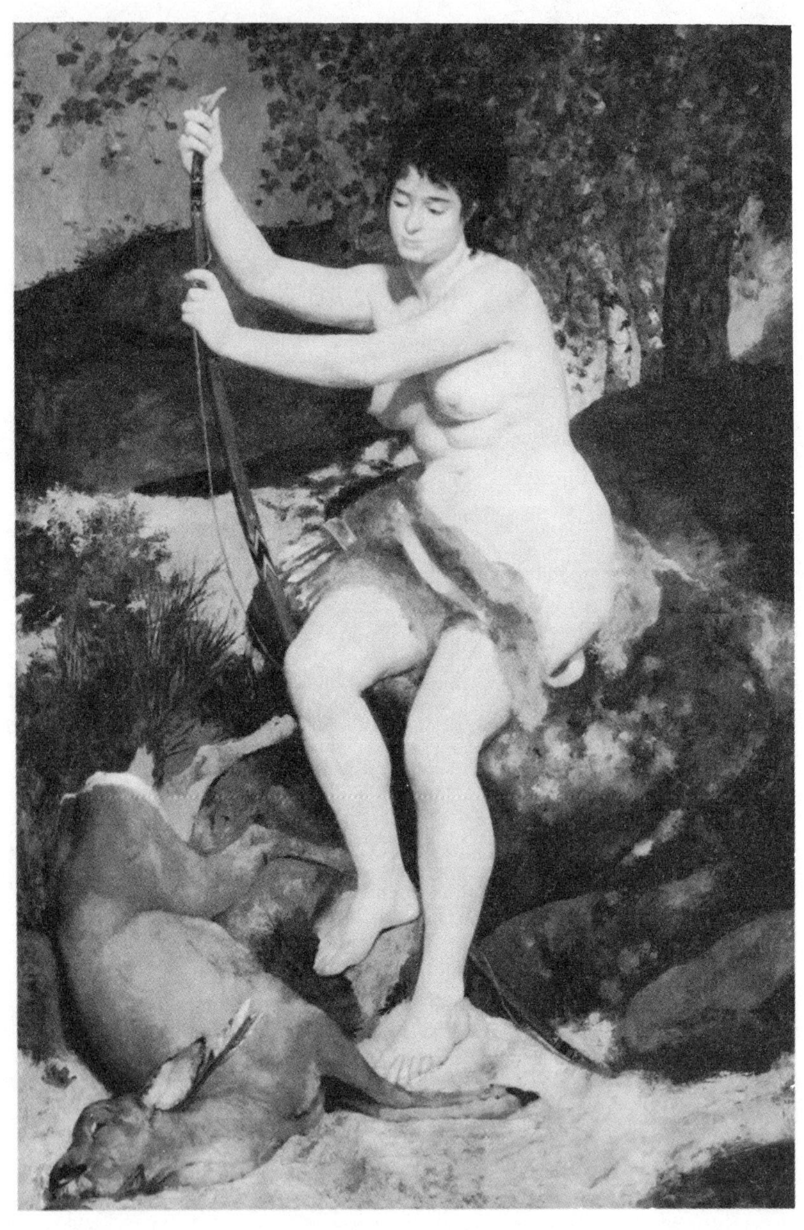

DIANA (1867)

See p. 13.

CHAPTER SEVEN

THE EXHIBITIONS OF THE IMPRESSIONISTS

RENOIR: When order was restored in Paris, I took a studio in the Rue Notre Dame des Champs. About the same time I got some decorations to do in the house of Prince Bibesco, which enabled me to spend the summer at Celle-Saint-Cloud. I did the *Henriot Family* there. On returning to Paris with the first cold weather, I commenced my big equestrian canvas, for which the wife of a certain Captain Darras had consented to pose. I sent it to the Salon and it was refused.

"I told you so," said Captain Darras triumphantly. "Now if you had only listened to me . . ." The colour had literally taken his breath away. While the sittings were going on, he was for ever saying: "Who ever saw a blue horse!"

But in spite of the sorry opinion he had of my painting, he was none the less of great service to me in every way. It was due to him, in his capacity of aide-de-camp to General Barrail, that I secured the Salle des Fêtes in the Military School to paint the picture in. *The Spring* and the *Mounted Trumpeter,* which has disappeared, were of about the same period.

It was in 1873 that one of the most important events of my life took place: I made the acquaintance of Durand-Ruel, the first dealer—the only one, in fact, for many a long year—who believed in me. At that time I left my studio in the Rue Notre Dame des Champs to go over to the Right Bank, where I have since lived permanently. It is true that, through many associations, I had a strong attachment to the Left Bank; but I instinctively foresaw the danger of absorbing too much of that atmosphere which Degas defined so well when he said: "No doubt Fantin-Latour's work is all right, but it is a little too Latin-Quarter!"

In 1873, feeling that I had really "arrived," I rented a studio in the Rue Saint-Georges. It was certainly a great success. The same year I went to Argenteuil, where I worked with Monet. I did quite a few studies there, among them *Monet Painting Dahlias.* At Argenteuil I also met the painter Caillebotte, the first "protector" of the Impressionists. He did not buy our pictures as a speculation. His sole idea was to help his friends as much as possible. And this he did admirably, for he took only the things which were unsalable.

Vollard: What about the exhibition organized in 1874 under the name of "Society of Painters, Sculptors and Gravers?"

R.: The title in no way indicated the tendencies of the exhibitors; but I was the one who objected to using a title with a more precise meaning. I was afraid that if it were called the "Somebodies" or "The So-and-Sos" or even "The Thirty-Nine," the critics would immediately start talking of a "new school," when all that we were really after, within the limits of our abilities, was to try to induce painters in general to get in line and follow the Masters, if they did not wish to see painting definitely go by the board. "Getting in line" meant, you understand, relearning a forgotten craft. Except for Delacroix, Ingres and Courbet, who had flourished so miraculously after the Revolution, painting had fallen into the worst sort of banality. Everyone was busy copying everyone else, and Nature was lost in the shuffle.

V.: If it was as bad as that, Couture must have seemed like an innovator.

R.: I should say so—almost a revolutionary! Those who flattered themselves on being "advanced" hailed Couture as their leader. His famous *Roman Orgy* had come on the scene in 1847 like a thunderbolt. They believed they had found in Couture a combination of Ingres and Delacroix, which the critics had vainly hoped for from Chassériau.

For, in the last analysis, everything that was being painted was merely rule of thumb or cheap tinsel—it was considered frightfully daring to take figures from David and dress them up in modern clothes. Therefore it was inevitable that the younger generation should go back to simple things. How could it have been otherwise? It cannot be said too often that to practise an art, you must begin with the ABC's of that art.

V.: But how did the "Society of Painters, Sculptors and Gravers" become the "Impressionists"?

R.: The name "Impressionists" came spontaneously from the public, who had been both amused and angered by one of the pictures on exhibition: an early morning landscape by Claude Monet entitled *Impression.* By the name "Impressionists," they did not intend to convey the idea of new researches in art, but merely a group of painters who were content to record impressions.

In 1877, when I exhibited once more with a part of the same group in Rue Lepeletier, it was I again who insisted on keeping this name "Impressionists" which had put us in the limelight. It served to explain our attitude to the layman, and hence nobody was deceived: "Here is our work. We know you don't like it. If you come in, so much the worse for you; no money refunded."

We were full of good intentions, but as yet were groping in the dark. Our struggles would perhaps have gone unnoticed, to the immense good of all, if it had not been for the critics and their "literature"—born enemies of the plastic arts. The public, even some of the painters themselves, were finally made to swallow a lot of nonsense about a "new art"! What on earth is the difference whether you paint in black and white, as Manet did under Spanish influence, or light upon light, as he did later under the influence of Claude Monet? Of course I do not mean to say that the artist's temperament has nothing to do with the method he employs. There is no doubt that Manet was surer of himself with black and white than with high-keyed colours.

V.: I have never heard of a single person who prefers Manet's dark manner to his light. But how did Manet come to be regarded as a pioneer, when his first canvases were so directly inspired by the galleries?

R.: He was the first to establish a simple formula, such as we were all trying to find until we could discover a better.

V.: The "Impressionists" had less luck in 1877 than with their first exhibition in 1874, didn't they?

R.: Yes, much less. The first exhibition was dubbed an art student's joke; the next time the public declared that the joke had gone too far. Perhaps if we had been shrewder we might have been able to conciliate the "connoisseurs" by painting subjects borrowed from history. What shocked people most of all was that they could find nothing in our pictures that was reminiscent of the galleries. To learn our craft, you see, we had to place our models in an atmosphere which was familiar to us. Can you see me painting a *Nebuchadnezzar* at a café table, or *The Mother of the Gracchi* in a box at the opera?

Nothing is so disconcerting as simplicity. I remember the indignation of Jules Dupré at one of our exhibitions. "To-day," he said bitterly, "one paints what one sees. . . . One doesn't even prepare the canvas. . . . Are these the great masters?"

V.: How *did* the "great masters" prepare their canvases?

R.: Dupré was referring to the minium preparations so much in vogue with the Barbizon School. It was believed that preparing the canvas in this way gave "sonority" to the painting, which was quite true in principle; but the "great masters" of that time, for all their minium, only succeeded in producing work which lacked sonority, and which cracked all over into the bargain. What will pictures such as the *Angelus*[1] look like fifty years from now? The Duprés are already melting down over their frames.

What an amazing period that was! Those people spent three quarters of their time with their heads in the clouds. The subject had to crystallize in their minds before it could be put on canvas. One continually heard such

[1]I arrived one day at Lewis Brown's (about 1888) to find him in a state of great excitement. "I used to know Millet's *Angelus* when it was all cracked from top to bottom," he declared. "And now I have just seen it again, and it looks like new." But recently (1920) a newspaper again raised the alarm that the *Angelus* was "beginning" to crack. So much for the work of the picture-restorers. (Author's Note.)

nonsense as: "The Master is overworking himself; he has been dreaming away in the forest for three days now!"

They couldn't even make a living with their literary pictures! Aside from a few like Dupré and Daubigny, and especially Millet, who were successful, what about the gang of poor devils who took the artist-legend of "dreamer" and "thinker" seriously, and sat with their heads in their hands in front of canvases that they never touched? You can imagine how those people scorned us, because we were getting paint on our canvases, and because, like the old masters, we were trying to paint in joyous tones and carefully eliminate all "literature" from our pictures.

V.: Didn't the Impressionists allow themselves to be too much influenced by foreign schools? Japanese art, for instance?

R.: Unfortunately, yes, in the beginning. Japanese prints are certainly most interesting, as Japanese prints . . . that is to say, on condition they stay in Japan. No people should appropriate what does not belong to their own race, if they don't want to make themselves ridiculous. If they do, they produce nothing but a kind of bastard art, with no real character. Certain critics are beginning to claim me as a true member of the French School. I am glad of that, not because I think that that school is superior to the others, but because, being a Frenchman, I ought to represent my own country.

V.: You were talking just now about the exhibition in 1877. You have said nothing about the pictures painted from 1874 to 1877.

R.: I recall the *Dancing-Girl,* the *Moulin de la Galette* and *La Loge*—the latter done I think in 1874, and then, let me see . . . *The Woman with the Cup of Chocolate.* I'll try to remember others for you some time again. I have painted so many pictures in my life, that I cannot always recall what year I did them.

V.: I remember once having seen two amateurs at an exhibition of your work at Durand-Ruel's. One of them was explaining to the other the qualities, and no doubt the faults, in each canvas. But when he came to *La Loge,* he said: "There's nothing to do but take off your hat to that."

R.: Oh, yes, I know all about those protectors of the arts who have the greatest respect for pictures after the artist has nearly died of hunger while painting them. In the case of *La Loge,* in fact, I had gone everywhere trying in vain to get five hundred francs for it, when I stumbled on Père Martin, an old dealer who had at last been won over to Impressionism. I could only squeeze four hundred and twenty-five francs out of him, but I was only too glad to get that! Père Martin considered the price far and away too high—but it wasn't possible for me to come down a *sou,* for it was just the amount I needed for my rent, and I had no other resources in sight. And as the dealer had a prospective purchaser for the picture, he had to accept my terms. But he never forgave me for having taken advantage of the situation on that day by making him hand over so much money for a single canvas!

His luck soon went from bad to worse. His protégé Jongkind, who had heretofore sold him canvases at the uniform price of ten francs apiece, suddenly became famous. One day, all unsuspecting, Martin went to see him. "Well, Martin, my friend," said Jongkind, rubbing his hands, "no more pictures in the hundreds, you know. I'm in the thousands now."

Poor old Martin went off fairly gasping. Suddenly he discovered that he had forgotten his famous black bag which was always with him on his peregrinations, for he was perpetually on the look-out for old iron and other "bargains" that could be picked up *en route.* You can imagine his indignation when he returned and found Jongkind in the midst of a most elaborate meal. "The bastard!" he said to me afterwards. "He eats asparagus in the dead of winter!"

My friendship with Jongkind is one of the pleasantest memories of my youth. I have never in my life met such a gay, happy-go-lucky fellow. His great height and his beatific smile permitted him to do eccentric things without in the least offending people. One day we were sitting quietly in front of a café, when Jongkind suddenly jumped up and planted his ponderous form in front of an astounded pedestrian. "You don't know who I am?" he cried in his ridiculous Dutch-French jargon. "Impossible! Why, I'm Jongkind the Great!"

There was another dealer in Montmartre besides Martin who handled very fine pictures. His name was Portier. Did you ever know him, Vollard? He had an ingenious way of disposing of his wares.

"Don't buy that picture!" he would say. "It's much too expensive!"

Of course the collector usually bought it. It must be said that two thousand francs was still considered expensive in 1895 for a first-class Manet.

Portier had a second floor in the Rue Lepic, and Père Martin a ground floor at the foot of the Rue des Martyrs. They were both wretched places, but what magnificent canvases they had to show!——all the Impressionist School, not to mention Corot, Delacroix, Daumier, and what not! Rouart bought the greater part of his collection through Père Martin, among them Corot's famous *Woman in Blue,* for which he paid three thousand francs. It was a scandalous price at the time. And it was this picture that the Friends of the Louvre later bid up so high at the Rouart sale.

Among the pictures I painted in the Rue Saint-Georges studio, I remember a *Circus,* with little girls juggling oranges; a life-size portrait of Félix Bouchor, the poet; a pastel of Madame Cordey; and, finally, *The Wife and Children of Monet,* in Monet's garden at Argenteuil. I arrived at his house just at the moment that Manet, who was also a guest, was making preparations to do the same subject; with the models all ready, I could not let such a fine chance slip. When I had gone, Manet turned to his host and said:

"You're a good friend of Renoir; you ought to advise him to give up painting. You can see for yourself that he hasn't the ghost of a show."

Chapter Eight

"SERIOUS" PURCHASERS

Renoir: My first "serious" patrons came from among my friends—friends like S., whom you used to know. There's a real friend for you! He bought my pictures for the sole purpose of being agreeable; he cared very little about my painting for its own sake, and besides, he always ran the risk of incurring the displeasure of his wife if he spent three or four hundred francs for a thing which was useless—and ugly to boot. You remember that canvas of a *Woman with Her Finger on Her Lips*? S. must have paid me about 250 francs for it. For a long time it was relegated to a hallway by Madame S. She found the picture a little expensive, a little vulgar, and, furthermore, she felt that the pose was not quite in good taste. But one day when Madame S. repeated to me for the twentieth time, "That picture! . . ." I had the satisfaction of being able to reply:

"Madame, you will soon be rid of it, for my friend Caillebotte has commissioned me to offer your husband three times the price he paid; and as I believe Monsieur S. isn't exactly keen about it either——"

"But I never said that *I* didn't like the picture," protested Madame S. "Except for certain little things—quite unimportant . . ."

I should like to have known what those "unimportant little things" were, but Madame S. sent for the butler without further explanation, commanded him to bring hammer and nails, and had my picture hung in the best light in the drawing-room!

Not that Madame S. was the kind of person to be lured by the prospect of making a profit. She was not like her friend, Madame N., for instance. Madame N. had bought a little *Head of a Child,* for five louis. A few years afterwards, someone said to her:

"Ah! you have a Renoir, I see."

"Yes," replied Madame N.; "that is to say, five louis not working."

"Five!" echoed the other. "You can add a zero to that."

Madame N. was prostrated to think that so much money lay unproductive. So when her husband came home, the picture was already down off the wall.

"Quick! Take that to Durand-Ruel's as fast as you can!" and she put it under his arm.

Dear old Madame N.! I remember one day finding her in tears. "Would you believe it, Monsieur Renoir? My husband has deceived me after thirty years of fidelity!"

Thirty years! I felt that was a bit extravagant. . . . But, however that may be, I agreed that it was a magnificent record.

"But that isn't all," she wailed. "I've just found out that during our vacation in the country the creature received her five hundred a month regularly . . . and for doing nothing, too!"

It was through S. that I got to know some of my other "patrons," such as Deudon, Ephrussi, and Bérard. . . . Bérard came to my studio one day with the banker Pillet-Will, who happened to be seeking a portraitist. He said I wouldn't do.

"I don't know anything about art, you understand, but even if I did, my position is such that I am forced to have pictures in my home by artists who sell at high prices. So I shall have to try Bouguereau, unless I can find a still higher-class artist."

Fortunately there were other amateurs, such as Monsieur de Bellio, who didn't mind having less expensive pictures about them. But they were so exceptional that we always had to "touch" the same ones. Every time one of us was in urgent need of a couple of hundred francs, he would run to the Café Riche at lunch-time with a picture. One was sure to find Monsieur de Bellio there, and he would buy it without even looking at it. Of course his apartment was soon full to overflowing at that rate, so he finally had to rent a vacant room to put his canvases in. If Monsieur de Bellio left behind him an enormous fortune in pictures that cost him next to nothing, at least you can be sure it was no fault of his. Like Caillebotte, he used to buy all the stuff we had in our studios that had been ordered and never called for.

Some other pictures come to my mind from the Rue Saint-Georges days—the *Déjeuner,* which is now in the Frankfort Museum, and the *Woman with a Cup of Chocolate,* a type of woman that I used to love to paint. Her name was Marguerite. About the same time I had another model called Nini, a beautiful girl too, and very charming; but I preferred Marguerite. Nini always seemed to me a sort of Belgian counterfeit.

Vollard: What kind of dress do you like to paint best?

R.: Of course I prefer the nude. But when I have to paint a woman clothed, I like the "princess" gown——it gives such a lovely, sinuous line to the body.

I haven't spoken to you about the *Moulin de la Galette.*[1] That dates back to the Rue Saint-Georges days also [1875]. One day Franc-Lamy, while looking over the canvases which were stacked against the wall in my studio, discovered a sketch of the *Moulin de la Galette,* made from memory.

[1]A famous dancing-place of former days in Montmartre. It is still in existence but has lost much of its charm. Renoir's painting is one of the principal canvases in the Caillebotte collection in the Luxembourg Museum. (Trans. Note.)

"You really *must* do this picture!" he cried.

It was a complicated business . . . models to find, and a garden. . . . I had the good luck just at this time to secure a commission that was royally paid: a portrait of a woman and her two little daughters. It brought me 1200 francs. So I rented a house in Montmartre, surrounded by a large garden, for a hundred francs a month. It was there that I painted the *Moulin, The Swing, After the Concert,* the *Torso of Anna.* . . . Lord knows how often I have been taken to task for the violet shadows in the last picture!

"Your model must have had the small-pox!" one art critic said to me. Somehow one felt that he used the word "small" to keep from being thought indecorous.

It was also in this garden that I made the various portraits of Mademoiselle Samary. She was a charming girl. And what a beautiful skin she had! She positively radiated light from within!

As luck would have it, I found some girls at the Moulin de la Galette, like the two in the foreground of my picture, who asked nothing better than to pose. One of them used to write to me about her appointments on gilt-edged note-paper. I used to see her delivering milk in Montmartre. One day I learned that she had a little apartment which a box-holder at the opera had furnished for her. But her mother had made her promise that she would not give up her job. At first I was afraid that the more or less serious lovers of these models whom I had taken from their nest at the Moulin de la Galette would forbid their "wives" to come to the studio. But they were good sports too; I even got some of them to pose. But you mustn't think that these girls gave themselves to anyone who happened along. There was fierce virtue among some of these children of the street. I recall one little girl, just the type I liked, who had stopped in front of a jewellery shop on the Rue de la Paix, her eyes wide open with ecstasy. I was with Deudon and Baron Rothschild, a friend of his. Rothschild said:

"Watch me make that child come to terms."

He went up to her.

"Mademoiselle, would you like to have that ring?"

At this the girl began to scream so loudly that a gendarme appeared and escorted the lot of us to the police station. When she had explained her grievance, the *commissaire,* after making all sorts of excuses for his officer's stupidity, gave our little ingénue a scolding of the first order. As we went off we caught such snatches as:

"Little goose! . . . The idea! . . . Just as the baron was . . ."

V.: I saw your picture of *Needle Women* at a recent exhibition. You never found such queens as those at the Moulin de la Galette. When was it painted?

R.: That picture is not so very old. [About 1900–1905.] As for your "queens," they're nothing but our housemaids. . . . I remember another canvas of the *Moulin de la Galette* period representing a *Girl in a Blue Apron.* It was also painted in the garden at Montmartre.

V.: And the dance panels in the Durand-Ruel collection?

R.: Those were done later than the *Moulin.* My wife posed for one of the figures. The other woman was a model, Suzanne Valadon,[2] who later went in for painting herself. My friend Lauth posed for the two male figures. He appears also in the *Boatman at Bougival* with Lestringuèz and Ephrussi.

V.: The sale that you organized at the Hotel Drouot along with Claude Monet, Sisley and Berthe Morisot, took place about this time, did it not?

R.: When I received the twelve-hundred-franc commission which enabled me to rent the garden on Rue Cortot, I said to myself: "Perhaps there are some other good people who might be disposed to pay us twelve hundred francs for our pictures, if we only knew where to find them! Let's make a bold move and have a sale at the Hotel Drouot!"

The others shared my enthusiasm for the plan. We got together twenty choice canvases—at least *we* thought them choice. The auction brought 2,150 francs! After it was over, the expenses had not even been covered; we actually owed money to the auctioneers! A certain Monsieur Hazard had had the courage to bid one of my pictures, a *Pont Neuf,* up to three hundred francs.[3] But nobody followed his example.

But that sale turned out well for me in the end. Through it I made the acquaintance of Monsieur Chocquet. He was a ministry employé, with only very modest resources, who had succeeded in getting together a most remarkable collection. It is quite true that at that time—and even much later—it was not necessary for a collector to be very rich. A little taste was sufficient.

Monsieur Chocquet had dropped in at the Hotel Drouot by chance during the exhibition of our pictures preceding the sale. He felt that he found some resemblance to the work of Delacroix, his god, in my canvases. He wrote to me the very evening of the sale, paying my work all sorts of compliments and asking if I would consent to do the portrait of Madame Chocquet; I accepted immediately. Not that I often refuse portrait commissions. When there is too much sham about the sitter, I take it by way of penance; it is good for a painter to do some dull job from time to time. Take the portrait of Madame L., for example. I told her I didn't know how to paint wild animals! But that was not the case with Madame Chocquet. If you have seen that portrait, Vollard, perhaps you have noticed a copy of a Delacroix at the

---

[2]One of the best-known of the present-day French woman painters. See the monograph on her work in the *Peintres Français Nouveaux* series, published by *La Nouvelle Revue Française.* Her son, Maurice Utrillo, is one of the leaders among the younger artists. (Trans. Note.)

[3]At the Hazard Sale (1919), this same *Pont Neuf* brought nearly 100,000 francs. (Author's Note.)

top of the picture? It was part of Chocquet's collection. Chocquet himself asked me to put it in.

"I want to have you both together, you and Delacroix!" he said.

I need not tell you that as soon as I knew Monsieur Chocquet well enough, I got him to buy a Cézanne. I took him to Père Tanguy's, where he bought a little study of *Nudes.* He was delighted with his acquisition, and while we were going back to his home, he remarked:

"Won't that look well between a Delacroix and a Courbet!"

But just as he was about to ring the bell, he stopped short.

"I wonder what Marie will say?" he said dubiously. Then: "Listen, Renoir, do me a favour. Suppose you tell my wife that the Cézanne belongs to you, and when you leave, forget to take it with you; that will give Marie time to get used to it before I confess that it belongs to me."

This little ruse met with complete success, and Madame Chocquet, to please her husband, took to Cézanne's work very quickly.

As for Monsieur Chocquet, his admiration for Cézanne, whom I soon brought to him in person, became so great that before long one could not mention the name of any artist in his presence without his crying: "And Cézanne?"

If you only could have heard Chocquet tell how, during a stay in his native city of Lille, he "educated" his fellow citizens, who were at that time very proud of the Parisian laurels of another native of their town, Carolus Duran!

"Carolûsse Dûran?" he would say, blankly, if anyone mentioned the author of the *Woman with a Glove. "Carolûsse Dûran?* Good Lord, no! I never heard of that name in Paris. Are you *quite* sure you're not mistaken? Cézanne, Renoir and Monet are the artists all Paris is talking about. But your Carolûsse——Surely you must have made a mistake."

As for my other patrons, Vollard, have you ever seen the collection of Monsieur de Bellio, of whom I was speaking a while ago? He has a little portrait that I did of myself. For some reason or other, everybody praises it nowadays. It's an unimportant little sketch. I had thrown it in the trash-basket at the time, but Monsieur Chocquet asked me to let him take it. I was ashamed that it wasn't better. But a few days later he brought me a thousand francs. Monsieur de Bellio had gone crazy over that bit of canvas, and it was he who had given the thousand for it.

There you have the patrons of the day. Of course I must admit that they were the exception, even then. For every Chocquet, for every de Bellio, Caillebotte or Bérard, there were I don't know how many of the other kind. . . . And the downright ferocity of the general public!

V.: I nearly forgot to ask you about the portrait of Madame Daudet. Does that belong to the period of the *Moulin de la Galette?*

R.: 1876, to be exact. I went to spend a month with Daudet at Champrosay. At the same time I did the portrait of *Young Daudet in the Garden* and a *Banks of the Seine,* where the river skirts the town.

Franc-Lamy one day showed me a letter I had written to him saying: "I send you a rose plucked from the tomb of Delacroix at Champrosay." How long ago all that seems! . . .

Chapter Nine

THE CAFÉ GUERBOIS, THE NOUVELLE ATHÈNES, THE CAFÉ TORTONI

Renoir: Up to 1870 the Impressionists, and the men of letters who had appointed themselves champions of "plein-air" painting, used to forgather at the Café Guerbois, situated at the foot of the Avenue de Clichy. Fantin-Latour has painted a picture called *A Studio in the Batignolles,*[1] which shows some of the habitués of the Café Guerbois gathered about Edouard Manet, seated at his easel. The group consists of Zola, Maître, Astruc, Bazille, Claude Monet, Scholderer, a foreign painter and friend of Fantin, and myself.

After 1870 we abandoned the Café Guerbois, and along about 1878 we started going to the Nouvelle Athènes. The rival of the Nouvelle Athènes was the Café Tortoni, quite a celebrated place on the Boulevard. Every afternoon from five to seven Aurélien Scholl, Albert Wolff and other Parisian celebrities were to be seen there, among them Pertuiset, the lion-hunter. Have you ever seen Manet's portrait of Pertuiset? The lion looks as if he'd just fallen out of bed, and the great hunter has a pop-gun that wouldn't kill a sparrow! Everybody thinks Manet couldn't paint a lion, but the joke is on the public. Manet was just poking fun at a public hero.

Vollard: Did you know Albert Wolff?

R.: Very slightly. I remember one day a great discussion which took place at Tortoni's between Wolff and another man. . . . It was Robert-Fleury, I believe. . . . They were arguing about whether it was better to varnish a painting immediately, as Blaise Desgoffe did, or to leave it to time, as Vollon did!

V.: I can just see Cézanne getting up in the middle of such a discussion and growling: "Pack of milksops!"

R.: Cézanne scarcely ever went down as far as the Boulevards, and I did not see him even at the Café Guerbois or the Nouvelle Athènes more than three or four times. And even then he had to be dragged there by Cabaner.

V.: You haven't told me how Manet and Degas got along together.

R.: They were on very good terms. They admired each other as artists, and enjoyed each other's companionship. Beneath Manet's somewhat

---

[1]In the Luxembourg Museum.

"Boulevard" manners, Degas found a man of good education and of good middle-class principles like his own. But, as with all great friendships, theirs was not without frequent quarrels and reconciliations. After one dispute Degas wrote to Manet: "Sir, I am sending back your *Plums.*" And Manet returned the compliment by sending back the portrait of himself and his wife which Degas had just made. It was this portrait that caused their most serious quarrel. The picture represented Manet half stretched out on a sofa, and Madame Manet at the piano in a corner. Manet decided that he would appear to better advantage alone, and calmly removed all of Madame Manet except the edge of her skirt. You know how Degas disliked having his work tampered with; and what a fuss he used to make if his "garden frames," as Whistler called them, were ever changed for gold ones. . . .

Degas' picture, however, gave Manet the theme for his masterpiece, *Madame Manet at the Piano.* Everybody knows how easily Manet could be influenced. He has been called "an imitator with genius." But when he really let himself go . . . I saw in a window in Rue Laffitte one of those little sketches of a woman's legs that Manet used to dash off in the street. . . . It was unique!

As I said before, both Degas and Manet belonged to the respectable Parisian bourgeoisie. But there was another curious element in Manet, a strain of playfulness which made him constantly try to mystify his public.

They tell how a pompous member of the Institute was introduced to Manet one day and cried, "Ah, Monsieur Manet, indeed! How interesting! I am preparing an elaborate study of the modern masters, and perhaps you can help me. You knew the great Couture, I believe!"

"Why, yes," Manet replied. "There was a certain rite very highly thought of in the Master's studio, which particularly impressed me. The pupils had a flute which they were accustomed to play by inserting it in the rear. Whenever a notable visitor would come to the studio, they never failed to inform him that tradition required all those who were admitted to Couture's to blow the flute by this unique method!"

Degas liked to mystify people, too. I have seen him amuse himself like a schoolboy by puffing up a great reputation for some artist or other whose fame, in the ordinary course of events, was certain to perish the following week.

He fooled me badly once. One day I was on the driver's box of an omnibus, and Degas, who was crossing the street, shouted to me through his hands: "Be sure to go and see Count Lepic's exhibition!"

I went. Very conscientiously I looked for something of interest. When I met Degas again, I said: "What about your Lepic exhibition?"

"It's fine, isn't it? A great deal of talent," Degas replied. "It's too bad he's such a light weight!"

V.: I've heard Lautrec compared with Degas. . . .

R.: Ridiculous! Lautrec did some very fine posters, but that's about all. . . . Just compare their paintings of *cocottes* . . . why, they're worlds apart! Lautrec just painted a prostitute, while Degas painted all prostitutes rolled into one. Lautrec's prostitutes are vicious . . . Degas' never. Have you ever seen *The Patronne's Birthday*? It's superb!

When others paint a bawdy house, the result is usually pornographic—always sad to the point of despair. Degas is the only painter who can combine a certain joyousness and the rhythm of an Egyptian bas-relief in a subject of that kind. That chaste, half-religious side, which makes his work so great, is at its best when he paints those poor girls.

V.: One day I saw a *Woman in a Tub* by Degas in a window on the Avenue de l'Opéra. There was a man in front of it, tracing an imaginary drawing in the air with his thumb. He must have been a painter, for as I paused I heard him say to himself: "A woman's torso like that is as important as the Sermon on the Mount."

R.: He must have been a critic. A painter would never talk that way.

V.: Just then a carpenter came along. He also stopped in front of the nude and exclaimed: "My God! I wouldn't like to sleep with that wench!"

R.: The carpenter was right. Art is no joking matter.

V.: Did you ever have a chance to watch Degas make his etchings?

R.: I used to go to Cadard's, usually after dinner, and watch him pull his impressions—I don't dare say etchings—people laugh when you call them that. The specialists are always ready to tell you that they're full of tricks . . . that the man didn't know the first principles of *aqua-forte.* But they're beautiful, just the same.

V.: But I have always heard you say that an artist ought to know his craft from the ground up . . .

R.: Yes, but I don't mean that fly-speck technique they call modern engraving. Some of Rembrandt's finest etchings look as if they had been done with a stick of wood or the point of a nail. You can hardly say that Rembrandt didn't know his business! It was just because he knew it from start to finish that he was not obliged to use all those fancy tools which get between the artist's thought and his execution, and make a modern engraver's studio look like a dental parlour.

V.: What about Degas as a painter?

R.: I recently saw a drawing by Degas in a dealer's window—a simple charcoal outline, in a gold frame which would have killed anything else. But it held its own superbly. I've never seen a finer drawing.

V.: Degas as a colorist, I mean.

R.: Well, look at his pastels. Just to think that with a medium so very disagreeable to handle, he was able to obtain the freshness of a fresco! When he had that extraordinary exhibition of his in 1885 at Durand-Ruel's, I was right in the midst of my experiments with frescoes in oil. I was completely bowled over by that show.

V.: But what I'm trying to get at is what you think of Degas as a painter in oils. . . .

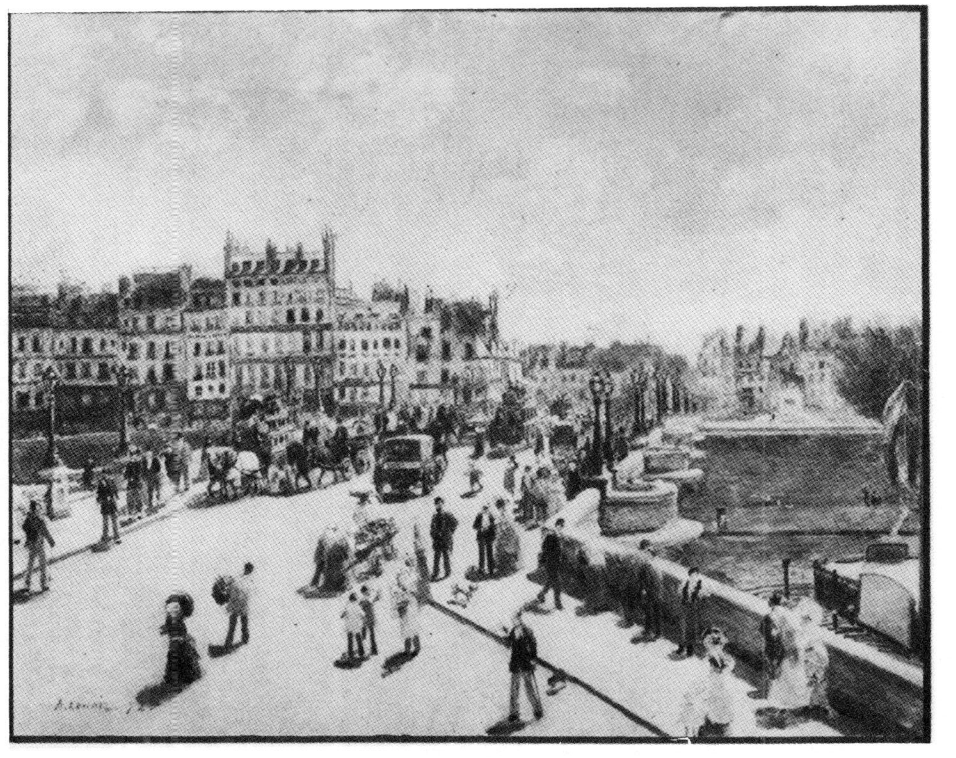

PONT NEUF, PARIS (1872)

See p. 33.

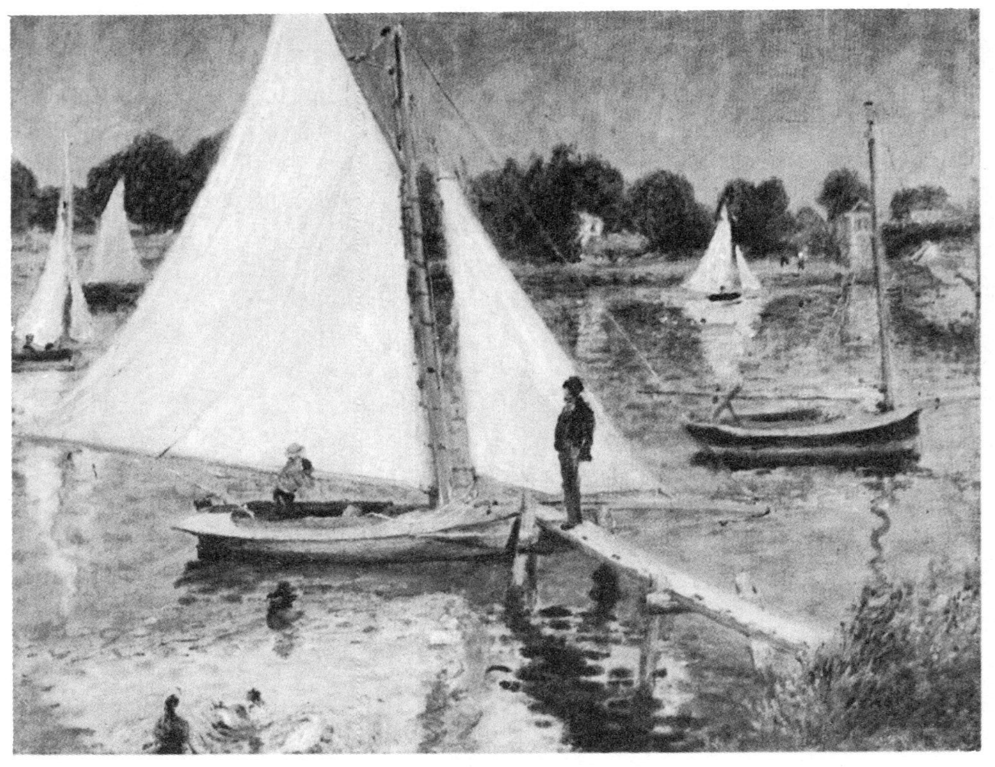

THE SEINE AT ARGENTEUIL (1873)

R. (interrupting): Look, Vollard.

(We had arrived at the Place de l'Opéra. He pointed to Carpeaux's group of the *Dance.*)

Why, it's in perfect condition! Who was it told me that that group was falling to pieces? I really haven't anything against Carpeaux, but I like everything to be in its place. It's all right to carry on about that kind of sculpture, since everybody likes it; I don't see any harm in that, but if they would only take those drunken women away and put them somewhere else . . . Dancing as taught at the opera is a tradition, it is something noble; it isn't the Can Can. . . . To think that we're living in an age that has produced a sculptor to equal the ancients! But there's no danger of *his* ever getting commissions. . . .

V.: Rodin has just had an order for the *Thinker.* And then there's his *Victor Hugo* and his *Gates of Hell* . . .

R. (impatiently): Who said anything about Rodin? Why, Degas is the greatest living sculptor! You should have seen a bas-relief of his . . . he just let it crumble to pieces . . . it was beautiful as an antique. And that ballet dancer in wax! . . . the mouth . . . just a suggestion, but what drawing!

What's the name of that old fool . . . that friend of Degas who does nudes that look as if they're moulded on a living model[2]—probably are, too. . . . I never can remember names! Well, never mind. He kept after Degas until he finished that mouth, and of course he spoiled it.

Have you seen his extraordinary bust of Zandomeneghi? Degas always pretended that it wasn't finished so he wouldn't have to show it. . . .

V.: I thought Degas had quarrelled with Zandomeneghi.

R.: They used to be intimate. But Degas offended him terribly one day. In asking him to come to pose, Degas remarked: "You have nothing to do, Zandomeneghi . . ." The Italian, on the contrary, felt that he had a good deal to do, and he replied haughtily: "That is no way to talk to a Venetian."

---

[2]Renoir was referring to Bartholomé.

Chapter Ten

THE SALON OF MADAME CHARPENTIER

Renoir: The salon of Madame Charpentier, the publisher's wife, was the rendezvous of all the celebrities that Paris had in the world of politics, letters, and art. The familiar figures of the house were such people as Daudet, Zola, Spuller, the two Coquelins, Flaubert, and Edmond de Goncourt. De Goncourt was cold, pretentious, and sour. The portrait of him by Bracquemond is very striking.

Vollard: I heard about Goncourt's quarrel with Zola from Guillemet. Goncourt suddenly stopped speaking to Zola, and even began talking about him behind his back. Zola was frightfully distressed, and had no idea what he had done to offend the Master. Charpentier, who was greatly upset because he could no longer get his two authors together at his house, tried to act as peacemaker. Goncourt was evasive. Charpentier therefore asked him bluntly: "Why don't you try to meet Zola half-way?"

At last a grand dinner of reconciliation took place; Goncourt was all the while very distant, so much so that, when the meal was over, Zola insisted on an explanation at any cost and dragged Goncourt into another room where they could be alone. Guillemet saw him emerge again looking very much perplexed.

"Well, what's up?"

And Zola told him that Goncourt had been absurd enough to accuse him of plagiarism in taking the title *Work* for his latest novel, after the brothers Goncourt had published their *Work of François Boucher!*

R.: I was going to tell you that I saw Cézanne also at Charpentier's. He had come with Zola, but the place was too "social" for Cézanne. Whenever painting was discussed there, I made a point of saying, like Chocquet: "and Cézanne?" I repeated it so often that Zola began to think that I was advertising talent from his native town just to please him. "You are very kind to say nice things about my old friend," he said. "But, between you and me, what's the good of trying to do anything for an obvious failure?"

When I protested, Zola replied: "Well, after all, you know painting isn't in my line."

At Madame Charpentier's I met Juliette Adam, Guy de Maupassant, and also that charming Madame Clapisson, of whom I did two portraits. Maupassant was then at the height of his fame, and his ever-increasing output filled Goncourt and even Zola with dismay. Their conversation always began something like this: "Ah, Maupassant! What a talented writer! But someone ought to warn him against the danger of producing too much."

I remember having seen Turgeniev at the Charpentiers', and many others whose names slip my mind. Then there was someone who always wore a red sash in order to attract attention. He was equally in evidence for his vehement assertions that museums are necessary for the education of the masses.

The masses in the museums! That's a good joke. One day I was sitting on a bench in the Louvre and I heard someone passing say: "Lord, what a face!"

I supposed they were talking about me, and I wondered what could be wrong. As I got up to go, other visitors came along, and I watched them self-consciously. They stopped right in front of the bench I had just left, and one of them exclaimed: "My God! Take a look at that mug, will you?"

It was the little *Infanta Margherita* of Velasquez!

V.: The man with the red sash you were speaking of makes me think of Barbey d'Aurevilly. . . .

R.: I met him once or twice. In spite of all the fancy costumes he affected, that man had a devilish charm. I remember that after seeing him for the first time I decided to get one of his books, but as soon as I saw that the illustrations were by that "Belgian Cabanel"—you know whom I mean, Félicien Rops—I could never get up courage enough to read the text.

To come back to Madame Charpentier: She did not stop at just inviting artists to her soirées; she got her husband to start a magazine for the defence of Impressionist art, called *La Vie Moderne.* We all collaborated. We were to be paid out of the earnings; in other words, none of us got a single *sou.* But the worst part about it was that they made us draw on a kind of paper which we had to scrape in order to produce the whites. I never could learn to use it properly. The editor-in-chief of *La Vie Moderne* was Bergerat. Later, when Charpentier deserted it, my young brother Edmond bought it out. But the paper was in its last throes and it was not long before it died completely.

V.: You were telling me a little while ago about Zola. What do you think of his books?

R.: I have always hated them. When you want to depict a certain *milieu,* you must, it seems to me, start by putting yourself in the shoes of your characters. Zola would glance out of the window and let it go at that. He imagined that he had described the common people once and for all when he said that they smelled bad. And as for the middle classes . . . He could have done a fine book, not only as a historic record of a unique art movement, but also as a "human document" (for that was the label under which he sold his goods), if he had only taken the trouble in *Work* to recount quite simply what he had seen and heard while he was with us in our studios; for in associating with us, he was really living the life of his characters! But at bottom Zola didn't give a rap about representing his friends as they were, or, at any rate, emphasizing their good qualities.

V.: Did you ever happen to meet Flaubert at Charpentier's?

R.: I remember him very well; he looked like a retired army officer turned insurance agent.

V.: What do you think of his writings?

R.: I've skimmed through *Madame Bovary.* I can't see anything in a story of an idiot whose wife doesn't know what she wants. After you have read those three hundred pages, you feel like saying to yourself: "Well, what of it?"

V.: Didn't you like the character of Homais, the apothecary?

Renoir shrugged.

V.: Guillemet told me how delighted certain friends of Flaubert's were when the famous author of *Salammbô,* in the latter years of his life, began to flout clericalism and rage about the influence of the Jesuits, taking over his druggist's whole political and philosophic baggage. . . .

R.: I think *Salammbô* is a very fine book——not so good, however, as Gautier's *Romance of the Mummy;* in my opinion, that is the most perfect thing of its kind ever written. I am aware of the fact that many people have criticized Gautier because he wrote easily and joyously, as if he were telling a story for the fun of it. I have heard the same thing said about myself many times. One would think the only way of giving pleasure was to be tedious. France has turned Protestant, I tell you! And I do believe the public is still afraid they won't get enough for their money. They insist on an artist sweating blood over a thing before they'll even look at it. What about those canvases Cézanne worked on a couple of hundred times? They look as if they'd been dashed off in a day!

V.: You have not spoken of Huysmans. Didn't he go to Madame Charpentier's too?

R.: I hardly ever saw Huysmans, even at the Nouvelle Athènes. He was a good fellow, but he was wrong in praising a picture for its subject rather than for its intrinsic merit. That is why he spoke of Degas, Rops, and Gustave Moreau all in the same breath. It's incredible that Gustave Moreau could have been taken seriously! Why, he couldn't even draw a foot! They talk so much about his scorn for the world——simple laziness, to my way of thinking. But he certainly knew what he was about when he conceived the idea of painting with gold colours to take in the Jews! He even fooled Ephrussi, who I thought had more sense than that. I went to Ephrussi's house one day and the first thing I laid my eyes on was a Gustave Moreau.

V.: Didn't you do a decoration for Madame Charpentier's salon?

R.: I have always enjoyed doing decorations, even those I painted on the walls of cafés when I was a youngster. Unfortunately there was not much space left at the Charpentiers', for the reception rooms were entirely decorated in Japanese style after the fashion of the day. Perhaps my horror of Japanese art comes from having seen so much of that kind of stuff.

During the World's Fair of 1889, my friend Burty took me to look at the Japanese prints. There were some very beautiful things, I must confess. But as I was leaving the room, I saw a Louis XIV arm-chair covered with a bit of the simplest tapestry imaginable; I could have hugged the thing!

As there were no walls to decorate, Madame Charpentier could only offer me two narrow panels on the staircase. I managed the job by doing two figures, a man and a woman, facing each other. When the work was finished, they asked for the judgment of the painter Henner, an old friend of the family. Taking me by both hands with that easy gentleness that Alsatians have, he said: "It's fery goot, *fery* goot; dere is only one vault. De man should always be browner dan de voman."

Madame Charpentier bore a certain resemblance to Marie Antoinette. Consequently there was never a fancy dress ball that she did not appear as the martyred queen, which made even her best friends sick with jealousy. Since she was rather *petite,* one of them observed, one day: "Poor Marie Antoinette has been beheaded at the other end this time!"

V.: Did you ever meet Gambetta at Charpentier's? There seems to be a great difference of opinion about him; he is either inordinately praised or violently criticized; apparently there is no happy medium.

R.: He was the simplest and most courteous man I have ever met. One day when he had been particularly nice to me, I got up courage enough to ask him to use his influence in getting me named as curator of some provincial museum or other, at two hundred francs a month. Spuller was present at the time—he thought I was really a bit too ambitious. But Gambetta was not so much surprised at my presumption as at the oddity of my request. He finally said: "My dear Renoir, you talk as if you had been born yesterday. Ask for a job as professor of Chinese or inspector of cemeteries—something at least that has nothing to do with your profession—and I will help you; but if we nominated a painter as curator of a museum, we would simply be laughed at."

But when Gambetta could do someone a service, he did it with the best grace in the world! During one of our exhibitions I had gone to *La République Française* to ask them to publish a little article in our behalf. I had to deal with Challemel-Lacour, who made short work of my request. "We can't do a thing for you," he said. "You Impressionists are nothing but a pack of rebels!"

On the way downstairs, however, I met Gambetta, who asked me what I was doing at the newspaper office. I told him my story, and he burst out laughing.

"Imagine Challemel-Lacour objecting to a rebel!"

So Gambetta had the article put in for us. He was the simplest and most straightforward of the whole crowd.

V.: But his head was turned later on, wasn't it?

R.: Perhaps, but don't forget that whenever he entered a salon he had to face a mob of people craning their necks to get a look at him. Such notoriety simply made him ill at ease, so he avoided the crowd and took refuge in the smoking-room, which was immediately invaded by the most fastidious women at the gathering. On those evenings, they declared that there was nothing they loved so much as the odour of cigars and pipes! You can imagine my astonishment, then, when one night I found Gambetta all alone in the smoking-room at the Charpentiers'. Not a female in sight. I then learned that on that very day he had given the Chamber of Deputies the dressing-down which proved to be a fatal set-back to his political career.

At the Charpentiers' I also met the musician Chabrier again, after an interval of several years. He is the man who owns my *After the Concert* (*La Sortie du Conservatoire*), which I painted in the garden in the Rue Cortot. We had been intimate for a long time. There's a musician for you! I remember an evening of music at my house in Montmartre, just after Chabrier had returned from Spain. After dinner he went to the piano and worked until midnight on the characteristic themes of his *España.* He played with his whole body; his hands and his feet worked together with the rhythm as he chanted *Ollé, Ollé!*

V.: When did you paint *Madame Charpentier and Her Children?*[1]

R.: In 1878. It was because of the personality of the sitter that they decided to admit this "revolutionary" work to the Salon of 1879. I sent the full-length portrait of Mademoiselle Samary to the same Salon. It is an absolute miracle that that canvas was ever preserved. The day before the opening, a friend came and told me that he had just been to the Salon, and that something queer seemed to have happened to my *Mademoiselle Samary.*

I dashed to the Salon and found the picture almost beyond recognition—it looked as if it were melting away. It seems that the framer instructed the delivery boy to varnish another picture that he was delivering at the same time. The boy had a little varnish left over and decided to give me the benefit of it. I didn't varnish mine because the paint was still wet, but he thought I was being economical! The result was I had to repaint the whole thing in an afternoon. You can imagine my state of mind!

V.: How much did you get for the portrait of Madame Charpentier?

R.: I believe it was about a thousand francs.

V.: A thousand francs! A huge canvas with three figures?

R.: That was an exceptional price at the time. Did you ever know a man named Poupin, a former employé at Durand-Ruel's, who bought up a business in *objets d'art,* and occasionally sold pictures on the side? I remember having seen one of my canvases, *The Page,* on the sidewalk in front of his shop. It was a life-size figure and it was marked in chalk "80 francs."

---

[1]In the Metropolitan Museum, New York.

V.: Did you ever paint Mademoiselle Samary in one of her rôles?

R.: No, I hardly ever saw her on the stage. I don't like the acting at the *Comédie Française.* One day I saw Ellen Andrée in a pantomime at the *Folies Bergère*—a tiny part, but how she played it! The next day I astonished Bérard by remarking that the State ought to subsidize the *Folies Bergère* instead of the *Comédie!*

V.: Then I don't need to ask you what you think of Hervieu's plays. . . .

Renoir made a vague gesture.

Franc-Lamy had entered the studio at this moment. "Were you talking about Hervieu?" he asked.

V.: Do you know him?

Franc-Lamy: I met him at tea at the château of the Duchess of X. There were a crowd of ladies around him raving about the living quality of his characters, the sincerity of art, etc.

"What is your secret, Master? How do you manage to know the human heart to its very depths?"

Hervieu replied: "My secret? I'll tell you. I rely on Nature." We were in the rose-garden of the château at the time; it was a wonderful sight, Renoir; thousands of rose-bushes in bloom. "Roses are my passion," the Duchess said to Hervieu. "Ah, you who love Nature so much . . ."

Some days afterwards the Duchess with her hundred thousand roses received a box by express from the lover of Nature. It was a sheaf of hot-house roses, forced in a florist's laboratory, all wrapped up in gold paper and mounted on wire stems!

V. (to Renoir): I have never heard you mention Sarah Bernhardt.

R.: What I like in an actress—and it's rare enough, Lord knows—is feminine charm.[2] Jeanne Granier had it to the *n*th degree. You should have seen her in *Barbe-Bleue!* I should love to have painted her.

[2]Renoir had seen Sarah Bernhardt in *Camille,* and as he detested the play, he always disliked the actress on account of it. (Author's Note.)

Chapter Eleven

EARLY TRAVELS

Renoir: After the Salon of 1879, I took a six weeks' trip to Algeria with Lestringuèz. There I painted the *Banana-Trees, Garden at Essai, Arab Mounted on a Camel,* and *Arabs and Donkeys. . . .* The *Arab Mounted* gave me the most trouble on account of the crowds that collected about me. But for curiosity the Arab is nothing compared to Frenchmen in general and the Parisian in particular.

That reminds me of the time I was painting in a field near Beaulieu. I was surrounded by a whole family which had just got off the train from Paris. I never realized before how ignorant city people are about the country! While the mother and children were hanging on my neck giving me advice, the father, who had walked off a little way to tend to Nature's needs, began shouting back at them excitedly:

"Hey, come over here; I've just found a field of wild artichokes!" *Wild* artichokes!

The layman seems to have an insatiable curiosity about an artist at work. Animals too, for that matter. One day when I was working in the Forest of Fontainebleau, I heard a whistling noise behind me. I turned and saw a couple of deer craning their necks to watch me paint.

Upon returning from Algeria, I took a studio in the Rue de Norvins (1880). From there I moved to the Rue Houdon. The following summer found me in Guernsey, where I did several beach pictures. It is a charming place, with such patriarchal customs! . . . at least, they were patriarchal then. The English left their Anglo-Saxon prudery behind them on their vacations. Bathing suits were unheard of, and the little English misses, so proper at home, thought nothing of bathing side by side with a naked boy. I did my *Nude Bathers* that summer.

My wife and I occupied the first floor, and our friend Lauth the third, of a house in which the second and fourth had been rented by a Protestant minister from London. One day when I was passing the second-floor rooms, what should I see through the wide-open doors but the whole family of the pastor, including Mary, the maid, standing in Indian file, naked as the day they were born! They had just come in from swimming, and in order to get warm everyone was spanking the bottom of the person in front and singing:

"He runs, he runs, the ferret . . ."

They used to go naked up and down the stairways, from the second to the fourth floor. Lauth, who was near-sighted as a mole, one day saw a bare bottom directly in front of him on the staircase. He gave it a resounding thwack, and shouted in high good humour: "Hey there, Mary!"

It was the pastor himself! How we laughed!

Not long after returning to Paris, I decided to visit Italy. I went first to Venice, where I painted several *Nudes,* a sketch of the Grand Canal, a *Gondola,* the *Doges' Palace,* the *Piazza San Marco.*

My greatest surprise at Venice was the discovery of Carpaccio, with his fresh and gay colours. He was one of the first who dared to paint people actually walking in a street. I remember especially a dragon in one of his pictures which looks as if it were a merry-go-round beast on a leash—one of those dragons you expect any moment to offer you his paw. And his *Saint George* is baptizing the Gentiles in the midst of a gay crowd playing huge drums and trombones! Carpaccio must have got his models at the fairs! One of his landscapes also interested me immensely, for it was neither more nor less than a view of Provence.

I really enjoyed Venice. How superb the Doges' Palace is! That white and rose marble may have been rather cold when it was first built, but it was enchanting to me, made golden as it was by several centuries of sunlight!

And then Saint Mark's. It was a welcome change from those cold Italian churches of the Renaissance, especially that cathedral at Milan which the Italians are so proud of, with its roof made of marble lace. Lord, what stupidity! As soon as you have entered Saint Mark's, you feel that you are in a real temple; there is a soft and mysterious air about it, and the mosaics are magnificent—especially the Byzantine Christ with the hollow eyes. It is impossible to imagine how beautiful it is if you haven't been there and seen its heavy pillars and twisted columns.

The cold finally drove me from Venice, and I went on to Florence. I don't know when I've been so annoyed by a place. It is such a mournful city, with its black and white buildings. I felt as if I were walking about among chequer-boards! So I did nothing at Florence, or at Rome either, for that matter, but visit museums. I liked immensely Raphael's *Heliodorus Driven from the Temple* in the Vatican. It is full of innocent little flames that can hardly be said to set you on fire, but are satisfying none the less. In the midst of the endless variety of masterpieces both at Florence and Rome, I must confess that my greatest joy was Raphael. Especially at Florence. . . . I can't begin to tell you how I felt when I first saw the *Virgin of the Chair!* I expected to have a good laugh; but I found the freest, the most solid, the most marvelously simple and living kind of painting that it is possible to imagine. The arms and legs were of real flesh! And what a touching expression of maternal tenderness! When I came back to Paris, I spoke to Huysmans about the *Virgin of the Chair.* He exclaimed:

"Well, well! Another victim of Raphael's *bromure!*"

There was a painter, Gervex I think it was, who would say, whenever I spoke of my admiration for Raphael:

"What! Are you going in for *pompier* art?"

The frescoes of the Farnesina delighted me, too. You know how fresco-painting has always interested me. I had read somewhere that these were the first experiments in oil frescoes. No matter how they were painted, they're the most exquisite pictures in the world.

V.: Did Michael Angelo come up to your expectations?

R.: I prefer Donatello. His people are more varied than Michael Angelo's. In spite of his genius, Angelo's figures are all alike. His muscles are always too much the same; he studied anatomy too much, and, for fear he would forget the least little muscle, he put in so many that the poor things would never have been able to get about.

From Rome I went on to Naples. It was restful to find so much of the art of Pompeii and the Egyptians. I had begun to tire a little of Italian painting—for ever the same draperies and the same Virgins. The priestesses in their silver-grey tunics looked just like the nymphs of Corot. What I like so much about Corot is that he gives you everything in a mere sketch of a tree. And it was Corot himself that I found again, body and soul, in the Naples Museum, in the simplicity of workmanship that was characteristic of Pompeii and the Egyptians.

One picture in Naples which impressed me very much was the portrait of *Pope Julius III* by Titian. You should see the head of the Pope—with his white beard and his terrible mouth!

During my stay in Naples, I painted a large canvas, a *Woman with a Child on Her Knees;* also some views of the city, among them a *Quai with Vesuvius in the Distance;* and a *Woman's Torso,* which I sold to Vever; there is also a replica of it which I did at Paris for Gallimard.

V.: What about the portrait of Wagner?

R.: When I was at Naples, I received several letters from Wagner enthusiasts, among them Lascoux, the *juge d'instruction,* who was one of my best friends. He urged me to make every effort to bring back at least a sketch of Wagner. I decided to go to Palermo, where the composer was staying at the time. The very first day I went to his hotel, I ran right into a young painter named Jonkofsky, one of the most amiable souls in the world, who followed Wagner wherever he went, trying to do his portrait. In the meantime, he was painting the small models for Wagner's stage sets. Jonkofsky informed me that, for the time being, Wagner was busy completing the orchestration of his *Parsifal,* and was seeing nobody. But he agreed to let me know when the work was finished. When I got word that he was ready to present me to Wagner, I found that I had lost the letters of introduction sent to me by friends in Paris. But I took the chance and presented myself with empty hands—except for my paint box.

"I have only half an hour to give you," were his first words. He thought he would get rid of me that way; but I took him at his word. While I was working, I did my best to keep him interested, talking of Paris. He made no attempt to conceal that he hoped for much from the French, and when I told him that the aristocracy of French intellects was with him, he was very flattered.

"I have always wanted to please the French," he said, "but I always thought they liked nothing but German Jew music." (A reference to Meyerbeer.)

After posing twenty-five minutes, Wagner got up abruptly.

"Enough! I'm tired!" he exclaimed.

But I had had time enough to finish my study. I later sold it to Robert de Bonnières, and made a replica of it, which figured in the Chéramy sale. The Palermo portrait was done in 1881, the year before Wagner's death.

V.: Was that the only time you ever met Wagner?

R.: Yes. Of course I hardly knew Wagner at all personally, but I have been able to count as very good friends some of the first pilgrims to Bayreuth, such as Lascoux, Chabrier, and Maître, whom I have spoken to you about.

V.: And Saint-Saëns?

R.: I never knew him. They say that at one time there was no more ardent Wagnerian than he.

V.: So I have heard. Maître told Wyzewa an amusing story about Saint-Saëns. He and Maître were seated in a café in Bayreuth in 1876. In the course of the conversation, Maître was indiscreet enough to insinuate that the Tetralogy contained, perhaps, some rather long passages. . . . On hearing this harmless criticism, Saint-Saëns smashed his glass on the table and left the room in a rage.

R.: At all events, Saint-Saëns seems to be vigorously condemning his former idol at the present moment. Someone read me an article about it in a Nice paper.

V.: One day I met the director of some musical review at Wyzewa's house, Monsieur Ecorcheville I think it was, who had heard the story of the disagreement that arose between Wagner and Saint-Saëns, from a friend of the latter.

This time the scene was Wagner's home in Bayreuth, the doors of which had been opened to him by his fanaticism for the German master. One evening Frau Wagner asked the French disciple to play something by her husband on the piano in the drawing-room. Instead, Saint-Saëns launched into his own *Funeral March* written in honour of Henri Regnault. Whereupon Wagner, with friendly malice—or perhaps it was just ingenuousness—cried out: "Ah! a Parisian waltz!" And he seized one of the ladies by the waist and began to whirl around the room!

"But how about yourself, Monsieur Renoir? Are you a Wagner enthusiast too?" I asked.

R.: I used to like Wagner very much. I was quite carried away by the kind of passionate fluidity that there seemed to be in his music; but a friend took me once to Bayreuth, and I need hardly tell you that I was frightfully bored. The screams of the Walkyries are all right for a short time, but when they last six hours on end, you go mad. I'll never forget the scandal that I created when, in an excess of boredom, I lighted a match in the theatre while the performance was still going on.

I decidedly prefer Italian music; it is less pedantic than the German. Even Beethoven has sometimes a professorial side that makes my flesh creep. But there is nothing that can touch a little air by Couperin or Grétry—any of the old French music, in fact. There's fine "drawing" for you!

I couldn't stand it very long at Bayreuth. I'd had my fill after three days, and I felt the need of a change to compensate for it. So one fine morning I took the train for Dresden. I had been wanting for quite a while to see the big Vermeer called *The Courtesan.* In spite of the title, the lady looks like the most respectable of creatures. She is surrounded by a group of people. One young man has his hand on her breast, so that you will be sure to know that she is a courtesan. The hand, full of colour and youth, in sharp contrast to the citron-yellow corsage, is very beautiful.

There is another Vermeer at Vienna, which has an enormous reputation, *The Painter in His Studio.* I would love to have seen that! . . . All my life I have dreamed of going there . . . like Athens. . . . But to return to Dresden: There is also a Watteau with a marvellous landscape in the museum. . . . As to architecture, Dresden is rather weak, aside from the Catholic church and the Museum, two buildings of a charming kind of rococo.

V.: I suppose you are not a great devotee of the Opera, if you have so little patience with long pieces of music.

R.: You would hardly call me an habitué. I have only put my foot in the place two or three times in my life, and then I was always dragged there by friends. Just recently Mrs. Edwards took me there to see the Russian Ballet. It's not bad. The Opera ought to get some new women, though. You see the same ones they had there thirty years ago.

Coming back from Italy, I went to the Midi. I looked up Cézanne and proposed that we should go to Estaque together to paint.

"Oh, don't go there!" cried Cézanne, who had just come back. "Estaque is done for! They've put up parapets. I can't bear it!"

I went just the same, a little saddened by the thought of how they must have spoiled it; but I was encouraged when I found the same old Estaque, and if Cézanne had not told me, I would never have noticed any change. His parapets were just a few stones one on top of another.

It was on this trip that I brought back a magnificent water-colour of *Bathers* by Cézanne, the one you see there on the wall. The day I found it, I was with my friend Lauth. He had been suddenly taken with a violent diarrhœa.

"Do you see any good leaves around? No, I don't want pine-needles."

"No, but here's some paper," I replied, picking up a stray piece at my feet. It was one of the finest of Cézanne's water-colours; he had thrown it away among the rocks after having slaved over it for twenty sittings.

Nothing is so treacherous as the climate of the Midi. I caught the inevitable cold in my chest at Estaque, which decided me to make a second trip to Algeria. There I made a life-size portrait of a young girl named Mademoiselle Fleury, dressed in Algerian costume, in an Arab house, holding a bird. I also painted the canvas called *Algerian Women,* a little *Arab Porter—Biskra,* some studies of Mosques, and a *Fantasy.* When I delivered this last canvas to Durand-Ruel, it looked like a pile of palette scrapings. But Durand-Ruel had confidence in it, and several years afterwards, the colour having worked sufficiently, the picture came out on the canvas in just the way I had conceived it.

There you have my principal travels while my legs were still good, and when travelling meant lodging in real native taverns, and spending whole days tramping in the country. . . .

Later I visited other countries, among them Spain, Holland, and Germany. I recently went to Munich again, but this time I had to be carried to the museums.

Ah! if I had only met Doctor Gautiez[1] before I was completely done up! Have you heard about that woman who couldn't take a step without twisting her ankle? He cured her simply by showing her how to put her foot down on the ground properly. I told a famous physician about it once, but he interrupted me with: "Yes, but Gautiez cures without operating. That's only empiricism!"

---

[1]Doctor Henri Gautiez. Bernheim-Jeune had brought him one day to the studio. Renoir had already been confined to his wheel-chair for several years. Doctor Gautiez succeeded in getting him to take several steps unaided. He said that if Renoir would exercise every day, and give his best efforts to it . . .

"But my painting!" cried the artist.

And he sat down, never to leave his wheel-chair again.

Chapter Twelve

THE IMPRESSIONIST THEORIES

I HAD been wanting for a long time to know what Renoir thought of the theories of Impressionism; but I was positive that if I were to ask him bluntly, he would reply at once: "Oh, don't bother me!" Therefore I set about reading what the critics of modern art had written on the subject, and, taking note of the statements which had struck me as the most significant, I said one day:

"The modern painters are very fortunate to have colours that the ancient never even dreamed of!"

Renoir: Fortunate ancients, you mean; they had only the ochres and browns. What a pretty spectacle progress is anyway!

Vollard: At least you cannot deny that the Impressionists have made real progress by discarding "flat tones, which destroy transparency."

R.: Who told you that flat tones destroy transparency? That sounds like Père Tanguy.[1] He thought that you had to paint "thick" to be modern.

At first I was tempted to reply that I had got it from a book of advanced modern criticism;[2] but I thought it would be more prudent not to mention it. However, I continued: "Then the only innovation of Impressionism, so far as technique is concerned, is the elimination of black, the non-colour?"[3]

R. (startled): Black a non-colour? Where on earth did you get that? Why, black is the queen of colours! Wait. Look in that *Lives of the Painters.* Find Tintoretto. Here, give me the book!

(He read.) "When Tintoretto was asked what his favourite colour was, he replied: 'The most beautiful of all colours is black.' "

V.: How is that, when you have substituted Prussian blue for black?[4]

R.: Who told you so? I have always had a horror of Prussian blue. Once I

---

[1]For further information about Père Tanguy, see *Paul Cézanne, His Life and Art,* by Ambroise Vollard, translated by Harold L. Van Doren. (Nicholas L. Brown, New York, 1923. Reprinted by Dover as *Cézanne.*)

[2]Georges Lecomte, *Impressionist Art,* Chamerot and Renouard, Paris, 1892, page 22.

[3]*Ibid.*, page 16.

[4]Camille Mauclair, *Impressionism* (*Librairie de l'Art Ancien et Moderne*), Paris, 1904, page 117.

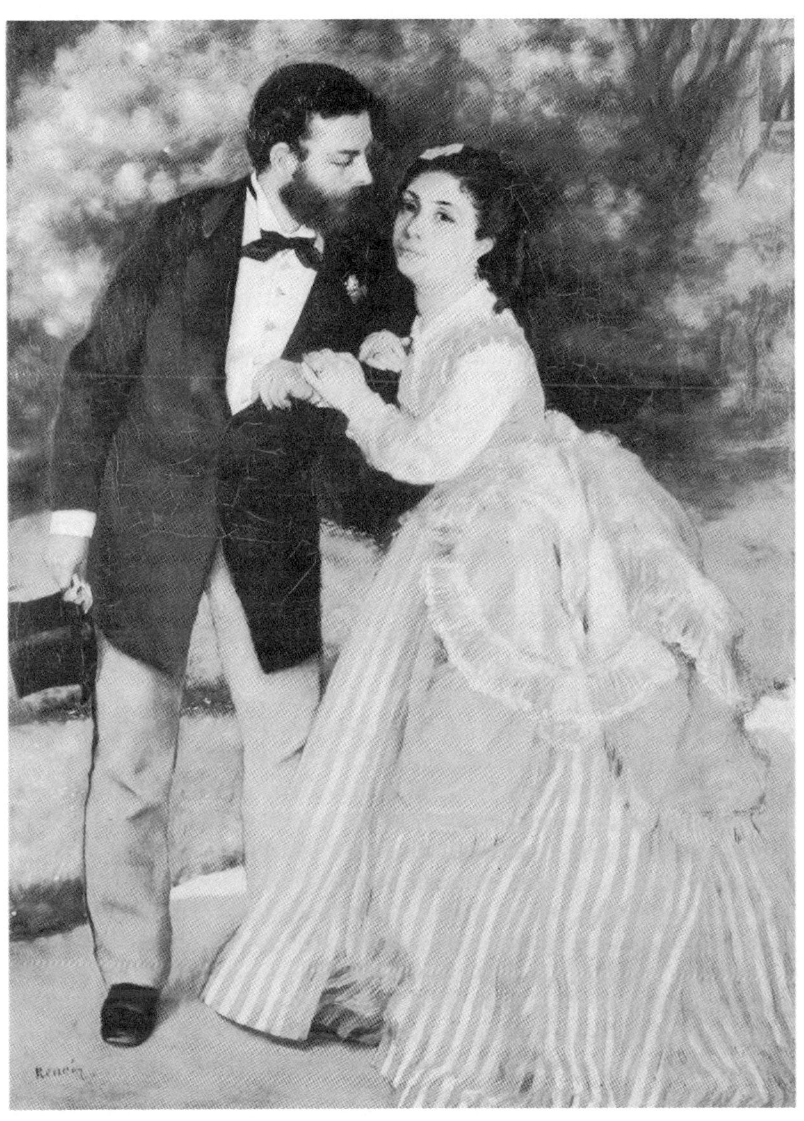

THE SISLEY FAMILY (1868)

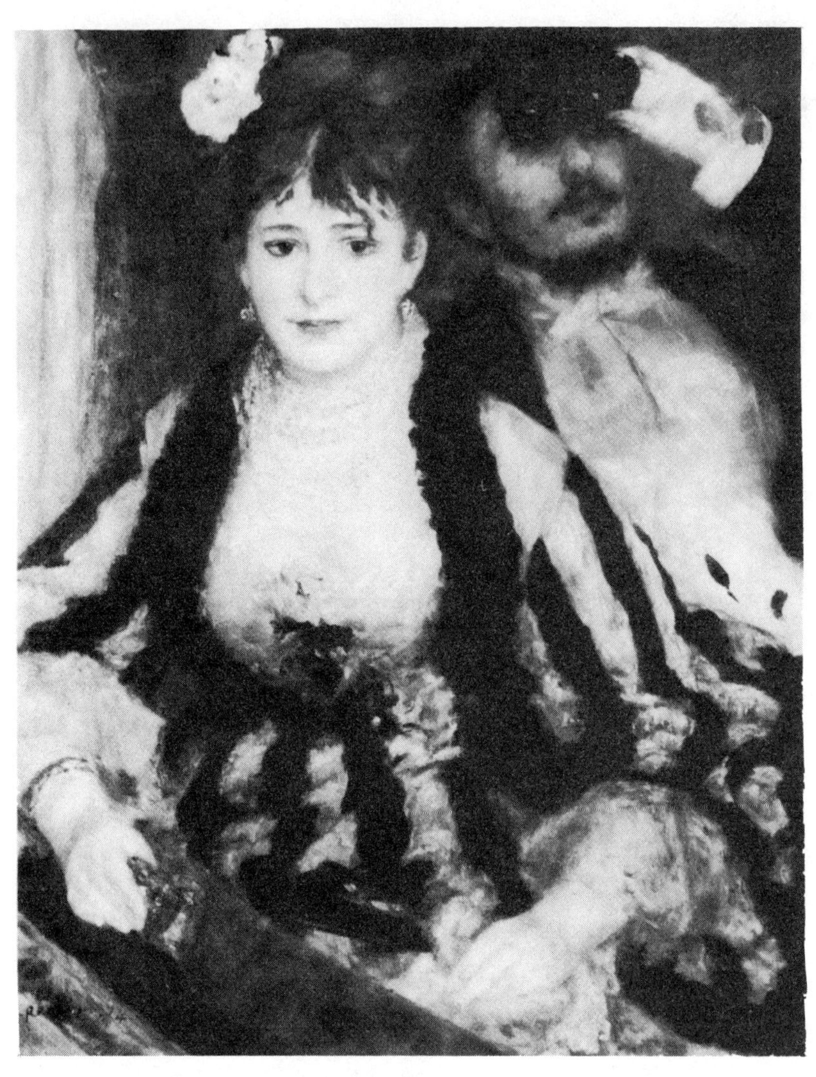

LA LOGE (1874)

See p. 28.

tried to use a mixture of red and blue instead of black, but then I used cobalt-blue or ultramarine, only to come back in the end to ivory-black.

(I was decidedly not having any luck with my quotations. I began to think that my authorities, not being painters, might be ignorant of questions of technique, but I supposed that their professional standing as critics would at least guarantee their competence on other points: the influence of one artist upon another, for example. So I led the conversation by degrees to Monet, and I asked Renoir if Watteau, in his *Embarkation for Cythera,* had not anticipated Monet's manner even as early as the eighteenth century with his "division of tonalities by touches of juxtaposed colour, combining at a distance in the eye of the spectator to give the effect of the local colour of the objects painted."[5])

R.: No more of that, I beg of you! I remember having heard something like that before. Have you never even looked at the *Embarkation for Cythera?* You can take a magnifying-glass to it and you will find nothing but mixed tones.

V.: Then Turner, in his "luminous" period, was the only one before Monet who used prismatic colours.

R.: Turner? Do you call that luminous?—just like bon-bon colours. . . . It would be exactly the same thing if he painted with his morning chocolate!

V.: But Claude Monet and Pissarro were Turner's disciples, were they not?

R.: Pissarro tried a little of everything, even *petit point,* but he gave it up like the others. As for Monet, someone told me that on returning from one of his trips to London, he said: "Turner makes me sick!" The only man who influenced Monet was Jongkind. He was Monet's point of departure.

I can give you a personal example of influences in painting. At the beginning, I used to put paint on thick, thinking I would get more "value" that way. One day, at the Louvre, I noticed that Rubens had obtained more by a simple rubbing than I did with all my heavy layers. Another time, I discovered that Rubens produced a silver with black. I learned my lesson, of course; but does that necessarily mean that I was influenced by Rubens?

(I began to ask myself if all the things which had impressed me so much were not simply "literature." I made one last try:)

At any rate, the Impressionists excel in "painting by chance sensations and by the powerful clairvoyance of instinct. . . ."[6]

R. (interrupting): "Chance sensations"! "Power of the instincts"! Like the animals, eh? That sounds like the fools who congratulate us on giving our models "expressive poses."[7] Those good people do not realize that Cézanne called his compositions souvenirs of the museums; for my part, I

---

[5]*Ibid.,* page 16. See also Georges Lecomte, *Impressionist Art,* page 23.

[6]Georges Lecomte, *Impressionist Art,* page 22.

[7]See Appendix I, A.

have always tried to paint human beings just as I would beautiful fruit. Look at the greatest of modern painters, Corot, and see if his women are "thinkers." But if you try to tell those people that the most important thing for a painter is to know good colours, just as the mason ought to know the best mortar——[8] And the first Impressionists worked away without ever even thinking of a sale! It is the only thing our imitators have forgotten to copy.

(I saw a little book on the table with the pages still uncut, called *The Laws of Impressionism, a Selection from the Masters of Criticism.*)

R.: Always this mania for imposing a lot of rigid formulæ and processes on the painter! To conform with the rules, we would all have to have the same palette—socialism in art, eh? Painting in twenty-five lessons!

(I had started to turn the pages of *The Laws of Impressionism,* and I read aloud: "Manet died before he was able to take advantage of the luminosity derived from the division of tones."[9])

R.: He was lucky to have died in time.

V. (continuing to read): "The majority [of Impressionists], especially gifted artists, would certainly have left glorious works, even if they had kept to traditional methods."[10]

R. (silencing me with a motion of his hand): But it was just when I was able to get rid of the Impressionist theories, and came back to the teaching of the museums. . . . (He gave a slight shrug.)

V.: So even the best of the Impressionist "theories" is simply literature "putting the hooks into painting," as Cézanne would have said. But you cannot deny that certain painters profited by Chevreul's work on the spectrum. Now when the Neo-Impressionists applied their scientific discoveries . . .

R.: Their what?

V.: You know what I mean, pure tones juxtaposed. . . .

R.: Ah, yes, *petit point.* Octave Mirbeau took me one day to see an exhibition of that. But the worst of it was that, on entering, you were informed that to be able to tell what the pictures represented, you must stand two and a half yards away from them. You know how I love to walk close to a picture, and even take it in my hands! You remember the large picture by Seurat, *Models in a Studio,* that we saw together—a canvas painted in *petit point,* the last word in science! Lord! that picture was ugly in tone! Do you remember the chap beside me who said: "What difference does it make how the picture turned out, so long as the artist enjoyed doing it?"

Can you imagine Veronese's *Last Supper* painted in *petit point?*

But when Seurat paints without tricks! . . . you know those little

[8]Monsieur Mauclair does not approve of the tendency of the Impressionists "to insist on a painter's being, above all, a good craftsman."

[9]Georges Lecomte, *Impressionist Art,* page 27.

[10]*Ibid.,* page 24.

canvases of his, unpretentious, no "pure tones"; how beautifully they are preserved.

The truth is that in painting, as in the other arts, there's not a single process, no matter how insignificant, which can reasonably be made into a formula. For instance, I tried long ago to measure out, once and for all, the amount of oil which I put in my colour. I simply could not do it. I have to judge the amount necessary with each dip of the brush. The "scientific" artists thought they had discovered a truth once they had learned that the juxtaposition of yellow and blue gives violet shadows. But even when you know that, you still don't know anything. There is something in painting which cannot be explained, and that something is the essential. You come to Nature with your theories, and she knocks them all flat.

The door bell rang.

"Is Monsieur Renoir at home?"

I got up to go.

R.: You can stay; I recognize the voice. It is Z. You know, he is the only one at the Beaux Arts who likes what we are doing, except, of course, Roger Marx.

(I congratulated Monsieur Z. on the courage with which he was battling for modern art, risking, at every turn, his excellent position of chief Under-Inspector at the Ministry.)

Z.: Behold a man who has not wasted his day! By going over the head of my minister, I have just succeeded in obtaining from the Ministry of Commerce the formal promise of a *rosette* for Ernest Laurent. His "open air indoors" is doing more than anything else to popularize Impressionist art.

(When he had left the studio, I echoed: "Open air indoors"!)

R.: The popularization of art, indeed! That's enough to make you give it all up! Fortunately there is no stupidity in the world that can make a painter stop painting.

CHAPTER THIRTEEN

RENOIR'S DRY MANNER

RENOIR: I was going to tell you last time, when Z. called, about a sort of break that came in my work about 1883. I had wrung Impressionism dry, and I finally came to the conclusion that I knew neither how to paint nor draw. In a word, Impressionism was a blind alley, as far as I was concerned.

Vollard: But what about all the effects of light that you rendered so well?

R.: I finally realized that it was too complicated an affair, a kind of painting that made you constantly compromise with yourself. Out of doors there is a greater variety of light than in the studio, where, to all intents and purposes, it is constant; but, for just that reason, light plays too great a part outdoors; you have no time to work out the composition; you can't see what you are doing. I remember a white wall which reflected on my canvas one day while I was painting; I keyed down the colour to no purpose—everything I put on was too light; but when I took it back to the studio, the picture looked black.

Another time I was painting in Brittany, in a grove of chestnut-trees. It was autumn. Everything I put on the canvas, even the blacks and the blues, was magnificent. But it was the golden luminosity of the trees that was making the picture; once in the studio, with a normal light, it was a frightful mess.

If the painter works directly from Nature, he ultimately looks for nothing but momentary effects; he does not try to compose, and soon he gets monotonous. I once asked a friend, who was exhibiting a series of *Village Streets,* why they were all deserted.

"Because," he replied, "the streets were empty while I was at work."

V.: Corot painted all his life in the open, didn't he?

R.: His studies, yes, but his compositions were done in the studio. He *corrected* Nature. Everybody used to say that he was wrong to work his sketches over indoors. I had the good fortune to meet Corot once and I told him of the difficulty I had in working out of doors. He replied: "That's because you can never be sure of what you're doing. You must always paint over again in the studio." But that did not prevent Corot from interpreting Nature with a realism that no Impressionist painter has ever been able to equal! How I have slaved to paint the colours of the stones of Chartres cathedral and the red bricks of the houses at La Rochelle as he did!

V.: Weren't the Old Masters working for these same effects of light? Duranty, I think, says that the Venetians foreshadowed them.

R.: "Foreshadowed" is good! Just look at the Titians in the Prado. You don't even have to go back as far as Titian——take Ribera, a painter who has the reputation of being the last word in black. Do you remember the rose colour of the child and the yellow of the straw in his *Infant Jesus* in the Louvre? Have you ever seen anything more luminous than that?

V.: Allow me one last question. I read somewhere that "when we study the pictures in the museums—even those which exhibit the utmost science in the disposition of the planes, the use of perspective, the forms of clouds, the drawing of objects, the play of light, we observe one convention, or, rather, a lack of knowledge. In Ruysdael, and especially in Hobbema, the stippled, metallic foliage is the colour of ink. It is as if the sun had been blotted out."

R.: Yes, but long before Ruysdael there were painters who filled their pictures with sunlight. Your author chooses his examples badly. In Italy, which is a warm country, Nature is more prodigal than in Holland. In the *Marriage at Cana* and the nudes of Titian, there is finer light than in any modern canvas.

V.: What about their landscapes?

R.: Look at the *Villa d'Este* of Velasquez, or the *Concert Champêtre* of Giorgione, to mention only two. Even Rembrandt——would it ever occur to you to wonder whether his pictures were painted out of doors or in the studio?

I'm sick and tired of the so-called "discoveries" of Impressionism. It isn't likely that the Old Masters were ignorant of them; and, if they did not use them, it was because all great artists have despised mere effects. By making Nature simpler, they made it more impressive. For instance, if the magnificence of a sunset were permanent, it would wear you out, whereas the same scene, without that special effect of light, is not at all fatiguing. With the ancient sculptors, action is reduced to a minimum. Yet you instinctively feel that their statues could move if they wanted to. When you look at Mercié's David, you almost want to help him put his sabre in its sheath!

I was looking at a nude on the easel, which had just been begun.

"From the way you talk, Monsieur Renoir, one would think that ivory-black is the only colour that counts, but how do you expect me to believe that you painted flesh like that with 'mud'?"

R.: I don't mean to compare myself with Delacroix, but do you remember that phrase of his, "Give me some mud, and I will paint you a woman's flesh"?

V.: But by that he meant it to be understood that the complementaries should be added, did he not? At least so the critics say.

R.: Please don't ascribe things to Delacroix that he never even thought of! If he spoke of complementaries, it was probably when he was making experiments for a ceiling which had to be looked at from a distance. In that case, perhaps, you might reasonably speak of colours mixing in the eye of the beholder. The only thing I remember from the Journal of Delacroix, is that he is forever talking about red-brown. At the very mention of passing for an innovator, Delacroix would have . . . why, when he was painting the ceiling of the Chamber of Deputies, an employé of the library tried to compliment him by saying:

"Master, you are the Victor Hugo of painting."

And Delacroix returned dryly:

"You don't know what you're talking about, my dear friend! I am a classicist, pure and simple."

V.: Did you know that his distrust of innovations in art also extended to music? Guillemet asked Corot one day what he thought of Delacroix. Corot replied:

"A great artist! He's the greatest of them all! But there is one thing we have never been able to agree upon, and that is music! He doesn't like Berlioz—revolutionary music he calls it—and I feel very sorry for him."

R.: I have told you how I discovered, about 1883, that the only thing worth while for a painter is to study the museums? I made this discovery on reading a little book that Franc-Lamy picked up along the quays; it was a treatise on painting by Cennino-Cennini, and gave some precious information on the methods of the fifteenth-century painters.

The public is always convinced you are a fool if you abandon one style to which it is accustomed and adopt another; even my best friends complained of these new leaden colours of mine "after such pretty tones!"

I had undertaken a large picture of *Bathers* and slaved away at it for three years. (The portrait of Mademoiselle Manet with a cat in her arms is also of this period.) The best that people could find to say about it was that it was a muddle of colour!

On the other hand, I must admit that some of my paintings of this period are not very soundly painted, because, after having studied fresco, I had fancied I could eliminate the oil from the colour. The surface then became too dry, and the successive layers of paint did not adhere well. I did not know at that time the elementary truth that oil-painting must be done with oil. Of course none of those people who established the rules of the "new" painting ever thought of giving us this precious hint! Another reason that induced me to dry the oil out of my colour was my search for a means of preventing the paint from blackening; but I later discovered that oil is the very thing which keeps colour from becoming black; only, one must know how to handle the oil.

At this time I also did some paintings on cement, but I was never able to learn from the ancients the secret of their inimitable frescoes. I remember also certain canvases in which I had drawn all the smallest details with a pen before painting. I was trying to be so precise, on account of my distaste for Impressionism, that these pictures were extraordinarily dry.

After three years of experimentation, the *Bathers,* which I considered as my master work, was finished. I sent it to an exhibition at the Georges Petit Galleries (1886). I got roundly trounced for it, I can tell you. This time, everybody, Huysmans in the lead, agreed that I was a lost soul; some even said I was lazy. And God knows how I had laboured over it!

Apropos of the Exhibition at Georges Petit's, I might mention an article by Wyzewa, who was then the book-reviewer on the *Independent Review.* He wrote an article about my exhibition which was very comforting. I met Wyzewa shortly after, and through his good offices Robert de Bonnières later gave me a commission for a portrait of his wife. I can't remember ever having painted a picture which gave me more trouble! You know how I hate to paint skin that does not take the light! What was worse, it was the fashion then for women to be pale. And Madame de Bonnières, of course, was as pale as wax. I used to say to myself: "If I could only get her to swallow a good beefsteak, just once!" No such luck! I worked at her home every morning until lunch-time, so I had a chance to see what they brought her to eat; a miserable little morsel in the centre of the plate. . . . Can you imagine *that* giving her any colour? And such hands! She put them in cold water before each sitting, in order to increase their whiteness. If it hadn't been for Wyzewa, who spent most of the time cheering me on, I'd have thrown it all out of the window, brushes, colour-box, canvas—the whole infernal business! Fancy my getting one of the most charming women in the world to paint and—well, she simply refuses to have colour in her cheeks!

But when I say that I have never done a portrait which annoyed me more, I am forgetting Madame Chartier, a beautiful young woman whose husband kept a little inn near Paris.

V.: I suppose her hands were used to house-work, anyway.

R.: Yes, but there were other things that were not so pleasant. She was not what you expect an innkeeper's wife to be, the placid and docile kind of woman I like to paint. On the contrary, she was fidgety and impatient. One day, more exasperated than usual, I shouted at her: "For God's sake, what's going on behind that face of yours!"

"Oh, *là là,* Monsieur, you're a nice one! I was just thinking that while I've been sitting here doing nothing, the stew has probably burned to a crisp!"

Chapter Fourteen

THE TRIP TO SPAIN

RENOIR: After having finished the portrait of Madame de Bonnières, I went to Spain with Gallimard. I had wanted to see the Prado in Madrid for a long time. But what a country Spain is! I didn't see a single pretty woman the whole month I was there. And there's a total lack of any vegetation. But at least Spain hasn't become a republic like France, and doesn't have to put up with that delightful régime which has abolished the right of inheritance by the eldest son, and obliges a man to divide the smallest bit of land among all his surviving children. Before long we won't have a single tree left in the fields, or a fish in the rivers, or a bird in the air.

Vollard: Did you see any of the famous Spanish dances?

R.: I saw some in Seville. But in general they were no longer considered fashionable, so I had to go out into the toughest parts of the suburbs to find out what they were really like. The women are enormous! And these cigarette girls that writers talk so much about are perfect frights. If it hadn't been for the Prado, I should have turned round and come right home the same day. But I couldn't miss Velasquez.

V.: And the Grecos?

R.: It's commonplace enough to say that El Greco is a very great painter, in spite of the studio lighting in his pictures, and his hands, which all look alike, and his "chic-ed" draperies. His faults only serve to strengthen my natural preference for Velasquez. What I love so much is that aristocratic quality that you find over and over again in Velasquez, in the smallest detail, the simplest ribbon. The whole art of painting is in the little pink bow of the *Infanta Margherita* in the Louvre! How lovely the eyes are and the skin in the hollow of the eyes! There is not the slightest shadow of sentimentality, either.

I know that the critics find fault with Velasquez for his too great facility. But what better proof that Velasquez knew his craft to perfection? Only the painter who knows his business thoroughly, can create the impression that a picture was done at one stroke. His work looks so easy, but think of the experimentation it must have taken! His blacks are magnificent. The older I grow, the more I love black! You break your neck trying to find the right colour; then you put in a little touch of ivory-black—and there you are!

V.: Did you know that Emile Bernard was expelled from Cormon's class[1] at the Beaux Arts for not using black? Cormon said to him: "What, you haven't any ivory-black on your palette? If you think you are going to make black with blue and red, I can't have you in my class. You might stir up trouble with such ideas."

But recently a young painter who had taken his first lessons from Emile Bernard, who, by that time, had changed his mind about ivory-black, went to study under Cormon. One day Cormon stopped in front of the newcomer's easel.

"What's that dirty stuff you have on your palette? Whom have you studied with, anyway? Don't you know that black is a non-colour and that nowadays everyone agrees that it must be made with red and blue?"

But tell me more about the Prado, Monsieur Renoir. Which Velasquez did you like the best?

R.: Lord, it would be hard to choose among so many marvels! The workmanship in those pictures is superb! He gives you thick and heavy embroideries with a simple rubbing of black and white. I know nothing more beautiful than *The Spinners!* The background of that picture is sheer gold and diamonds.

Wasn't it Charles Blanc who said that Velasquez was too matter-of-fact? Why do people always look for ideas in painting? When I look at a masterpiece, I am satisfied simply to enjoy it. It takes a professor to find defects in the masters. The very defects may be necessary. Raphael's *Saint Michael* in the Louvre has a thigh half a mile long! But it might not be so fine otherwise. Take Michael Angelo himself, the supreme anatomist. The other day, I was afraid that the breasts of my Venus were too far apart. Just then I happened upon a photograph of the *Dawn* from the tomb of Julian de' Medici. Then I saw that Michael Angelo had not hesitated to put the breasts even farther apart than I had. And look at the *Marriage at Cana.* If that picture were in proper perspective, with the figures in the background proportionately small, it would look empty. It is full because the figures in the back are nearly as large as those in the foreground. What is more, the floor doesn't recede according to the rules. Perhaps that's why it's so fine.

There is another thing in Velasquez which delights me: his painting radiates with the joy the artist had in doing it.

It is not enough for a painter to be a clever craftsman; he must love to "caress" his canvas too. That's what was lacking in Van Gogh. "What a wonderful painter!" people say. But his canvases do not show the light, tender touch of the brush. And there's his rather exotic side too. . . . But try to tell your critics that art is not only a question of craftsmanship, but also that there must be a certain something that the professors can't give you—finesse, charm, perhaps—that can't be taught.

---

[1]Cormon, Fernand. French painter born in 1845. He is remarkable for his colour. (Larousse Dictionary.)

You ought to see Velasquez's pictures of the Spanish nobility! Doubtless they were all as common as dirt; but they have a supreme dignity. Velasquez has given them his own dignity. . . . Take *The Surrender at Breda* for example. Aside from the quality of the painting, there is infinite nobility in the gesture of the conqueror. A lesser artist would have made him pretentious. I went back again and again to look at that canvas. I almost felt like kissing those horses!

If a painter has real temperament, he can paint his characters just as they are, and still give the picture an indefinable charm. Goya's *Royal Family* is worth the trip to Madrid alone. As painting it is magnificent, but the king looks like a butcher, and the queen, well—she looks as if she had escaped from a brothel, if not worse. She is fairly dripping with diamonds! Nobody ever painted diamonds like Goya. And how delightfully he has done the little satin slippers!

Somewhere in Spain there is a little church with a ceiling by Goya. It shows people looking down from a balcony above. I was marvelling at it, when a guide informed me that a "great painter from Paris" (Jules Ch . . .) had been there some time earlier and, after one look at the ceiling, had departed with a shrug of his shoulders!

V.: You haven't told me about the Titians in the Prado.

R.: Ah! Titian has everything. First, mystery; then depth. Rubens is just a shell beside him, nothing but surface. You almost feel like trying to open the cuirass of Philip II to find out what is inside; but there is nothing photographic about it; and the flesh is fairly alive. In the *Venus* and in the *Organist,* the limpid quality of that glowing flesh is amazing. You actually feel the joy he had in painting it. . . . I have really lived a second life through the pleasure I have had from the work of the masters.

You see how I love Titian; but in spite of everything I always come back to Velasquez. Far be it from me to put him above Titian, but at Madrid, you get the full force of Velasquez because nearly all of his work is in one place, whereas most of the fine Titians are in other places. Take the portrait of Francis I in the Louvre, for instance; what richness it has, what simplicity and distinction! There is a man who looks every inch a king. How perfect the sleeves are, and the slashes in the satin! . . .

Another thing which struck me particularly at the museum in Madrid was a Poussin which has remained as fresh as a Boucher, whereas in the Louvre and the other galleries, the Poussins are so dirty. . . .

V.: How do you account for that?

R.: I used to think it was because Madrid is situated on a plateau where the air is pure; the air is good in Munich too, and the paintings are well preserved, but in the Louvre, which is near the Seine, the paint becomes rancid. Yet I think the real reason is that they have no *conservateurs* in Spain.

(Renoir noticed that I was astonished, and went on:)

I see that you take *conservateur* in the usual sense of the word. Roujon, the Minister of Fine Arts, interpreted my remark in the same way, and was offended——naturally! By *conservateur* I don't mean the gentleman who does nothing but walk about in the halls looking important. He can't do any harm. I mean *conservateur* in the real sense of "restorer." Spain is a poor country and probably can't afford them; so once the pictures are hung, they are left alone.

V.: In your capacity as executor of the Caillebotte estate, you must have had more than one quarrel with Roujon when the question of admitting the Impressionists into the Luxembourg came up.

R.: To tell the truth, Roujon and I never could agree about anything. Not that he is lacking in intelligence, or that he is not a pleasant enough person. But to keep from quarrelling with him, I had to be careful never to mention any of the painters I really admire.

You can imagine our discussions about the Caillebotte Collection. Roujon was quite ready to accept the Degas, and also the Manets, though not all, however, for he rejected one or two of the latter. But he was suspicious of my pictures and didn't try to hide it.

The only canvas of mine that he accepted with confidence was the *Moulin de la Galette*—because Gervex appeared in it.[2] He regarded the presence of that master as a sort of moral guarantee. On the other hand, he was rather disposed to like Monet, Sisley and Pissarro—not overmuch, though. The amateurs had begun to buy them. But when he saw the Cézannes! Those landscapes of his . . . composed with the precision of a Poussin! The colours in the *Bathers* seem to have been ravished from some ancient pottery. What supremely wise art! . . . I can still hear Roujon saying:

"If that chap Cézanne only had the vaguest notion what painting is!"

On leaving the studio, I stopped to look at a study of *Roses* lightly brushed in. "That's an experiment I'm making in flesh tones for a nude," Renoir said.

---

[2]Gervex, Henri. A painter who has never decided whether he belongs to the school of Cabanel or to the Impressionists. He is a popular portrait-painter who has attained to considerable success and the usual number of decorations. (Trans. Note.)

Chapter Fifteen

LONDON, HOLLAND, MUNICH

VOLLARD: You have never spoken to me about the English School.

Renoir: The English School? It doesn't exist. They copy everything: one minute they're doing Rembrandts, the next Claude Lorrains. There is only one interesting English painter, Bonington, and you seldom hear about him.

It is a curious fact that it was the Turners which attracted me to London for the first time. Long ago I had seen a reproduction of a *Portrait of Turner* as a young man. It looked exactly like me! But the original was awful. What a difference between him and Claude Lorrain, whom he tried so hard to imitate! Turner knew nothing about construction. As for his so-called audacities—gondolas under a London sky! There isn't a penny's worth of sincerity in the lot of it. I infinitely prefer a primitive who stupidly copies a bit of drapery. Imagination doesn't go very far when you don't rely on Nature. Fortunately the Claude Lorrains in London make up for the Turners, the Lawrences, and even the Constables.

I read somewhere that Lorrain painted from instinct—as a bird sings. That would be very extraordinary in a man who had such a profound knowledge of his craft. Everything you read about Claude Lorrain is strange; people have even gone so far as to pretend that he got others to paint the figures in his pictures. Sometimes his figures don't seem to be very much in the picture, but usually they are quite up to scratch. And his ships are marvellous too! He was lucky to have lived in an age when ships were much more picturesque than they are nowadays. . . . What wonderful things to paint——those old galleons!

A painter in those days was a painter pure and simple. He didn't even bother about appropriate titles for his pictures. Look at that Lorrain in the Louvre, the *Siege of La Rochelle.* Nothing but a few soldiers chatting in the shade of some beautiful trees!

That reminds me of a canvas of mine called *Wash-House.* There wasn't even the shadow of a wash-house in the picture. I wrote those words on the back of the canvas because it was painted near a wash-house and I wanted to be sure to remember the spot, and I forgot to scratch it out afterwards.

There is a picture by Claude that I recommend if you go to London some day: the *Embarkation of Saint Ursula* in the National Gallery. It's a beautiful thing!

Those who claim that Lorrain knew nothing ought to realize that everybody who came after borrowed wholesale from his work . . . any one of his pictures will furnish an example. You know his *Ox-Driver* in the Print Museum. Why, Rousseau's drawings are nothing but imitations, although some of them are quite fine. Constable, as well as Turner, knew everything Lorrain had to teach. Corot also. But I must admit that I like Corot even better than Lorrain. He had so much personality. There's a man who created trees for himself, whereas Claude's trees smack a little of the conventional. But there is nothing finer than the still, pure air of his landscapes, the profound depths of his skies.

V.: When you went to Holland, did the Rembrandts impress you as much as the Velasquez at Madrid?

R.: You know how I love Rembrandt; but I find him a little "stuffy." For my part, I have a predilection for painting that lends joyousness to a wall.[1] In fact, when I look at *La Finette* . . . People are always telling you that Rembrandt is greater than Watteau in other ways. Good Lord, I know that, but the pleasure a picture gives you can't be measured. . . . When I'm looking at one picture, I simply forget all others. Gallimard will never let me alone when we're in a gallery together. At Madrid he was always at my elbow, murmuring: "I like Rembrandt better."

"You and your damned Rembrandt made me tired!" I finally burst out. "While I'm in Spain, let me look at Velasquez to my heart's content. When I go to Holland, it will be time enough to enjoy your Rembrandt."

V.: What about the *Night Watch?*

R.: If that picture were mine, I'd cut out the woman with the chicken, and I'd sell the rest as rubbish. It can't approach the *Holy Family,* or even the *Carpenter's Wife,* in the Louvre, the woman nursing a child. There is a glorious beam of light that shines through the bars of the window and gilds the breast. . . .

V.. My favourite Rembrandt is the *Jewess Betrothed.*

R.: That's a Rembrandt after my own heart. But the pleasure of seeing the museums in Holland comes high. I don't understand how there can be any healthy people left in such a country, with all those poisonous canals. And aside from three or four great artists, the rest of the school, such as Teniers and the "little Flemish painters," is a hopeless bore. Old Louis the Fourteenth showed his good sense when he ordered "all that truck" out of his sight!

---

[1]Renoir said to me one day: "There is a *mot* of Joyant's that gave me a lot of pleasure. Someone was looking at my picture called *The Spring.*

" 'Ah, that man Renoir! He's never serious, always on a holiday. . . .'

" 'Right you are,' said Joyant. 'Painting a woman excites him more than embracing her.' "

Nevertheless, I have gloomy Holland to thank for producing the model who posed for that picture there on the wall. She was a perfect Madonna. And what a virginal skin! You simply can't imagine the breasts that girl had; they were so heavy and firm . . . and the golden shadow made by the fold underneath! Unfortunately she could give very little time to posing, because she did not want to give up her work; but I was so delighted with her gentleness and with that skin which took the light so well, that I wanted to take her to Paris with me. I said to myself: "I only hope she doesn't get ruined right away, and that she keeps her lovely complexion!" So I asked her mother to confide her to my care, and promised to see to it that her daughter was not molested.

"But what will she do in Paris, then, if she doesn't 'work'?" the mother asked, dumbfounded.

Then I realized the kind of "work" my virgin did! Needless to say, my plans went no further.

V.: You have not told me about your trip to Munich.

R.: That was the last of my travels. I went to Munich about 1910 to paint some portraits.[2] They have a very famous Rembrandt there, the *Descent from the Cross*. But in spite of the great reputation of that picture, I must admit I found it a bit chalky. And I don't like the black effect at the bottom of the canvas. . . . However, I saw a thing at the Pinakothek which interested me tremendously: a *Head of a Woman* by Rubens, painted thickly instead of with his usual thin rubbings. But then as far as Rubens goes, there is no need for France to be jealous of any other nation as long as the *Helena Fourment and Her Children* is in the Louvre! The white dress is full of dirt, due to the layers of filthy varnish they've put on, but it's magnificent, just the same. There's painting for you! Nothing can spoil splendid colours. . . . Ah! what a generous painter Rubens was! He would put a hundred figures in a picture without turning a hair! Speaking of Rubens, you have no idea the surprise I got when they opened the new Rubens room in the Louvre! Someone told me they'd put a lot of bright gold frames around the pictures. But there is no use talking, they are better than before in spite of all the gilt.[3] And hanging them straight like frescoes, instead of at an angle, has helped them immensely.

---

[2]Renoir was invited to Munich to paint portraits of the Thurneyssen family. On his arrival, he was amazed to find a colour-guard and a military band at the station to escort him with regal pomp through the streets to the home of his host. (Trans. Note.)

[3]Renoir always recommended frames of bright gold for his own pictures.

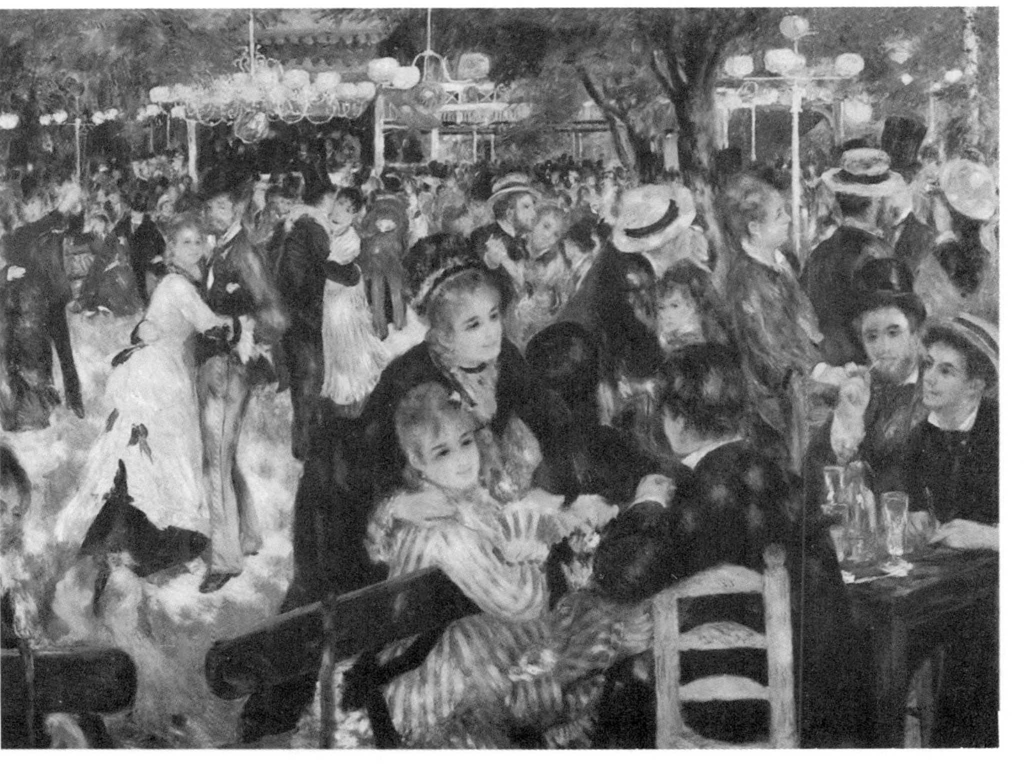

LE MOULIN DE LA GALETTE (1875)

See pp. 31–33.

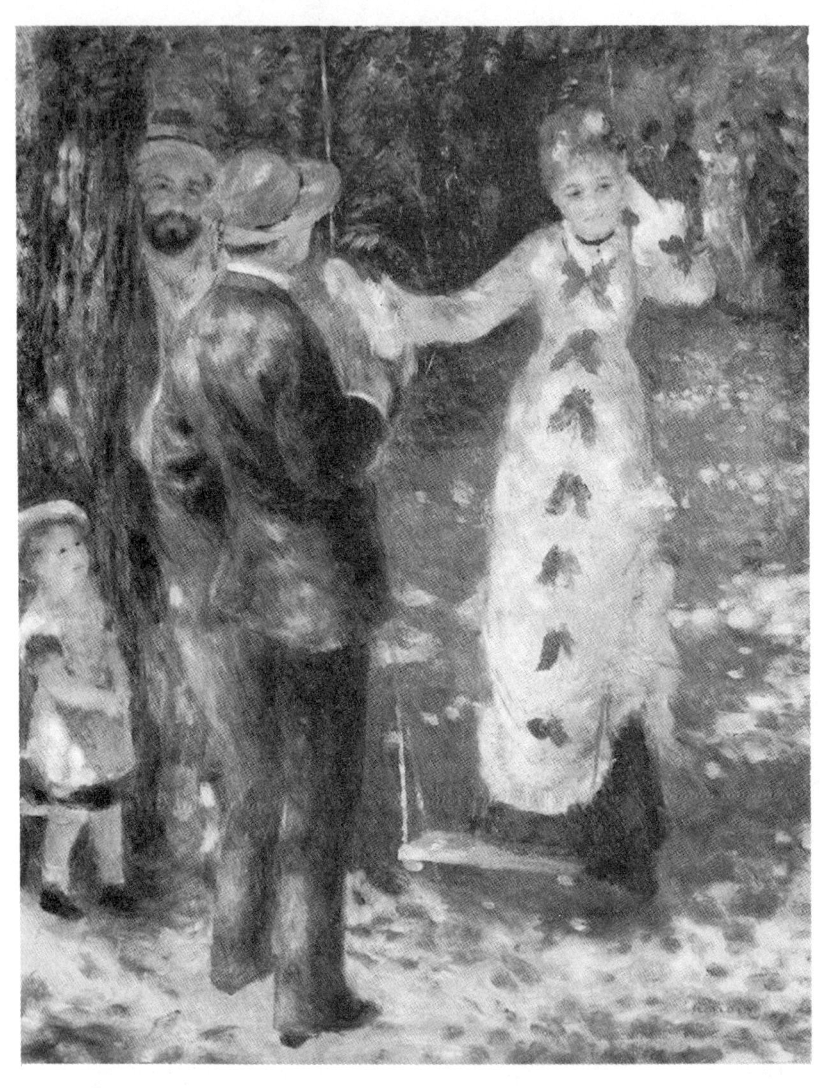

THE SWING (1875)

See p. 32.

Chapter Sixteen

RENOIR AT PONT-AVEN

Renoir: About 1892 Gallimard and I went to Pont-Aven. I had been told it was one of the most beautiful spots in Brittany and quite far from the sea. The sea air has never agreed with me, you know; in fact it was during a summer by the sea that I began to be seriously troubled with rheumatism.

I thought that so far away from Paris, I would have a few days of rest without hearing a word about art. Well, we arrived at Pont-Aven right in the midst of an International Exhibition! And never did an exhibition better deserve the name, for there were painters from every corner of the globe at Julia's and at Gloannec's, the two inns of the town.

At Gloannec's I observed a young man working on some very curious tapestries. It was Emile Bernard. Gauguin was there too; he had somehow got the idea that he ought to put all the artists who were "painting black" on the right track. There was a poor hunchback named Haan—who up to then had made his living doing Meissoniers—whom Gauguin dragged into the maelstrom of the painting of the future. But his pictures stopped selling the very day that he yielded to Gauguin's imperious advice and substituted the vermilion on his palette for bitumen. The most astonishing person I met at Pont-Aven was a Monsieur—well, never mind the name. He was one of those funny little bourgeois who still dressed after the fashion of the time of Louis Philippe. He had heard painting talked about so much that he wanted to try it himself. But due to his natural ineptitude, he had to content himself with putting his name to the unsuccessful pictures that others had given him. One of his "works" figured in the International Exhibition: a landscape in which someone for a joke had painted a boat on the top of a tree. The poor chap was never able to explain the phenomenon, for he was certain that he had handed over to the committee a landscape with no sign of a boat in it.

At Julia's there was an American woman who dabbled a little in painting, and who had already come to me for criticism in Paris. I could be of no help to her, for she felt herself attracted more towards Puvis de Chavannes; but she held me responsible for her lack of progress. She was perpetually rummaging around in my colour-box.

"I'm positive you're hiding something from me . . ." she would say.

One day I cut myself with a palette knife. I have never been able to stand the sight of blood, my own particularly. I was afraid I was going to be sick. My "pupil" came to the rescue, but just as she was about to wrap up my finger, she happened to glance at my palette; she dropped the bandage, and cried in a voice full of indignation:

"What! Venetian red? You never told me you used that!"

Chapter Seventeen

THE PORTRAIT OF MADAME MORISOT

I WAS looking through the racks where Renoir kept his pictures.

"The pastel you have in your hand, Vollard, is in the very middle of the 'dry' period," said Renoir. "I have had more than one chance to sell it, now that the collectors don't care a rap how a thing is done, and think of nothing but the signature. But I really couldn't sell that: it is the portrait of Madame Morisot and her daughter."

"Did you know Madame Morisot well?" I inquired.

"Yes. My friendship with her has been one of the finest I have ever had. I remember the wonderful evenings Mallarmé and I used to spend at her house. It was a great treat to hear Mallarmé talk, but I never could understand much of his writing.

"And as for Madame Morisot herself—what a curious thing fate is! A painter with such a definite temperament born into the most austerely bourgeois *milieu* that ever was, and at a time when a child who wanted to be an artist was considered little short of a dishonour to the family! And what an anomaly too, in our age of realism, to find a painter so impregnated with the grace and delicacy of the eighteenth century; she was the last elegant and 'feminine' artist that we have had since Fragonard, not to mention that 'virginal' something that she had to such a high degree in all of her painting.

"Madame Morisot's first teacher was Corot. He had conceived a great friendship for her; so much so that one day when she asked him the price of one of his pictures—a Corot which to-day would be worth a couple of hundred thousand francs—he replied: 'For you it will be a thousand francs!"

"You can imagine the long faces of the parents when the young girl, all excitement, came to announce this 'favour' from her teacher. . . .

"Papa Corot had an immense respect for Nature. One day his pupil showed him a copy that she had done of one of his pictures, and he said: 'You must do that over. Your tree has one branch less than mine.'

"Will you do me a favour, Vollard?" continued Renoir. "I have been told that the Society of Friends of the Luxembourg would like to buy something of mine. I know that the majority of those people don't think much of what I paint. One of them, a very well-known collector, told me frankly that my pictures made him positively ill!

"The society deserves all the more credit—don't you think?—for wanting to make me one of its protégés. . . . Well, I would make them a present of the *Portrait of Madame Morisot,* if it didn't look too much as if I were trying to force the doors of a museum. Do you know Monsieur Chéramy, the president? He has a lot of Corots. I remember, incidentally, having seen the *Terraces at Genoa* at his house; it's a gem; it is painted like a Titian.

"Would you mind taking my pastel to this Monsieur Chéramy and telling him that I will sell it to the society for . . . well, let us say a hundred francs? Then I won't have anything on my conscience."

I did as Renoir requested. Hardly had I mentioned the painter's name when Chéramy exclaimed:

"Lots of talent! Perhaps he would like me to recommend him to the patrons of our society? Tell him he can count on my good will; I am familiar with his fine drawings in the *Illustration.*"

"But this is a question of one of his paintings," I protested.

"Lots of talent, too, as far as colour goes. Please assure him of my interest! I am familiar with the *Moulin de la Galette,* and I have even encouraged your Renoir by a personal purchase, a *Portrait of Wagner.* Ah, Wagner! What a magnificent talent!"

I explained the object of my visit. When I had mentioned the price, a hundred francs, Monsieur Chéramy replied:

"Obviously a hundred francs is not the devil of a lot. But of course the purchases of our society cannot be decided like that, on the spur of the moment. Have Monsieur Renoir make a formal request. Doesn't he know somebody who knows Bonnat? Bonnat is the final judge on our purchases. And he is very strict about drawing!"

As I bade him good-bye, someone brought in a picture, carefully done up, which Monsieur Chéramy himself helped to place on the easel. Turning to me, he said:

"Now you shall see the work of a master who knows how to combine colour and drawing!"

With meticulous care the president of the Society of Friends of the Luxembourg uncovered the picture, and I beheld a *Group of Nudes* by La Touche. . . .

Chapter Eighteen

THE FAMILY

"Do you need Gabrielle and La Boulangère this morning?" Renoir asked his wife. "I want them to pose for a picture of bathers."

Madame Renoir managed to get along without them.

"Caillebotte, the brother of the collector," Renoir continued, turning to me, "said to me once: 'It's extraordinary, but I have never been able to have *bouillabaisse* made at my house the way they make it at the Renoirs'. . . . And I have a real cook too. All that Renoir asks of a cook is that she have a "skin that takes the light"!' "

That was all very well, but he forgot that Madame Renoir could cook too. . . .

I wonder if it is generally known that it is largely due to his wife that Renoir painted all his wonderful still-lifes of flowers. She knew what pleasure it gave him to paint flowers, but she realized that the trouble of going to get them was too much for him. So she always had them about the house in those pretty fifteen-cent green pots that Renoir used to like to look at in the shop windows. And she would laugh when Renoir, seeing a new bouquet which she had carefully arranged, would say:

"Flowers are so pretty when they are put in any old way. I must paint that."

Another no less important part of Renoir's work was the studies of his own children. It is doubtful if he ever would have painted them if they had been like the little rich children, brought up by a nurse or fed on the bottle, that he used to paint when he had to accept commissions!

I used to go to see Renoir as a rule on Sunday morning. About eleven o'clock Madame Renoir would say: "Is there anything you want, Renoir? I am going to mass."

"It is marvelous how you manage everything!" I said. I had found her shelling peas, with little Jean on her lap. He was teething and therefore not behaving very well. "To think that you even find time to go to mass!"

Madame Renoir got up brusquely.

"Oh, dear, the brushes haven't been cleaned!" And, dropping the peas and little Jean, who suddenly stopped crying—for he realized, with the intuition children have, that it would do no good to make a noise if his mother could not hear him—Madame Renoir flew into the next room. She came back with a handful of brushes.

"Renoir says that I clean his brushes better than Gabrielle. . . ."

Finally fame, prosperity, even fortune came to Renoir.[1] But at the same time came the scourge of rheumatism, which, before very long, was to nail him fast to his chair.

"How I long for those days!" Madame Renoir said to me one day, referring to their trip to Italy. I was on the point of remarking: "But Renoir wasn't selling then, was he?" I checked myself in time, however, realizing the meaning of her regret: in those days her husband was still in good health.

Renoir finally devoted himself wholly to his art, which expanded and developed in spite of his infirmities, or, paradoxically, because of those infirmities, for, having to keep perfectly quiet, there was nothing to distract him: he thought of nothing but painting. He turned the knotted hands and the legs, which each day became a little stiffer, to account.[2] . . . Finally the acute suffering of the first days nearly vanished, his general health even improved, and Madame Renoir could almost say that she was happy again; then the war broke out.

The two eldest sons, Pierre and Jean, enlisted immediately.

I had gone to the Renoirs' to ask for news of them. There were other callers. Everybody was optimistic.

Dorival, the actor, a friend of the family, had just brought an "extra" which announced a thunderous advance in Lorraine.

Everyone was discussing the event, when Monsieur Z., a deputy, arrived with further tidings.

"I have just left the War Ministry," he said, still a little out of breath from having run up the stairs four at a time. The ministers have just had a conference, and the government thinks that the Russian steam-roller will reach Berlin by the first days of October [1914] at the latest. . . ."

When the visitors had departed, Renoir said:

"For the first time I am really beginning to feel uneasy. Everybody seems to be going mad."

"But the Germans are retreating," I protested.

"That's just the trouble——"

"Well, the Russian steam-roller is no joke!"

Renoir shrugged his shoulders. "Just look at the distance they have to go on the map. . . . It reminds me of my friend Norvin, who wanted to shoulder a gun and run to Berlin. Well, one day before the war I met him

---

[1]At the Doria sale in 1899, *La Pensée* brought 22,100 francs. Renoir had sold it less than twenty years before for 150 francs. (Author's Note.)

[2]Monsieur Bérard, the collector, found Renoir one day in terrible pain. He never got over his astonishment because Renoir had said: "Really, I am a lucky man. Now I can do nothing but paint."

near the Opera and suggested that we take a little walk to Asnières, about five miles beyond the city walls.

" 'What!' he replied, aghast. 'Do you think you can go on foot to Asnières?' "

Renoir had taken up his brushes, but he was so tormented by the thought of his sons that he was unable to finish the little still-life—a cup and two lemons—that he was working on.

"I can't paint any more!" he said of a sudden, letting his arms fall.

Madame Renoir, who was knitting a soldier's muffler, took off her glasses, looked at her husband, and, without saying a word, stifled a sigh and lowered her head again over her work. Renoir, in an effort to hide his apprehension, started to work again, but mechanically—it was the first time I had seen him paint without passion. He began to hum one of his favourite airs, a tune from *La Belle Hélène*. But there was no life in it.

Nevertheless, news from the "children" arrived regularly. The graphic letters they wrote to their parents confirmed what the papers said about the joyous life of the *poilus*. Renoir and his wife were beginning to breathe freely again, when out of a clear sky came the news that Pierre, the eldest, was in a hospital at Carcassonne, his forearm fractured.

"I suppose I ought to think myself lucky, considering what might have happened," said Madame Renoir when she came back from Carcassonne; "I hope that Jean——"

But Jean, unable to bear the inactivity which was the fate of the cavalry, secured a transfer to the Chasseurs Alpins.

"Just think, mamma, I have a *béret*. . . ." The *béret* was the cap the Blue Devils were so proud of.

And then word came that Jean was in the hospital at Gérardmer.

"At least he isn't fatally wounded," said Madame Renoir, reading the letter to her husband.

"I suppose not," said Renoir, forcing himself to be calm.

Jean took it as a joke. His thigh had been punctured by a bullet. "The doctor," he wrote, "tells me my leg will be stiff for a time. What luck! They'll be taking me for an officer now!" Madame Renoir left for Gérardmer the same day.

"You'll see," said Renoir. "I know perfectly well that if I receive a telegram with too many details, it will be because they want to hide something from me."

A short and optimistic dispatch arrived; but Renoir was not in the least reassured.

"I am sure they are going to cut off his leg. I think I'll write to Clémentel. You laugh because I'm thinking of asking the Minister of Commerce to keep them from cutting off a leg? You know very well that nobody is in his right place in this war. Think of the director of a theatre as chief surgeon of a hospital! Doctor Abel Desjardins was reprimanded by the Under-Secretary of State of Hygiene because his report, in proportion to the number of beds in his ward, did not show as many amputated arms and legs as the ward next door."

My bedroom was next to Renoir's; I could hear him moaning all night. The least distraction kept him from sleeping, and in his restless condition, his infirmities gave him particular trouble, but did not lessen his energy. When he was seventy-eight, he was carried groaning to the studio, after a sleepless night, and his strength came back under the stimulus of his work.

The telephone rang. It was the Cagnes post office, which was rather far from *Les Collettes,* calling to give the contents of a telegram that had just arrived for Renoir. Jean was to keep his leg. He had fallen into the hands of a major who preferred to let the leg get well rather than cut it off—an ambitionless major, who got nothing for his forbearance but reprimands.

After all the excitement Jean and Pierre had caused, peace settled again upon *Les Collettes.* Madame Renoir could go back to her chickens and her rabbits with a tranquil heart.

It was the season for gathering orange-blossoms. I recollected that Renoir had told me when he bought *Les Collettes* that one could make a good living from the fruit alone. I asked Madame Renoir if the property was making a good return.

"Well, if Renoir were younger," she replied, "and we could work the garden together . . . But I suppose we have done best to count on his painting!"

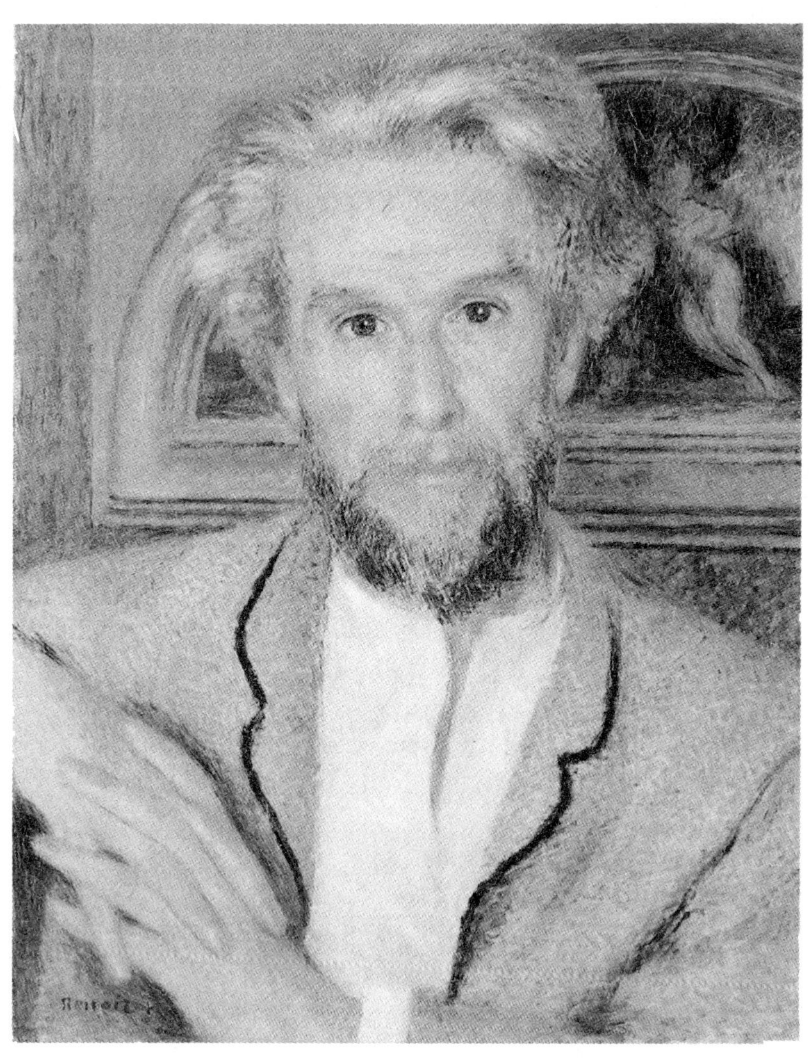

PORTRAIT OF VICTOR CHOCQUET (1875)

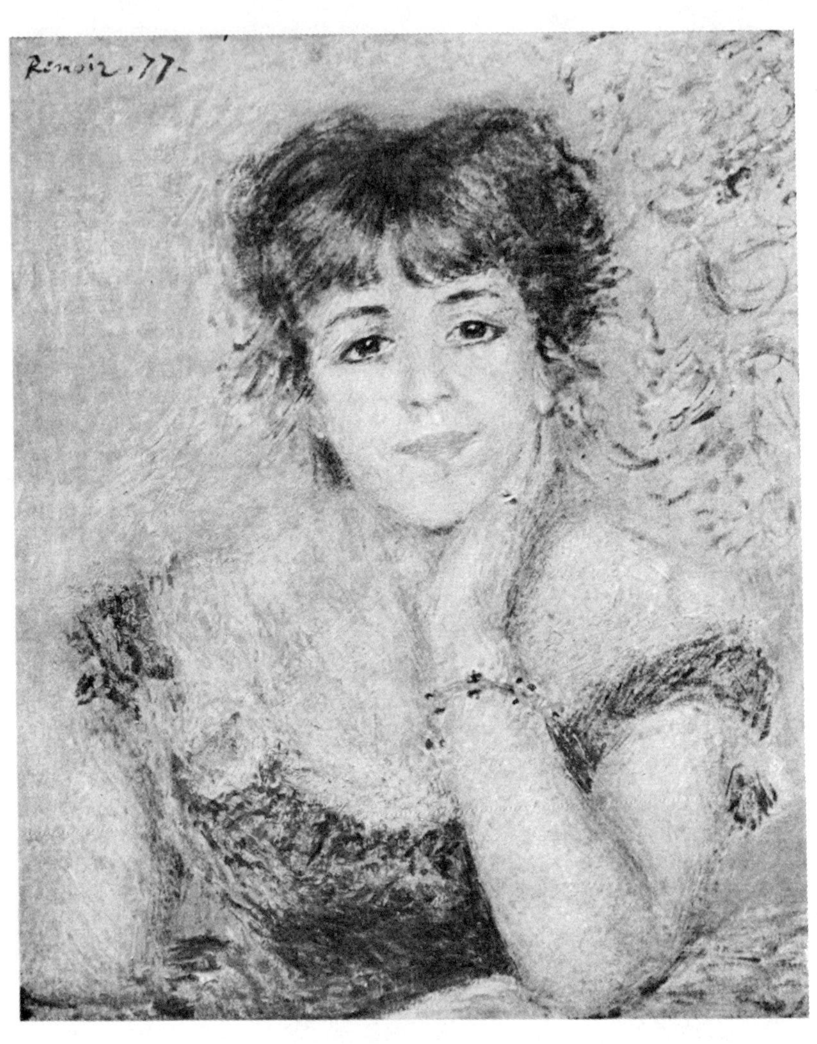

PORTRAIT OF JEANNE SAMARY (1877)

Chapter Nineteen

ESSOYES, CAGNES

On a day in 1912, Renoir spoke to me about a marvelous spot only two or three steps from Paris.

"But you mustn't tell about it," he said. "It is a unique place for a painter: there's a pond with sand—real sand, you understand—and lilies on the water! And there's hardly anybody at the hotel, and a very good hotel it is, too. It's a wonderful place to knock off masterpieces!"

This place, which he thought so well hidden, was none other than Chaville, a rendezvous for Parisians on Sunday. I went out there to visit Renoir, who by this time could no longer use his legs, and found him at an inn, where the staircase was so narrow that the servants had to carry him down in their arms in the morning, and, what was still more painful, hoist him up again in the evening.

Decidedly he had no instinct for comfort or for making himself at home. But fortunately his family and friends had it for him; so in 1898 he became the owner of a house in Essoyes, Madame Renoir's native town.

"A real bargain!" she told her husband. "A fine old peasant house built of real stone."

Renoir always fought shy of bargains, in the belief that the sauce costs more than the fish. This time, however, with his old hatred for the bourgeois, he let himself be persuaded by the prospect of living in a peasant's house; but he soon learned to his regret that it was a bargain only because it had to be done almost all over from top to bottom to make it habitable.

But once he was a landowner in Essoyes, he spent one or two months out of each year there. And, with his ability to adapt himself readily to his surroundings, he was in a very short time considered by the townsfolk as one of themselves, which is the greatest mark of esteem that the country-bred man can show to the city-dweller.

Even though the good people of Essoyes were unanimous in their belief that Renoir was not able to "take a portrait" as well as the photographer in the neighbouring town, they were soon persuaded that for advice on country matters, such as vine-cutting, the artist knew quite as much as Firmin, the overseer of the château lands.

One of the qualities of the soil of Essoyes is that it produces a wine which rivals the very finest vintages of Champagne. When the law governing wine distribution was passed, the delight of the inhabitants knew no bounds; but the representatives of Essoyes ultimately found that to call their wine "champagne," even though it were distilled in the Champagne region, required more influence than they were able to wield. Consequently Renoir had all he could do to evade the entreaties of his new fellow-townspeople, who doubted not that such a well-spoken man could, by saying a word at Paris, have the real name of their wine bestowed upon it legally.

Another time, a delegation came from the neighbouring village to complain to the painter that their school-mistress was to be dismissed because she refused to accept the attentions of the mayor! Renoir felt that this time he could be of service, for he was acquainted with a Member of Parliament who had asked if he could do him any favours. Once back in Paris, Renoir explained the facts to the representative of the people, and that gentleman replied, rubbing his hands: "Why of course! I'll get my friend Briand[1] to give your mayor the sack!"

But a few days later, the Member of Parliament came to call.

"Can't do anything for your school-teacher! The mayor belongs to the Party!"

Up to the time when the doctors ordered Renoir to live in the Midi during the winter, he went to Essoyes every summer. But when he was forced to live from October to June in a sunny climate, he divided his summers between the Champagne country and the capital.

"I have to go back to Paris from time to time," he said to me one day. "Otherwise . . ."

"But when you are in Paris, you can't eat," I protested. "And you can't work there, the air is stifling. . . ."

"Yes, I know . . . but it's Paris air, just the same. . . ."

When he returned to the Midi, he loved to loiter along the way, stopping at any place that took his fancy. Once, after he had seen two little arches of an old Roman bridge at Saint-Chamas from a train window, he could not be happy until he had gone there to paint.

When Renoir found himself obliged to live almost completely in the South, Magagnosc was his first choice. Magagnosc is a Provençal village strangely perched on the side of a mountain, with vestiges reminiscent of a Spanish town. At that time, he was still able, although with difficulty, to use his legs. We took walks together on the mountain, and ate vine-thrushes which Madame Renoir used to roast on a spit turned in front of a hot fire made from vine-branches.

After two or three years of Magagnosc, Renoir complained of the cold in the mountains, and went to live at Cannet. Finally he moved to Cagnes,

[1]President of the Council.

which had been recommended for the purity of its air. But the pure air existed only in upper Cagnes, and Renoir did not find the swampy plain of lower Cagnes at all to his liking. Once settled, however, he could never bring himself to break away. He would have continued to spend his winters there, if a certain piece of land called *Les Collettes,* which was half-way up the hill and planted with fine old olive-trees, had not been put up for sale. Was it not said that these olive-trees (they were at least a thousand years old, so the people round about affirmed) were soon to be converted into wooden spoons, napkin rings, paper weights and other "souvenirs of Jerusalem"? Such an idea was unbearable to Renoir, and he bought *Les Collettes* to save the trees. When the property was purchased, he decided to build a house. The result was that charming home which Madame Renoir designed and supervised herself.

Arriving one day at the old house in Cagnes, while the new one was still under construction—the "Château des Collettes," as it was called in the town—I found Renoir sitting in his wheel-chair at the window. He could not take his eyes from the landscape before him.

"Would you like to do a picture from here?" I asked him.

"I wasn't thinking of that," he replied. "But they promised me that by to-day I would see the roof of my house above the trees up there!"

There was a note of apprehension in his voice at the thought of settling down to a "bourgeois" life. But who can escape from the fatality of things?

When the "château" was finished, Renoir found, little by little, that it was good to have his ease, and that *Les Collettes* in no way resembled the house of lower Cagnes, which he had been obliged to share with the post office. But though his new home was well arranged, it was so isolated that he later regretted the life and movement that made the post-office house interesting.

In spite of his horror of things mechanical, the new "châtelain" resigned himself to owning an automobile. It proved to be the most convenient means of getting out to paint in the country, which he persisted in doing to the end, even when he could no longer use his legs.

"You see all the worry my husband gives himself," said Madame Renoir one day when the painter came back from the fields in a push-cart, which jolted at every pebble in spite of its rubber tires. "The public appreciates his work; dealers are always coming down from Paris to buy his pictures. . . . Then why, when they write about him, do they say such ridiculous things! Somebody just showed me another paper—they don't know what they're talking about. When I arrived yesterday, I said to myself: 'How gloomy the dining-room is!' I had brought back from Paris three or four little canvases, some *Roses,* a *Head of Gabrielle*—things he had worked on for barely an hour. When I put them up on the wall—*voilà,* the dining-room was a different place; it was bright again!"

Madame Renoir relapsed into silence; I had never heard her talk so much about painting before!

Chapter Twenty

THE MODELS AND THE MAIDS

Renoir: Gabrielle! Gabrielle! She's gone already! And my palette isn't set yet.

Vollard: Will you permit me to help?

R.: Zut! I won't work this morning.

An elderly lady who had come to call: Isn't that girl *ever* in?

R. (after the lady's departure): These housewives! They're extraordinary!—even the best of them. That Madame Jaurès for instance. Everybody will tell you she's a perfect angel. Well, just try to make an angel understand that a housemaid is human like any other woman!

I must say, though, that Gabrielle does take it easy. If she only wouldn't put me out so! When she comes back I'll ask her why she stayed out so long. Then she'll say: "But, sir, I didn't go anywhere. I only wanted to get some news of Mother Thingumbob who is just getting out of the hospital to-day." You know my housekeeper, Mamma Thingumbob, and her husband, Papa Thingumbob, with his red belt and Tyrolese hat.

There was a sound of footsteps on the stairs.

R.: There's Gabrielle now! I'll give her a piece of my mind this time.

Gabrielle (on seeing her master trying to look severe): Please, sir, I didn't go out, sir. I just went over for five minutes to see Mamma Thingumbob. I hear she's back from the hospital, but she wasn't in.

R.: Five minutes! Well, of all the cheek! Gabrielle, I've told you a hundred times, if I've told you once: you're no different from the rest. Now I don't want to make a prisoner of you . . .

But just then who should come in but Mamma Thingumbob herself, and while she was down on hands and knees in the studio setting up Claude's leaden soldiers, Renoir said: "Well, your daughter ought to be pleased with the place I got for her with that friend of mine."

Mamma Thingumbob: No, sir. He didn't act like a gentleman. The other day he said to my daughter, right to her face, too: "To-morrow you must make some jam." My daughter was taken right off her feet, so she spoke right up to him and said: "I'll do it some other time. I'm going on a picnic in the country tomorrow." Then the gentleman said: "Oh, no, my girl, you won't do anything of the kind, because you're fired right here and now!" That isn't the way to speak to a decent young girl, is it, sir?

Gabrielle (to Mamma Thingumbob): Things must be awfully slow for your husband, without anything to do, now that the roofing-workers are on strike.

Mamma Thingumbob: No, he's working himself to death right now, seeing as how they have given him the job of looking after the interests of the widows and orphans during the strike; and that's no laughing matter, with the way the "cops" are murdering the poor defenceless workmen. But when Papa Thingumbob comes round, the police are mighty respectful, because he doesn't look like a workman. He has the same tastes as rich people, he has! Every Sunday he has his leg of mutton with plenty of garlic.

Renoir (alone with me, Mamma Thingumbob having followed Gabrielle): Did you hear the old woman! But I must say I'd rather put up with a hundred Mamma Thingumbobs than one "intellectual" female! . . .

The door-bell rang, followed by Gabrielle's voice calling: "Louise, if that's a young man with a funny face who talks through his nose, kick him out! He's always asking to see Monsieur Renoir. He looks like an artist."

Renoir: Go and see who it is, Vollard. No, never mind. It's the cook. Gabrielle has a perfect mania for chasing away anyone who looks like a painter. If I let her do as she pleased, I'd have an even worse collection of bores on my hands. Did you hear the fine trick she played on me just the other day?

"Somebody came who insisted on seeing you," she said, "but even though he had cut off his beard and put on his Sunday clothes, I knew who it was, all right—it was the *garde champêtre.* I wouldn't let him in."

Who do you think her *garde champêtre* was? Monsieur Joulon, the prefect himself!

And another time she wrote to Zoller, who had just been decorated, that we had all learned with great pleasure that he had been made a Knight of the Foreign Legion! . . .

Just at this point a visitor arrived; it was the little fellow who talked through his nose. He carried a lily in one hand and a lorgnette in the other.

Visitor (addressing Renoir): I would like to have you paint my portrait. I don't care about the likeness so long as my character is preserved.

Renoir: Don't go, Vollard. There is somebody coming that you would enjoy seeing. (Then, turning brusquely to the man with the lily:)

You wouldn't like the kind of portraits I paint.

The young man, somewhat discomfited by the fact that the studio had so little of the museum about it, was taking his leave with one of those sententious "Master . . ." phrases on his lips, which always made Renoir's flesh creep. Just then the friend that Renoir was expecting arrived. He turned out to be the poet Léon Dierx, my compatriot of the Isle of Bourbon, whom I had never met before.

Renoir had said to me one day:

"The only trouble with Dierx is that he has never desired anything for himself,[1] nor been envious of anybody. Only once did I ever hear him speak ill of anyone——he said of Madame de Sévigné: "She's the most terrible bore I know of!"

Dierx fully accepted Renoir's earlier manner. "What a fine picture *The Loge* is!" he said one day. "If only Renoir didn't have such a weakness for red nowadays! . . ." But when someone pointed out that this new manner of Renoir's was much appreciated by the public, the poet replied: "I know another painter who uses a great deal of red like Renoir, so I suppose it will soon be his turn to sell."

Dierx came into the studio beaming:

"Renoir, I've just heard the funniest thing! A young poet recited to me some verses about an adolescent boy . . . a virgin. My housekeeper suddenly stopped her work and looked up from the floor in ecstasy. 'Monsieur, I beg your pardon for interrupting, but I hear you talking about a young man who still has his virginity, and it reminds me of the most beautiful memory of my life! Just as you see me kneeling here, except for its being more than forty years ago, I once took the virginity of a young man!'

" 'And what did it feel like to take a young man's virginity?' I asked her.

" 'Well, sir, it's something you really can't talk about, but it was gorgeous!' "

Gabrielle did not appear entirely disposed to share the sentiments of the poet's housekeeper; she apparently held all men for deceivers, but she liked the stronger sex none the less.

One evening I went to take dinner with Renoir at Louveciennes.

"Look at Gabrielle and her soldiers," Madame Renoir said to me. I saw two soldiers perched on the kitchen window-sill, and Gabrielle was handing them jam-tarts through the grating. A moment later, Madame Renoir went into the kitchen and found Gabrielle giving them soup.

"Gabrielle, you're crazy! Soup after sweets!"

The girl began to be uneasy; she hesitated with a spoonful of soup in the air behind the grilling. I reassured her by saying that there were some people who ate soup for dessert, and that it was especially popular around Lyons.

"That's fine," answered one of the men; "the regiment is booked to go to Lyons next."

So Gabrielle extended the waiting spoonful to the soldiers, with no further fears for their health.

---

[1]After more than thirty years in government offices, Dierx never rose above a clerkship. When someone remarked what a pity it was, the "Prince of Poets" replied with a smile: "Believe me or not, a poet isn't good for much. I'll never forget the letter somebody in the service asked me to write one day. We got an indignant protest in short order. The letter was intended for an *Archiviste;* I had written, *Monsieur Anarchiste!* . . ." (Author's Note.)

Renoir had called for a liqueur after the coffee; but the carafe was empty.

"I gave a drop or two to the soldiers," explained Gabrielle.

"But how do you expect them to find their camp in the forest if you've given them drinks?" asked Madame Renoir.

Gabrielle snatched up a handkerchief and wrapped it around her head.

"Where are you going?" inquired Renoir.

"Eh? I'm going after them. It won't be so hard to find the camp road if there are three of us."

Gabrielle was very fond of bright colours. One day Renoir asked her for a neckerchief, and Gabrielle fastened around his neck a large red affair with white polka dots. Thus arrayed, Renoir went to the bank accompanied by Gabrielle, who was also rather conspicuously dressed.

When Renoir presented the cheque which he had come to cash, the clerk refused to honour it.

"But it's Monsieur Renoir!" Gabrielle protested. "Why, he's even been decorated!" and, opening her purse, she took out a red rosette of an Officer of the Legion of Honour. . . .

I happened in at that moment. Renoir still held the cheque in his hand, but he was looking at a little working-girl who stood in line at the teller's window.

"Look, Vollard, she's exactly like Marie, do you remember? When her cheeks were still ripe peaches! I'd give anything to paint that child. Won't you go and see if she will pose for me?"

Gabrielle had already started forward, but Renoir held her back. He was afraid that too much haste would frighten the girl away.

I was rather at a loss to know how to make the proposal. All I could think of to say was: "Mademoiselle, I come with the best of intentions . . ."

"What do you mean?" she asked, on her guard.

"That gentleman you see over there would like to take a picture of you in colour."

"Well, sir, I'm still pretty young, you know . . ."

I assured her that her virtue would be in no danger.

"That's what they all say at the start. I'll come with my big sister."

I was in the studio when she arrived; she stood stiff as a poker.

"I'll never be able to do anything with her," Renoir grumbled. "She's swallowed a ramrod."

But just then one of the models who was sewing on a hat pricked her finger and cried "*Merde!*" This exclamation apparently gave the newcomer confidence, for she immediately assumed a thoroughly natural pose.

I found Gabrielle one day examining a diamond ring on her finger.

"Look how it sparkles, Madame!" she said to Renoir's wife. "It came from the Rue de la Paix. It says so on the box."

"I've never had such a pretty ring as that myself," said Madame Renoir, who cared really very little for jewellery.

I was rather surprised to see Renoir examine the ring attentively.

"Just look, Vollard, they don't even know how to set a stone nowadays!" Then, turning to Gabrielle:

"Was it Monsieur Evrard gave you this ring? Yes? That's the way it goes! As a special favour I put his little boy into the picture he ordered, and you're the one who gets the ring!" He began to laugh.

"Vollard, I'll soon have to do like that Dutch painter, the fellow who painted a pasture scene with one more sheep than the number agreed upon, and when he couldn't get any extra money for it, he painted out the sheep before delivering the picture!"

Madame Renoir was the only one who was interested in the future of the ring.

"What are you going to do with it, Gabrielle? You will lose it, and it's worth quite a bit of money."

"He told me when he gave it to me," answered Gabrielle, "that if I took it to the jeweller he would buy it back for a thousand francs."

"Why, that's fine, Gabrielle! You must go right away to the Rue de la Paix; you can put the money in the savings bank, or else you can buy a grape farm near your home with it."

But Gabrielle:

"I don't trust the Government. I'm afraid of farms, too. There are too many kinds of bugs on the vines! Diamonds are so pretty to look at; see how it sparkles!" And, ring on finger, Gabrielle went back to polishing the furniture. . . .

But foresight was not one of Gabrielle's strong points. One day, at *Les Collettes,* she let two tramps into the kitchen, and cut them large slices of *pâté.*

"But you are not thinking what you're doing, Gabrielle," said Madame Renoir. "They won't be satisfied afterwards with just their bread and cheese, and they won't get any more *pâté.*"

Madame Renoir was mistaken. In the middle of the night, the vagabonds returned to the kitchen, which was locked with a simple bolt, and ate the rest of the *pâté.* But they were not a bad sort, and they did not set fire to the house on leaving.

One evening Madame Edwards came to call for Renoir to take him to the Russian Ballet. Renoir was already suffering from rheumatism, and could scarcely walk.

It goes without saying that people never asked Renoir to put on evening clothes. Even to see the Russian Ballet, he would never go so far as to get himself up in a costume which he found irksome and ridiculous.

But one can easily imagine the general surprise of the audience to see a man in a grey suit and bicycle cap in the front row of one of the boxes.

All at once the door of the box opened. It was Gabrielle.

"I couldn't see up there where I was. It's better here. Nobody can say I'm dressed too loud, can they?" And Gabrielle, in a high-necked black dress, seated herself beside her master.

If Renoir used his servants for his models, it was simply because he disliked nothing so much as the "professional." And after he had got a model well "worked into his brushes," it was a great annoyance for him to change. Age made no difference to him. One day he was greatly taken with a pretty girl whom he saw for the first time.

"I'm going to paint a wonderful nude!"

He executed the picture, but the pose was decidedly too rigid. So he got another very pretty model, and painted a second figure over the first, but still he was not satisfied.

"It's a long, hard job," he said to me. "I'm going to try to find Louison again. . . . The trouble is that her buttocks are all gone. . . . She has no breasts any more, and her belly has fallen. . . . When I think of the first time I met her on the Boulevard Clichy with a bit of blue ribbon at her neck . . . that was thirty years ago! What a curve her belly had!" So Renoir hunted up his former model, searched out the curve of the stomach again under the coarsening flesh, and painted his finest nude.

Gabrielle posed a great many times, either alone or with Jean in her arms, and, later, Claude. She figures also in the large picture of the family. One day I saw Gabrielle in the studio with a Phrygian bonnet on her head and her hair down her back.

Renoir: Doesn't she look like a boy, Vollard? I have always wanted to do a *Paris;* and I have never been able to find the right model. What a Paris she'll make!

In fact, he did make some drawings and two or three canvases from her representing *Paris Offering the Apple to Venus.* That is also how he came to make his bas-relief of *The Judgment of Paris* and a large statue, *Venus Victorious.*

Sculpture tempted him all his life. I once asked him, when he was working on a *Nude,* why he didn't do sculpture.

"I am much too old," he answered.

But when Renoir once got an idea into his head . . .

One day while I was with Renoir in the studio, he talked of the surprises one gets when the model first takes off her clothes. Some seem to be well formed but look like nothing at all, whereas others, quite hopeless at first sight, are veritable goddesses, once they are nude.

Somebody knocked at the studio door. A model presented herself—a regular cow! She stood there with her hands in the pockets of her apron.

"I 'do' the market district, but business is rotten, with all those broads on the loose. And there's too much competition with the married women. Somebody told me that posing was a good job, so I . . ."

"Well, we'll see, we'll see," said the painter impatiently, in order to get rid of her.

When she had gone, Renoir remarked: "I'm not hard to please, but there *are* limits! . . ."

Just then we heard a discreet cough from behind a screen at the end of the studio, and the potential model poked her head out.

"What are you doing there?" cried Renoir.

"Well, sir, you said you'd see, so I took off my clothes. . . ."

I departed. The next day, on returning to the studio, I found the painter at his easel.

"I'm waiting for the model; you know, the woman you saw yesterday."

"What! That horror!"

"Horror? Why, she's Venus herself!"

It had been some years since Gabrielle had left the Renoirs' service. Mamma Thingumbob had gone too, and had become a concierge. One day in Montmartre, I came upon her taking the air in front of the house.

"Your place looks nice and respectable," I said by way of complimenting her.

"No, Monsieur Vollard, you're mistaken. It isn't respectable. The lady on the sixth floor is deceiving her husband, and a fine man he is too; the gentleman on the first is an old goat, and the tenant on the third has left his wife. . . . Yes, sir."

"And have you ever seen anything more of Gabrielle?"

"No, sir. Gabrielle is living in Athènes, a nice little town. And I hear she has a maid and a velvet coat. . . . Yes, sir."

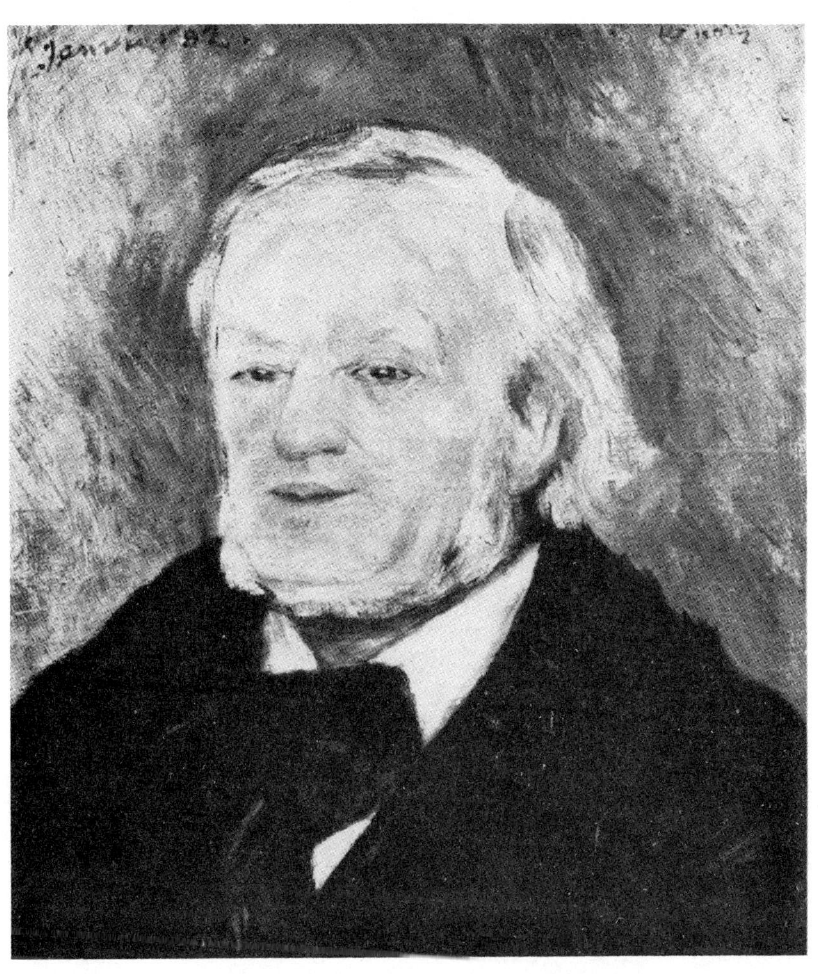

PORTRAIT OF RICHARD WAGNER (1881)

See pp. 48–49.

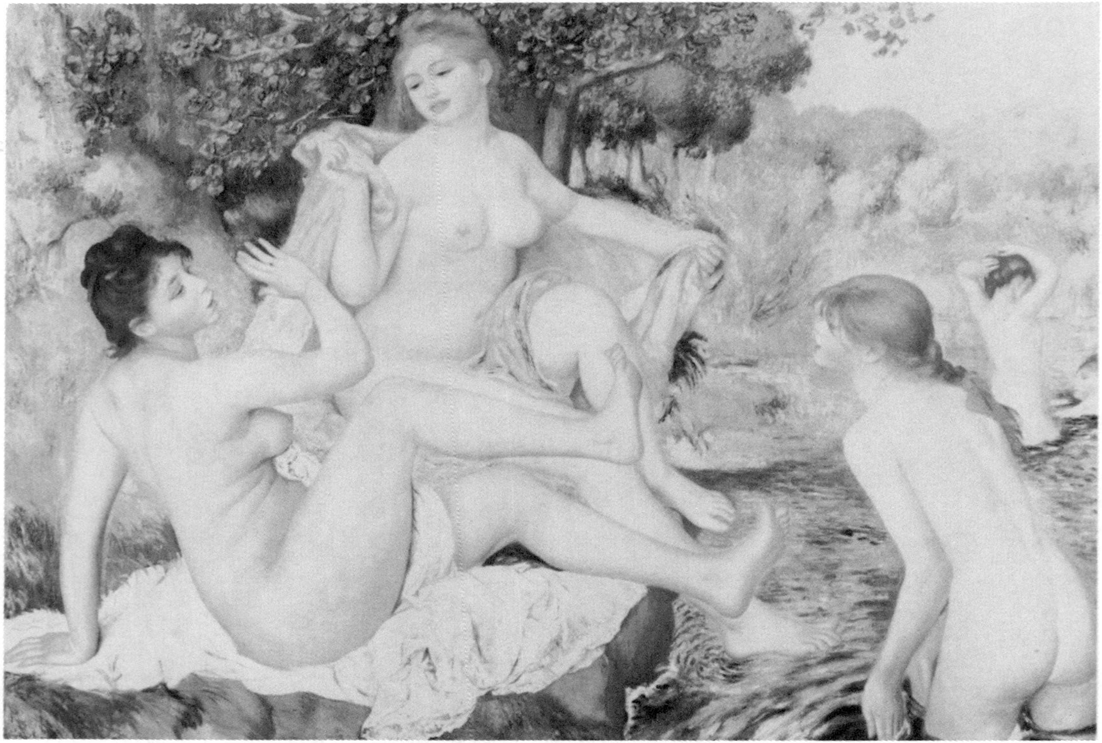

BATHERS (1887)

See pp. 58–59.

CHAPTER TWENTY-ONE

RENOIR AND HIS PATRONS

NOTHING distressed Renoir more than selling his pictures. Not that his desire to keep them was beyond bounds, but he wanted to see them again, touch them up, sign them. . . .

Sacha Guitry had come to take moving pictures of him, knowing the painter's inability to refuse anything.

"If I could only get you with a brush in your hand!" he said.

Renoir just happened to have a picture to sign. He had it put on the easel and called for his colour-box. From the far end of the room I could see his brush moving on the canvas. When the operator had stopped turning, Renoir put out his hand for little Claude to unfasten the brush from his fingers.

"But, papa, you didn't sign the picture!"

"I'll do that another time."

"From the movements of your hand," I remarked, "one would have thought that you had signed it two or three times."

"No, I just added a little rose!"

After Renoir had given his pictures the final touch, and the dealers believed them at last in their clutches, the amateur entered upon the scene . . . Inasmuch as Renoir had the reputation for disliking to sell directly to the buyer, the said amateur, in order to get into the studio, would begin by begging for the portrait of his wife or daughter—much less frequently his little boy, because paintings of male children do not sell so readily.

"Oh Monsieur Renoir!" he would say. "If you only knew how my wife has been saving on her wardrobe for more than three years to have her portrait in your new manner! She has just broken open her little bank and found three thousand francs! Of course, for that price, we don't dare to hope for a portrait in oil! But a little pastel would make us so happy!"

He would be perfectly well aware that with his paralyzed hands Renoir could no longer handle pastels, and that after having bargained for a drawing, the artist would take up canvas and brushes of his own accord.

The affair once arranged, I need not add that the lady invariably arrived in full négligée! The nearer the nude, the higher the price. Not to mention the likelihood that she would come accompanied by her "little daughter" (cases where the latter has been borrowed from a friend are not unknown), and a new campaign would begin to have the child painted along with her mother.

Thus, while the amateurs besieged the painter, the dealers were far from his thoughts. They did not turn up very frequently, for they knew that the first condition to observe in order to make sure of nabbing something by Renoir, was to leave him strictly alone. But when the maids, to make things more convenient, happened to leave the key in the door, thus passing on to the cook the responsibility of filtering the steady stream of visitors—the "amateurs" dropped in like grain into the mill.

Finally, if the dealers had been lucky, and the different lots were finished and signed, Renoir would say, rather with the air of giving a malediction:

"Get along, now! Take them away!"

And without even taking the trouble to look at the pictures, they always repeated the same phrase: "Another time, Monsieur Renoir, make the price higher and give us more pictures!"

"You don't like it, eh, when I sell to the collectors?"

"Well, we offer you a better price."

Then Renoir, who was never impressed by money, would retort:

"Wait a bit, then; at the rate they are going now, the amateurs will soon be stuffed to the gills with them!"

But the amateur was never stuffed to the gills, because a Renoir was to him nothing more than a bond in his safe-deposit vault. . . . If he was turned away empty-handed, he promptly sent another "amateur" to the attack, hired for the purpose.

They used to come to the studio primed with all his ideas about politics, religion, literature . . . they even exaggerated them if necessary. There was one fellow who thought that by ranking *La Dame de Monsoreau* above the *Iliad,* he would appeal to Renoir's passion for Dumas! In addition to his cargo of Renoiresque opinions, he thought he could manœuvre still more profitably by showing a profound knowledge of the "Master's" different styles. So he brought a canvas with him from which he had carefully effaced the signature and the date:

"Monsieur Renoir, here is a picture of yours unsigned! I found it at the Flea Market.[1] The moment I saw it, I cried: "A Renoir! And I'll bet my last *sou* that it was painted in such-and-such a year!"

---

[1]*Le Marché aux Puces,* a ramshackle market held every Sunday in the vacant lots just outside of the Porte de Clignancourt, Paris. In addition to legitimate dealers in cheap clothes and household utensils, there are many booths reputed to be the clearing-houses of thieves for stolen goods. Sometimes pictures and objects of great value find their way into this market, and are sold for a song. (Trans. Note.)

After Renoir had confirmed the statement and had re-signed and re-dated the canvas, the amateur poured out his gratitude with just the proper show of emotion!

"Just to think that I got hold of a Renoir that way! You permit me to say 'Renoir'? One gets in the habit of saying a Titian, a Velasquez, a Watteau! . . ." (A good collector must know the tastes of his victim; this one was not unaware that Titian, Velasquez, and Watteau were Renoir's gods. He was also not ignorant of the fact that if he had said "Master" instead of "Renoir," he would have made a very bad impression.) "After finding this picture, I came straight to your house, but when I got to the door my courage failed me. Once I even came up as far as your studio. I was just about to ring the bell, but I didn't quite dare. . . . To-day I took my courage in both hands, saying to myself: 'I'll bet anything I'll get thrown out.' "

How could Renoir have put such a brave fellow out! And the amateur talked on, with tears in his voice, of how happy his wife would be if he could come home some day with another Renoir. (The signal for the portrait.)

"Will you permit me to bring my wife with me? She simply hasn't been able to sleep since she saw the last exhibition of your pictures at Durand-Ruel's. 'If I could only have my portrait done by Renoir!' she keeps saying. I have told her many a time: 'Perhaps Renoir won't like you.' "

Disturbed to think that the poor lady could imagine that she might be distasteful to him, Renoir finally accepted the commission with the hope that the punishment would not be too severe—in other words, that the model would not be too old and would have a complexion that did not resist the light. . . . Need I say that such fears were quite vain? The amateur brought him a professional model, the finest kind of a blonde, the blonde that Renoir so loved to paint.

But these schemes were nothing to the astuteness of a Chinaman who wrote that his celestial happiness would be unbounded if he could obtain a mere line or two by the "Master" (Renoir could support "Master" better in writing than in conversation) for the modest sum of . . .

Renoir was reading the letter aloud. At this point, before turning the page, he said: "I'll wager, Vollard, that he will offer me something like three hundred francs. But it would be nice to have a picture in China, just the same." He read on.

The price suggested was five hundred pounds sterling. Renoir let him have a picture for which he had refused double that price.

"That chap has a very pleasant face!" I said one day to Renoir, speaking of a man who had just left the studio. He had just brought the painter a very beautiful Louis XIV frame. "It is an heirloom," he had declared. "Won't the portrait of my wife that you promised to do, look splendid in that!" (A smaller canvas had been agreed upon, as it happened.)

"Yes, Vollard, I am convinced more and more every day that he is a second Chocquet!"

The following day, in an antique shop, the same "amateur" came in with the same frame, the heirloom.

"I'm bringing back the frame that I took on trial," I heard him say to the dealer.

Since Renoir was for ever confined to his chair by rheumatism, the amateur ran no risk that the painter would drop in to see him to judge the effect of the canvas in the frame. But he did not count on another thing. Not long after, Renoir found the portrait that the "second Monsieur Chocquet" had got away from him, listed in the catalogue of a public sale.

Chapter Twenty-Two

PORTRAIT OF A GREAT COLLECTOR

Side by side with the collectors who are always on the look-out for a good bargain—and apart from certain "eccentrics" like Chocquet, de Bellio, and Caillebotte (to mention only those who are dead), who really loved the pictures they bought—there exists a species of collector who, in spite of his invincible indifference, even distaste, for the arts, possesses collections of pictures just as others have racing-stables. To this class of "grand amateurs" belonged Monsieur Chauchard, who, anxious to make a fine impression to the very last *sou* of his millions, ordered the pictures which had cost him the most to be borne before the bier at his funeral. But this grand old man died before the work of Renoir had attained high enough prices to be admitted to his "galleries."

Isaac de Camondo, however, shall have a special place in his history, not so much because he possessed several Renoirs (which he bought against his better judgment), but because of his desperate efforts to develop a taste for this kind of painting.

About 1910 Count Isaac de Camondo came into my shop. I imagined that the eye of the celebrated collector had been caught by a Renoir *Nude* exhibited in the window. It developed, however, that he had come to see a Degas drawing. He examined it with a bored air, and, between yawns, asked me the price. While I was wrapping up the drawing, which he had finally decided to buy, I hazarded:

"And the *Nude* by Renoir?" I turned around the easel which held the canvas. Monsieur de Camondo stepped back a few paces.

"If your Renoir were younger, perhaps he could be cured of that excess of colour, and learn how to draw; but when a painter is past sixty years of age and draws an arm like that, a thigh like this (with the point of his cane he indicated the parts of the canvas) . . . and just look at the colour of those cheeks! . . . And besides, do you know what Renoir lacks? . . . Tradition! You feel as if a man like that would not like the Louvre! Now Renouard, whom I met the other day at the museum, studying a Holbein, is made of different stuff!"

I happened at that time to have some drawings by the Renouard in question, especially a *Camérier du Pape,* which I showed to my client before bringing out some Degas drawings which he had asked to see.

"I have some much more important Degas than those," quoth Monsieur de Camondo, regarding the Renouard attentively, and he began to yawn again. This time, it was not difficult to divine that Monsieur de Camondo was yawning to simulate indifference, yet at the same time I could not for the life of me understand why he spoke of his Degas when I was showing him a Renouard.

However, I had visions of selling all my Renouards. And, reaching towards the racks, I said: "That is not the only one I have. I think you will agree with me that Renouard knows how to draw. . . ."

The yawning stopped short, and the visage of Monsieur de Camondo was suddenly overcast by an expression of discomfort. In spite of the signature, and in spite of the subject of the drawing, he had continued to mistake the Renouard for a Degas.

In order to change the subject, I asked him if he had always liked Impressionism.

"Certainly not. The old traditions of my family have made me a dyed-in-the-wool classicist from the cradle. Even though I am in modernism now up to my neck, I cannot repudiate my love for the works that our grandfathers have handed down to us,[1] such as our great cathedrals . . . even the less celebrated of our churches, for that matter. Take Saint-Germain l'Auxerrois, for instance. How many times have I stopped in front of it, on my way to the Louvre! When my friend Frantz Jourdain used to take me to see his Samaritaine,[2] we would pass Saint-Germain on the way, and my feet would fairly take root in front of it. He had all he could do to get me to move on.

"Although the very real relationship which exists between the old and the new was for long a mystery to me, it was not fully revealed to me until Frantz Jourdain took me up on the roof of the Louvre, and my eye fell simultaneously on Saint-Germain l'Auxerrois and the Samaritaine. . . .

"But to return to Impressionism: My first revelation came several years ago, at the home of a princess, . . . a friend of mine. I was looking at a sunset over a pond from the windows of her Henri II château. I had taken Frantz Jourdain with me; for a long time I had promised to present him to an authentic princess. At his request, the first valet of my amiable hostess brought in a Louis XVI frame of the purest style, which Jourdain wished to hold with his own hands between the sashes of the window. By stepping back a few paces, the portion of the pond cut out by the frame, gave the effect of an Impressionist picture! Not long after, I had the opportunity of

---

[1]Monsieur de Camondo's taste for French culture was such that he quite forgot his Turkish origin. (Author's Note.)

[2]*La Samaritaine* is perhaps the most atrocious building in Paris—a department store in the most flamboyant style of *nouveau art.* Frantz Jourdain was the owner. (Trans. Note.)

seeing some pictures by La Touche, which reminded me vividly of my framed glimpse of the pond. . . ."

"La Touche?" I queried.

"A great modern!" he pronounced. "I forget which critic said that. I came to Monet through La Touche, just as I began to like Saint-Saëns before understanding Wagner. 'You cannot reach Mecca in one day,' as the Turkish proverb goes. Once initiated into Impressionism, I no longer felt any desire to get out of it. But Impressionism must be *painting* too; and there is no such thing as painting without drawing!"

And he swore that he would never have a Renoir in his collection. But Monsieur de Camondo forgot that there is a proverb—not of Turkish origin—which declares that it is unwise to say: "Fountain, I shall drink not of thy water."

The day came when the art of Renoir began to trouble him. It was no longer a question of determining whether Renoir did or did not know how to draw, but whether a collection of Impressionist art could be complete without at least one Renoir. This much justice must be done to Camondo: he was capable, if worst came to worst, of sacrificing his personal tastes when he realized that certain names were necessary to a great collection.

"I shall end up by buying some samples of the wildest stuff that Renoir has done," he declared one day to an intimate friend. "If I can keep that down, I shall be able to swallow anything!"

The "wild" Renoirs were purchased.[3] However, Monsieur de Camondo could not always stomach their excess of colour and their lack of drawing. . . .

"How about trying another dish of Renoir?" I suggested one day.

"Perhaps. But none of your 1900's, nor your 1896's either," he protested.

I suggested a magnificent '89, the *Portrait of Madame de Bonnières.*

"I don't want any of your '89's either, for that is in the middle of the 'dry' period. A famous 'advanced' critic once remarked: 'Those Renoirs are like fruit that will never ripen.' But I have decided to have some Renoirs; so find me some good '70's, even '65's—women, of course. Watch out for the hands! None of those kitchen-wench hands of his. . . . Be very careful of the style of dress, too, and take care not to select any with that morbid note. I don't need to warn you, do I, that the Renoirs must not be too 'Renoir'? Keep in mind always that the pictures will go to the Louvre some day. . . . I won't object if you go back even as far as 1860! What I want above all is *drawing!*"

"I know an 1858, extraordinarily finished—in fact, the first picture that Renoir ever painted!"

"A woman?"

"No, a still-life."

"No still-lifes! I have just refused a *Fish* by Manet. . . . There's no more

[3]The Renoirs in the Camondo collection in the Louvre.

space in my dining-room. Do you happen to know off-hand if there still exists a *Nude* of a *grande dame,* in his earlier manner? I know his Faubourg ladies are not exactly . . . er. . . ."

"Not exactly appetizing," I was about to add, when Monsieur de Camondo continued:

"Not very easy to meet! I have heard it said, though, that Renoir was received socially by a relative of Rothschild—— Did you have something to say to me?"

I asked if I could offer to show him the work of some of the younger men.

"I see your game!" Camondo smiled. "And you're not the only one either! All you dealers seem to have passed the word around among yourselves. You all say: 'If you prefer the early work of the great painters, why don't you buy the work of some of the men who are still young?' You ought to know by this time that I won't have any works which are still disputed in my galleries. Oh, I know you're going to say 'What about Cézanne's *House of the Hanged?'* Well, yes, in that case I did buy a picture which had not yet been universally accepted. But I am protected; I have an autographed letter from Claude Monet, who gives me his word of honour that that picture is destined to become famous. If you come to see me some day, I will show you the letter. I keep it in a little pocket nailed to the back of the picture, for the edification of those malicious people who would like to have the laugh on me because of my *House of the Hanged.*"

With this security (as well as the prices they were bringing) Count Camondo felt that he was running no risk in buying Cézanne, and later acquired several others. He would have bought a good many more, but Cézanne painted too many still-lifes, which, as we have already seen, Camondo considered made specially to hang in a dining-room. And his dining-room was full of still-lifes.

Monsieur de Camondo was getting ready to depart; he turned for a last word:

"I would like to do something for your younger men just the same. They all adore Renoir, don't they? Well, you are at liberty to say that I asked you to show me some Renoirs."

"I have already given it out that you have taken a Degas," I answered indiscreetly.

"Ah! you must never make my purchases public without my permission! Don't you realize that the whole world has its eyes fixed on me, and that each time I buy a painting, the reputation of the painter goes up, and makes later acquisitions more difficult? The dealers are so *Jewish* these days!

"But if you promise to say nothing about what I buy, and also not to try to get the better of me, I will introduce you to some of my friends. For instance, to begin with, I will call over those two men whom you see going by there across the street. They never buy pictures; but it's something to have a baron and a marquis seen in your shop. . . ."

The two persons entered.

Camondo: Things not going very well, Marquis? You look as if . . .

The Marquis: I've just had a terrible blow! My son Jacques inherited over a million francs from his mother last year. Would you believe it, my banker has just informed me that there are only three francs and eighty-five centimes left in his account! And I was so proud of him too! On his eighteenth birthday I gave him a little farm to keep him in contact with the practical side of life. Well, sir, when fodder was high the cows nearly starved, I can tell you!

Camondo: If he had bought Impressionism instead of sowing his wild oats, he would have tripled his million in three years!

The Marquis: You know how interested I am in that kind of painting; you have never seen me miss an exhibition at Durand-Ruel's; but, frankly, I would rather see a crowd of harlots get the money than people like Renoir, Pissarro, and Sisley. . . . Have you ever really looked at a man who buys Impressionism? Your friend Florent, for instance. Why, he's a nervous wreck from the rumour that Sisleys might weaken. So the doctor has ordered him to sell his collection.[4] And Domergue, too, looks positively haggard when he is talking about the unhoped-for rise in Manets. My boy Jacques has gone through a million instead of making three. . . . Well, perhaps, but, he is just as gay as he ever was. He still throws his arms around my neck and says: "Good old dad, I love you." His eyes are still clear and there's not a line of worry on his forehead.

Someone had entered the shop. It was Viscount Jumelle. I recognized him from a caricature I had seen by Sem. He shook hands with the baron.

"Accept my compliments, Philippe, on your *Meat Pie* at the Epatant Exhibition. It looks good enough to eat!"

The Baron (modestly): Before painting a stroke, I went to study Bonnat's *Portrait of Coignet.* What a miracle it is to have created that harmony of red and black; the vermilion is enchanting and the bitumens amazingly rich. How marvelously the body is felt under it all!

The Viscount: I am very keen about Bonnat's drawing, and his colour too, although I feel that the Master has sacrificed himself a little too much to Impressionism in his latest works.[5]

The Viscount's remark rather astonished me, for he had bought a Cézanne at the Theodore Duret sale, ten years before. When I mentioned it, he answered: "It was not I, it was the Viscountess."

"But how do *you* like that canvas of Cézanne's?" I asked.

"I haven't seen it," he replied. "It has always hung in the Viscountess' bedroom."

Monsieur de Camondo was decidedly a man of his word. He arrived at my shop one day, bringing Monsieur B., a "serious" collector. The two

---

[4]See Appendix I, B.

[5]See Appendix I, C.

amateurs happened to find two of their confrères there: King Milan of Serbia, an eclectic (he went from Bouguereau to Van Gogh) and M. Sarlin, a "specialist" in the 1830's (the high-class 1830's). Someone had informed Sarlin (quite mistakenly) that he had seen a Daubigny in my shop—a Daubigny "with ducks."

Monsieur de Camondo (to Monsieur Sarlin): They were talking at the club of the new Corot you have bought. A Corot with water, of course?

Monsieur Sarlin (a little annoyed): No, a Corot without water.

Camondo and Monsieur B. (in unison): A Corot without water!

Monsieur Sarlin: No, there is no water, but the tone is magnificent.

Vollard: Good colour covers a multitude of sins.

Camondo: You have to watch out for colour! Once you have put your foot in it . . .

King Milan was looking with interest at a pair of field-glasses slung from Monsieur B.'s shoulders by a strap.

"Have you been to the races?" his Majesty inquired. "You haven't any good tips, have you?"

"These glasses," replied Monsieur B., a little haughtily, "are for examining the pictures that are submitted to me!"

King Milan had nothing further to say to such an unexpected explanation.

"I will show you," continued Monsieur B. "By looking at the canvas through the large end of the glasses—thereby reducing it—I can judge the drawing better. I don't buy pictures with my ears, you know. I'm not that kind. . . . One must always think of the sale later on."

"You are thinking of selling?" inquired Monsieur de Camondo.

"That will depend on the kind of marriage my daughter makes! It's not that we won't have enough to give her a dowry, even if she should marry a duke, or a prince—indeed, the son of a king. [At this point a slight grimace imperceptibly altered the placid features of King Milan.] But in the latter case, my Renoirs, my Meissoniers, my Besnards, my Rembrandts would no longer be of any use to me. With a royal son-in-law, can you see me keeping up a picture gallery to attract people to my house!"

With a curiosity which somewhat surprised me, especially after the wry face that I had just observed, King Milan inquired discreetly the age of the daughter.

"Oh!" exclaimed Monsieur B. "The little one hasn't started teething yet! So you see I haven't finished collecting!"

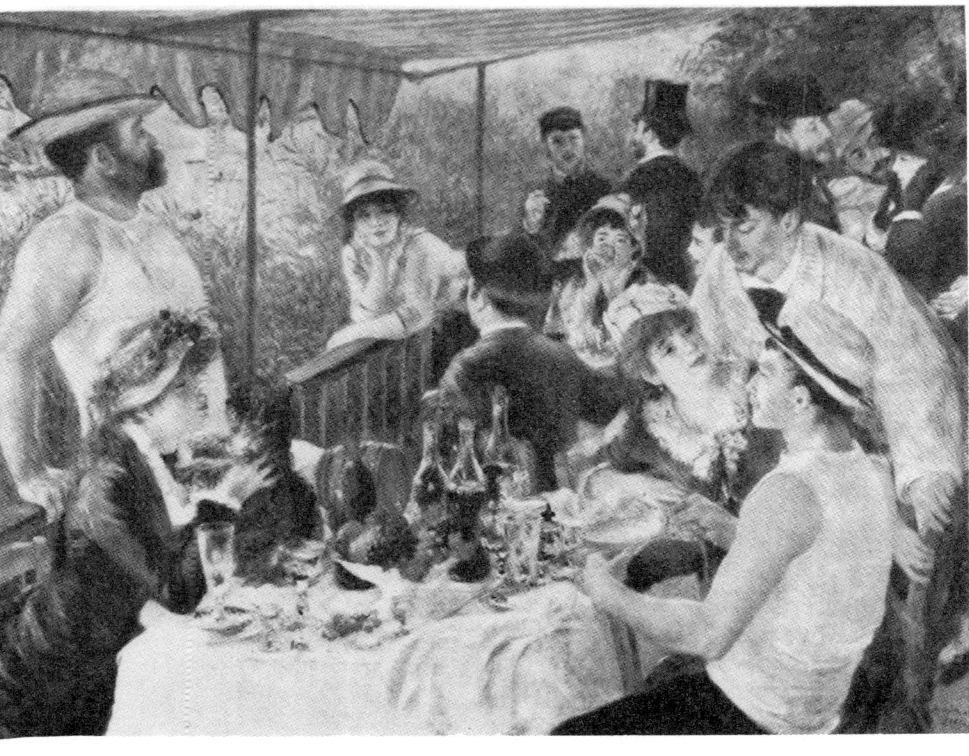

LUNCHEON OF THE BOATMEN AT BOUGIVAL (1881)

See p. 33.

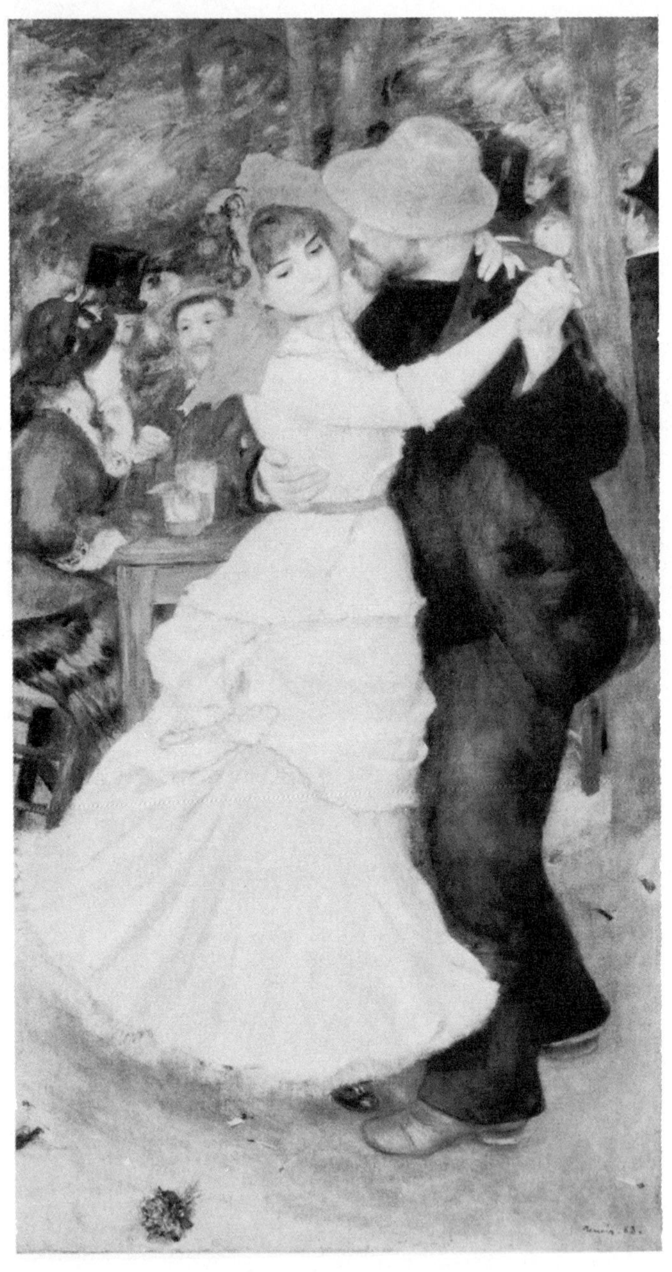

THE DANCE AT BOUGIVAL (1882–83)

Chapter Twenty-Three

RENOIR PAINTS MY PORTRAIT (1915)

I HAD already posed several times for Renoir. He had made one lithograph of me, and three studies in oil, one of which was carried rather far. It showed me with my elbows on a table, holding in one hand a statuette by Maillol (1908).

After that, I felt I had had my due. But at that time Renoir had not yet painted the portrait of Bernstein (1910), a canvas in a very extraordinary harmony of blue.

From that moment on, my greatest desire was to have a portrait of myself in a similar harmony. Renoir agreed, but he made one condition. "You must have a suit of the kind of blue I like," he said; "you know what it is, Vollard, that metallic blue with silver lights."

So I devoted myself to blue; but every time I ordered a new blue suit, Renoir would say: "That is not right yet."

In 1915 I had gone to spend a few days at *Les Collettes.* I had forgotten all about the portrait. As I was crossing the orchard of orange-trees, which extends from the road to the house, I heard someone call my name.

It was Renoir coming back from the fields, in an arm-chair borne by "Big Louise" and Baptistin, the gardener. The model was walking ahead, carrying the canvas.

The two porters stopped. "Don't walk so fast, Madeleine," Renoir called to the model. "I want to look at my picture." Then, turning to me: "I haven't been able to go out for two weeks; I certainly needed a change of scene. It would have taken only a few strokes to finish that picture; then I counted on starting something with Madeleine for a model; but they forgot to bring my sunshade. What a magician the sun is!

"One day when I was with Lauth in Algeria, we suddenly saw a fabulous personage advancing towards us, mounted on a donkey. As he drew nearer, he proved to be nothing but a beggar, but in the sun his tatters glistened like precious stones."

The model stood the picture up against a tree.

"Not bad, is it?" Renoir said to me with a slight wink. "The trouble is that indoors it will be all black, but after I've had a little skirmish with it in the studio, you'll see how brilliant it will be!"

When we had arrived at the studio, he said: "Vollard, will you call my 'doctoress'?"

"What?" I asked.

"I absolutely cannot get used to the word 'nurse'! What a nice hat you have got on! . . . I must do a picture of you. Sit down in that chair. You are in quite a peculiar light; but a good painter should be able to accommodate himself to any light! What are you going to do with your hands? Here, take Claude's cardboard tiger, or the cat sleeping by the fire-place, if you prefer."

I chose the cat, and did my best to assure myself of the good graces of the beast. Luck was with me, for after a few peaceful purrs, he went to sleep on my knees.

The "doctoress" prepared the palette. Renoir told her what colours he wanted, and she pressed the tubes. When the palette was set, and the nurse was about to slip the brush between his fingers, he exclaimed: "But you've forgotten my 'thumb'!"[1]

I was afraid there would be no portrait that day, but the nurse found the "thumb" in the pocket of her apron.

Renoir always attacked his canvas without the slightest apparent plan. Patches would appear first, then more patches, then, suddenly, a few strokes of the brush, and the subject "came out." Even with his stiffened fingers, he could do a head in one sitting as easily as when he was young.[2]

I could not take my eyes off his hand. "You see, Vollard?" he said. "One doesn't need hands to paint. They're quite superfluous."

Renoir's methods were exactly contrary to those of Cézanne, who never allowed his sitters to talk or move about. In fact Renoir had been known to dismiss a model if she were not animated enough. So we began to talk at once. Of a sudden we heard singing outside in the street:

"Liberty, dear Liberty,
Fight with thy defenders!"

Renoir: Do you hear that? They're always howling about liberty and putting it on monuments and writing about it in books. What a horror they have of it in the bottom of their hearts! One day I asked a friend to tell me frankly what he disliked about my work. He replied, "You take too many liberties. . . ."

Once I read in a paper how the United[3] Socialists, at one of their conventions, expelled a member in spite of his outraged protests. At first I thought it was some poor devil who was being robbed of his daily bread; but

---

[1]A band of rolled cloth which he habitually wore on his thumb.

[2]The portrait of Wagner was painted in twenty-five minutes. See pages 48–49.

[3]It is difficult to tell exactly what "united" means. The title implies unity of doctrine, but there are majorities and minorities within the party none the less. (Author's Note.)

then I learned that it was a rich socialist, and that he had been aiding the party out of his own pocket! What do you think of that? They gave him his liberty, and the poor man was lost when he found he had nobody to serve!

You can't have freedom except under a tyrant! The Pope took it as a matter of course that Raphael should paint the story of Psyche in the Vatican; but if he were living now, do you think the State would let him paint the story of the Virgin?[4] Just the other day I opened the *Fables of La Fontaine* which Claude had brought back from school: in the story of "The Little Fish Will Grow Up," the line "If God gives him life" has been changed to "If he has been given life." . . . It's really distressing! I see Liberty written everywhere, but underneath they put: "Lay instruction is compulsory." . . . In the old days, when there was no such thing as Liberty, there was no compulsory education. And they knew how to speak French, too . . . and write it!

(Renoir burst out laughing.)

The Impressionist School itself is a good example of the universal distaste for liberty. No sooner had we laid down the rules for our first exhibitions, and proclaimed that everyone was to paint just as he wanted, than we promptly forbade anyone to exhibit in the official Salon!

There was a knock at the door, and a physician from Paris entered. He was travelling in the Midi and had come to pay a call on Renoir.

"A funny thing has just happened," he said. "One of my patients just declared that he is not going to permit himself to be inoculated with salvarsan as long as the war lasts. Can you guess why? Because it is a German discovery!"

"Do you believe in all these modern remedies?" asked Renoir.

"Do I believe in them! Well, if salvarsan had been discovered in the time of Francis I, he would not have died so young as he did."

"That reminds me of a book of Geoffroy's about the Louvre," said the painter. "The way it treated poor King Francis!—'The old satyr,' 'the conceited old rascal.' . . . These republicans make me laugh. They don't think a king has any right to sleep with a woman!"

The doctor seemed to feel that Renoir was poking fun at the government, and with an air of superiority he declared:

"I'm not in favour of the Church."

"At Pierre's first communion," continued Renoir, "I saw a woman who had just drunk the wine of the Lord; as she returned to her place, her hat was all askew and she stumbled around among the chairs; she had lost all control of herself. I never understood until then the power the priests have, when they can put people in such a state. The freemasons, the Protestants, the whole crowd, in fact, would give anything to get the women out of the

[4]It is to be remembered here, and in the ensuing discussion, that the French State is anticlerical. (Trans. Note.)

clutches of the clergy, but they haven't the influence; that's what makes them so furious. I like things to be open and above-board. The clergy wear a definite costume; when you see them coming, you can take to your heels. But your damned socialists dress just like everyone else—they get hold of you before you know what's coming, and then they bore you to death!"

The door of the studio had opened, and Madame Renoir entered, a piece of blue paper in her hand.

"Here's a telegram from Rodin," she announced. "He is at Cannes. He is going to take luncheon with us to-day. You have a portrait of him to do for the Bernheim book, you know. He says that he will arrive about noon, and that he has very little time to spare. I have told Baptistin to get the car ready; I am going over to Nice to get a chicken, and some *pâté,* and a lobster. I'll be back in an hour."

Then turning to me, she added: "Renoir can say what he likes, but an automobile is a great convenience."

The doctor rose to go. "I'm going to Nice, and I would like to take advantage of the motor if I may."

Madame Renoir (to her husband): A letter came from the "Triennial" which I almost forgot to give you. They probably want you to send something to their exhibition.[5]

We were alone again.

Renoir: I suppose you agree with my wife. But just think a minute; if we knew nothing about motor cars or railroads, or telegrams, Rodin would have come by the diligence, we would have been notified a month ahead of time, the chicken would have been fattening in the poultry yard, the *pâté* made here; and it would have been a lot better than the tinned stuff my wife will bring back from Nice! Furthermore, I would never have found boric acid in my chicken, as I did the other day! Then, too, I wouldn't be always bothered by a swarm of people coming in to see me. If we lived in the good old times, without any railroads, tramways or autos, they would all have stayed at home.

Madame L. comes from Nice to our house on the tram in forty minutes. And she never misses her car either, the old hen! (Then imitating Madame L.'s nasal voice:) "When I left Paris, my husband made me swear that I would come to see you often." Bah! the old fool! And she has a nerve! She's a good Protestant, so she is always abusing the pomp of Catholic ceremonies. You know that I'm no sectarian, Vollard, but when I find myself with a Protestant, I become the most violent Catholic! I wish you could have heard Madame L. . . . "The Protestant religion has the virtue of being a simple religion at least." A simple religion! She thinks so, does she, the old idiot!

"Madame," I said to her, "I dare say you mean a sombre religion. You

[5]See Appendix I, D.

can't say that savages are simple. Just look at the brilliant colours they love to wear!"

After boring me to death with her "simple" religion, what does she do but start in to talk about music, especially the compositions of her friend B.? I can't help it if I don't like literary music. Gallimard once took me to see one of B's operas. He came to see me next day when I was painting a nude.

"How did you like the opera last night?" he said.

"Well," I replied, "it doesn't amuse me half as much as painting a behind!"

Renoir continued: Poor old Rheims cathedral! Have you seen the pictures of the decapitated angels in the papers? What a pity! But the worst of it is that after the war they'll go and rebuild it. Just look at the way they have arranged the façade of the church at Vézelay! That's enough.

In a row of Gothic columns, for instance, the motif of which is a cabbage-leaf, I defy you to find a single leaf exactly opposite the other, or carved in the same way. The same thing applies to the columns themselves: they are never squarely opposite each other, nor exactly alike. Not one of the modern architects, beginning with Viollet le Duc, has grasped the fact that the very spirit of Gothic is irregularity. Instead, they've decided that the early architects didn't know what they were about. I once remarked, in the presence of several architects, that the Parthenon was irregularity itself. I thought they would die laughing. It was a guess on my part, but I felt that it must be so. I found out later that I was right. No architect will ever admit that the regularity must be in the eye, and not in the object itself. There is a new church at Rome called Saint Paul's, which is atrocious because the columns were turned out on a lathe. When you look at the columns of the Parthenon, you are amazed by their regularity. But look closer, and you realize that they're all different. The same irregularity is to be found in all the primitives, even in China and Japan. It is the professors who have invented the modern compass regularity.

Have you read the article by Pelletan about Rheims cathedral? He proposes to have the German prisoners build a new one alongside the old! Deep down in his heart the good man is really persuaded that it would be more beautiful than the original!

I recall two of the prophets on one of the portals of the Rheims cathedral. There is a leaf motif above one of them; what astonishing fantasy that is! And there are two little heads on either side of the other prophet . . . such grace! . . .

The richness of those doors is unbelievable! Think of making such heavy material as light as lace! What an achievement to have given such a ponderous mass so much richness and at the same time such delicacy! . . . Tell all your Pelletans that with all the millions in the world they can't build anything to approach it, and they will reply in chorus: "What about Progress?"

Three figures stand out among all the masterpieces of Rheims: *Christian Religion,* the *Queen of Sheba,* and the *Smiling Angel.* It is beauty that maddens you!

When you see such things as that, you realize how depressing and, above all, how futile modern sculpture is! Look at those horses on the Grand Palais, each pulling in a different direction! Now if the Germans would only drop their bombs on that! No such luck!

They keep publishing those pastels by La Tour in the papers along with the sculpture of Rheims. As soon as a picture has suffered at the hands of the *Boches,* they at once make it out to be a masterpiece.

Vollard: But isn't La Tour a great painter?

Renoir: Well, perhaps. . . .

V.: About on a par with Nattier, for instance?

R.: Oh, better than that. . . . But I can't understand a painter who doesn't like to paint hands!

I was looking at a canvas propped up on a chair. It had several small subjects painted side by side: some figs, a small fine head, a little uncompleted nude.

R.: I started the nude with a model that Madame Frey had sent to me. "I can guarantee," she wrote, "that this young girl has a good moral character."

But when she had undressed, I could easily have dispensed with her moral character if her breasts had only been firmer! I kept that canvas for the little girl's head rather than for the figs or the nude. The model was a foreign woman of whom I made a large portrait later.

In the sketch I caught that cruel and yet gentle air which I was never able to get so well in the finished picture. There is an amusing story about that. The woman's husband kept repeating: "I vant you to make my vife qvite indimate!"

I painted the dress almost up as far as the neck. He repeated: "Still more indimate. . . ."

So I added a little collar.

"But, Monsieur Renoir," he protested, "I dell you *indimate, very* indimate! I vant to see at least one of the breasts!"

"I've run out of oil. Look in the little bottle in the corner of my box, Vollard.

"I can't keep that bottle full. I'm always afraid my pictures will be too thin! What a perpetual problem it is to paint rich and 'fat'——not thin like Ingres! Time has helped him out, but when he had just finished his pictures, they were very disagreeable. They stuck into your eyes like steel blades!

V.: Did you know Ingres?

R.: When I was about twelve or thirteen years old, my employer, the potter, sent me to the National Library one day to trace a portrait of

Shakespeare which was to be painted on a plate. In looking about for a seat, I came to a corner of the room where several gentlemen were gathered, among them the architect who designed the library. I noticed in the group a short man with impatient gestures who was busy doing a portrait of the architect. It was Ingres. He had a block of paper in his hand, and he would make a sketch, throw it away, begin another. Then all at once he made a drawing as perfect as if he had worked on it for a week.

Ingres must have appeared very tall when he was seated, but when he stood up, his knees seemed right next to his feet.

To return to his pictures, I don't know anything so awful as his *Œdipus and the Sphinx.* It has one good bit, however, a beautifully painted ear. His Napoleon seated on the throne is exceedingly beautiful too. What majesty it has! But Ingres' masterpiece is *Madame de Senones:* the colour is superb. . . . It is painted like a Titian. You must go to Nantes to see it. It's not like so many of the Ingres which look well in a photograph; you really have to see the original to appreciate it.

I like the *Martyrdom of Saint Symphorien* much less. There are very beautiful things about it, but a lot of sham also. Ingres has been tremendously ridiculed on account of paintings like that and the *Thetis Supplicating Jupiter.* But it isn't fair simply to say of a painter that he is absurd in this picture and brilliant in that; you ought to find out the reason why in each case.

It is a curious thing that when Ingres is carried away by his passion, he seems to run to imbecility. Look at the *Francesca da Rimini;* he tried to express so much passion in the attitude of the young man, that he made the neck twice as long as it should be; and Lord knows he knew how to draw a neck! Then the neck of *Madame Rivière,* in the Louvre, is another example! And the neck of the woman in *Roger and Angélique* . . . People usually think she has a goitre! That is because Ingres, in making her bend her head back so far to show pain, threw the muscles of the neck out of position. And yet people will tell you that he painted without passion.

I think I said that the *Madame de Senones* was his masterpiece. But I had forgotten about *La Source.* It is a superb thing. There are budding little breasts for you, and a lovely torso . . . and feet and a perfectly empty face!

V.: And the portrait of Bertin?

R.: Yes, it's magnificent, but I wouldn't take ten *Bertins* for one *Madame de Senones.* Compared to *Madame de Senones,* the other is so much confectionery.

V.: Guillemet once asked Corot what he thought of Ingres. Corot answered: "Lots of talent, but he got into a deplorable rut; he thought that life was to be found in outlines, but the truth is that outlines always elude the eye."

R.: Did you hear that idiot Z. the other day trying to compare Delacroix and Ingres, in order to make people think that he knew something about art?

V.: Guillemet told me also what Delacroix said one day, while he was walking with Chassériau in the Ingres room at the Hotel de Ville where he was then doing his own decorations: "It's good, very good. Of course Ingres has his limitations; Lord, so have I. My work is full of faults too, Heaven knows. When we are both dead, I suppose we'll stay in Purgatory a while for those faults. But if you were to give Ingres the job of doing my painting, and me his—well, I'll wager that I would come out ahead!"

But Delacroix is really more to your taste, is he not, Monsieur Renoir?

R.: By nature, of course, I have a preference for Delacroix. There isn't a finer picture in the world than the *Algerian Women.* How really Oriental those women are——the one who has a little rose in her hair, for instance! And the gait of the Negress is absolutely right. You can fairly smell the incense; it takes me back at once to Algeria. . . . But that is no reason for my not liking Ingres.

(Renoir had finished working for the day. He had half opened a newspaper which he found beside him, but he threw it down again angrily.)

R.: Oh, Lord, there they go again with their sports! To-day it's tennis. . . .

I haven't anything against tennis, you understand, but I was watching some people playing the other day, and they looked so silly and pretentious! In my day, we played battledore and shuttlecock, and if there was anybody who played tennis it wasn't considered anything extraordinary. And one managed quite well with a three-franc racket. The other day C.'s son had the gall to ask his father for seventy-five francs to buy a racket with!

The best game of all is "corks." You have to squat down all the time, and that squeezes your liver and expels the poisons. But who would think of playing corks nowadays? They've even got young girls playing modern games too. . . .

The other day I was doing a portrait of a girl of ten. I tried to interest her in the story of the little hunchback who turned into a prince charming and married the daughter of the king. . . .

"It isn't true," she said. "What good is it, if it isn't true?"

"Well, what do you read, then?"

"Instructive things, of course. *The Funeral Prayers* of Bossuet and *The Art of Poetry* by Boileau . . ."

By the way, Vollard, hand me that paper again; it seems to me that there was an article devoted to Art, with a big A, just above the one on tennis.

But Renoir had hardly laid eyes on it when he cried:

"Really, that's too much! Here they've got the same man who writes about run-away horses to do the articles on art! And yet you'd be considered a great fool if you tried to tell them that art is an indefinable thing, and that it would cease to be art if it could be defined."

Renoir had thrown the paper aside once more. He had not mentioned the

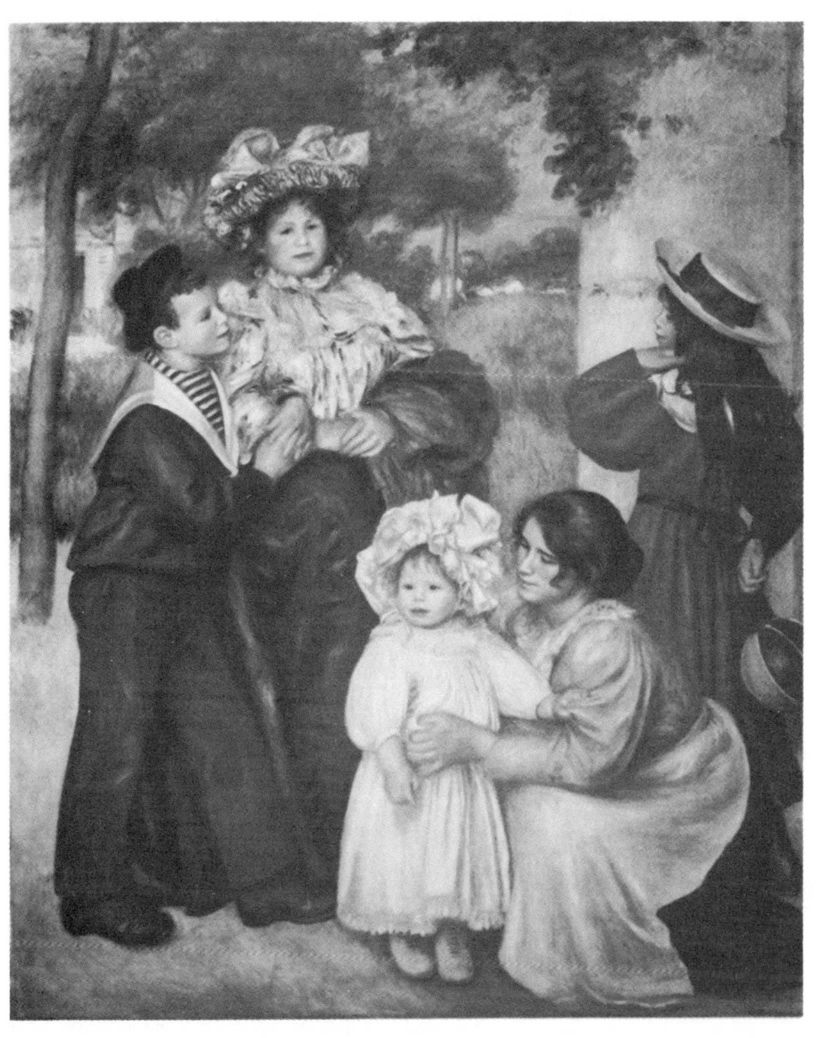

THE ARTIST'S FAMILY (1896)

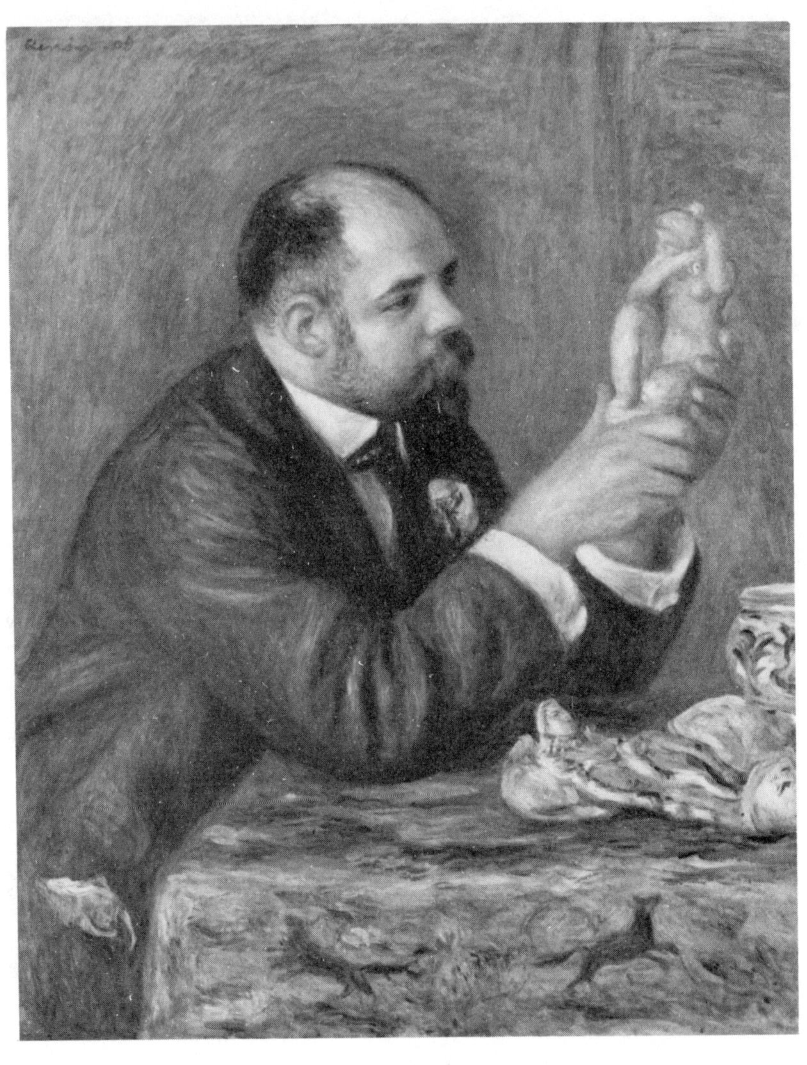

PORTRAIT OF AMBROISE VOLLARD (1908)

See p. 95.

author of the article, and without doubt he had not troubled to look at it. But I caught the paper just in time, for it had fallen into the fire-place and had started to burn. I saw that the article was signed "Henri Bergson." But the name meant nothing to Renoir.

Vollard: Here's something that will please you. I see an advertisement here for a new book by Anatole France.

Renoir: No, he has no feeling for simple sentiment.

We heard the sound of a motor-car approaching. It was Madame Renoir coming back from Nice. At the same moment the "doctoress" came in to announce that it was past noon. She arranged the brushes and closed the colour-box.

Baptistin and Big Louise, carrying the Sedan chair, followed the nurse. While he was being lifted in, Renoir said to me: "I must get a good likeness of Rodin; I have already done some drawings of him. But Rodin has a rather curious head—a combination of Jupiter and an office manager.

"Louise," he continued, turning to the maid, "don't forget to remind me about that pipe-manufacturer who said he would come in again. There's another man who says he can't live without some of my pictures! I said to that friend of his whom he always brings along when he comes to see me: 'Make him understand that I don't like to sell my pictures,' and the fellow replied: 'But, Monsieur Renoir, he is such a good man!'

"I loathe 'good' people. . . . I'd laugh if my pictures started to go down in price. The consternation among the Renoir speculators would be magnificent. I can just hear the pipe-maker wailing: 'That scoundrelly Renoir! Think of all the brier-root I could have bought with the money I spent on his pictures!' "

CHAPTER TWENTY-FOUR

LUNCHEON WITH RODIN

AS we were leaving the studio, we heard the sound of a motor-horn, and Rodin drove up, in high good humour.

Renoir: You haven't been able to give up your automobile either, have you? I am always complaining about mine, but I am very glad to have it when I want to go over to Nice.

Rodin: It belongs to one of my admirers, the Countess of X.

Renoir: A most remarkable woman, isn't she?

Rodin: Her heart and mind are one and the same. I must tell you her latest *bon mot*. The Countess was in the studio while I was having my hair trimmed. We were talking about the importance of proceeding with the utmost care in making restorations in cathedrals——meddling with any national property in fact, when a gentleman delegated by some of my friends came to tell me that the State was going to accept the donation of my works.

"Jules," the Countess exclaimed to the barber, "be careful you don't cut off too much; the Master is about to become national property!"

(Madame was showing Rodin some photographs of Jean and Claude as little children.)

Rodin: What handsome children, Madame! What did you feed them on?

Madame Renoir: My own milk, of course!

Rodin: If you nursed them yourself, what happened to your social duties?

Madame Renoir could hardly keep from laughing. "We can sit down at the table now," she said, changing the subject. "You are going to have some olives grown on our own place, Monsieur Rodin."

"The Greeks lived on these!" said Rodin, taking an olive between his thumb and forefinger. "All that they needed was a piece of black bread, some goat's milk, and water from a near-by stream! How happy the Greeks were in their poverty, and what wonders they left us! The Parthenon, for instance. . . . I believe I have discovered the real inspiration of their masterpieces. The secret of the Greeks lay in their love of Nature!

"Nature! On my knees before Nature I have always sculptured my finest pieces. People have often reproached me for not putting a head on my *Homme qui marche*. Does one walk with one's head?"

Renoir: Have you seen the Russian Ballet?

Rodin: The Russians are wonderful dancers. I got one of them to pose on top of a column—one leg bent back and arms stretched upward. I was trying to make a genie rising into flight. But that day my mind was somewhere else; I was dreaming of the Greeks. And presently I began to fall asleep with the lump of clay in my hands. Suddenly I woke up; my model had simply quit his pose; that was all. Oh, for the time when the artist had some rights of his own! Somebody once told me a story about an ancient sculptor who was doing an Actæon attacked by hounds, so he loosed a hungry pack of dogs on his model. But if I had done half of that to my Russian, there would have been a terrible uproar.

Renoir: Tell us about the Pope. How did you like him? Did he pose well?

Rodin (shaking his head): The Pope[1] doesn't know anything about art. I wanted, for instance, to work on the ear, but it was impossible to see anything of it. I tried moving around, but as I moved, he would turn too. A far cry from Francis I, who stooped to pick up the brush that had fallen from Titian's hand.

(Rodin was looking at a *Nude* on the opposite wall.)

Renoir, I understand why you make the right arm of that woman larger than the left; the right arm is the active one.

Vollard: Will you allow me to visit your hermitage at Meudon some day and your cell at the Hotel Biron?

Rodin: With pleasure.[2] People seem to know every detail of my artistic life. And Heaven knows I try to avoid publicity!

V.: They say that in spite of all your genius you are not afraid to handle a hammer and chisel the way the ancient stone-cutters did!

Rodin (running his fingers through his beard): The dream of the sculptor is to attack the stone or the marble always with his own hands.

V.: They also say that . . .

Rodin (good-naturedly): Well, what else do they say?

V.: That the Institute has made advances in vain——

Rodin (violently): The devil! Why don't they want me to be a member of the Institute?

V.: Your friends, Master, love you with such a jealous love. . . .

Rodin: Well, I wish they loved me less and would not keep me from being immortalized. That's the same crowd that wanted to keep the subscription for the Balzac commission among themselves. "Master, when one has your genius . . ." they all say. My genius! When you consider that in the ministries, at the cemeteries, everywhere, a mere Saint-Marceau has the

[1]Benedict XV.

[2]See Appendix I, E.

advantage of me! You'll even see Bartholomé himself some day . . . Do you think Clémenceau would have made me begin his bust over again fourteen times if I had belonged to the Institute?

At this juncture little Claude Renoir got up abruptly from the table and exclaimed: "*Zut!* I'm going to miss the ants again." And, paying no attention to a "Will you hush, Claude?" from his mother, he planted himself with his hands in his pockets in front of Rodin.

"Monsieur Rodin, won't you come to see the ants at work?"

"What a little goose!" said Madame Renoir, while Claude, without waiting for Rodin to answer, ran out of doors. "He's thirteen years old and he still spends his time watching the ants."

Rodin: At thirteen, Michael Angelo had already given great promise; and I did my first modelling at the same age. What a difficult thing sculpture is! Of course there have been great painters in every period, but is it really any wonder that sculpture should have fallen into decay by the time I came along?

Renoir (to Rodin): Vollard showed me some extraordinary reproductions of your water-colours.

Rodin: I did them with the help of Clot. When he is gone, lithography will be a lost art. But Clot has an annoying sense of humour. The other day I left him alone in the studio, and when I came back he had taken all my medals from their box and had pinned them all over his coat. There are some things that ought not to be trifled with.

Madame Renoir: Do you like flowers, Monsieur Rodin?

Rodin: I love them! Mirbeau once told me about a chrysanthemum of a unique golden brown which had been substituted for the evergreen in the mortuary chamber of Princess X. And I recently had the opportunity of seeing an exceedingly rare carnation at the house of Viscountess Z.: it was black as ink and had a very bad odour.

Madame Renoir: There are no rare flowers here, but the garden is very pretty nevertheless. Look at the daisies over there by the window next to the mimosa! My husband has a preference for common flowers.

Rodin: Like Mallarmé! There was an artist with an exquisite style! Yet I have seen him carried away by a bouquet of mere meadow flowers.

Renoir: Speaking of Mallarmé, Madame Morisot said to him one day when he was reading one of his poems: "Come, Mallarmé, why don't you write down to your cook, just for once?"

"But I wouldn't write in any other way for my cook," he answered.

Renoir continued: Even though certain of Mallarmé's poems are beyond my comprehension, I realize what an exquisite and original person he was! I remember the simplicity with which he told about a certain Negro pupil at the school where he taught English:

"I often send him to the board to write in chalk, and you can't imagine the voluptuous sensation I get when I see that black express himself in white!"

"Let us take our coffee in the garden under the rose-bushes," suggested Madame Renoir.

"But what about my portrait?" said Rodin. Then, taking a large gold watch from his vest pocket, he said: "It is five minutes to two. The Countess's motor is to come for me at three o'clock sharp, and my secretary informed me this morning that I would not have another minute to spare for the rest of my stay in the Midi."

"Quick, then," said Renoir. "Take me up to the studio. Vollard, will you fasten a sheet of paper on the board for me?"

I waited for a little in the studio, for I was curious to see how Rodin would pose. But I was not obliged to leave the room, for Renoir did not object to the presence of others while he was at work. Once Rodin was seated, he remained as motionless as the Rodin in the Grévin Museum. At ten minutes to three, Renoir put down his pencil and asked for a cigarette; the portrait was finished.

"I still have ten minutes left," said Rodin. "I will have time to see the garden." But at that moment a knock was heard and the footman appeared at the studio door.

"Madame la Comtesse's motor is awaiting the Master."

Then Rodin turned to Madame Renoir, who had just come in, and said: "If I ever come back to the Midi, I shall ask you to show me your garden. I love Nature so."

I went downstairs with the great sculptor. The chauffeur was cranking the machine but could not start the motor.

"The Master will have to wait about a quarter of an hour," said the footman.

Rodin: A quarter of an hour. Then I'll have time to see the garden after all. That will please Madame Renoir. (Then, looking down at his varnished boots, he shook his head.) But, on second thought, there's nothing remarkable about flowers you can see along any railroad track.

It occurred to me to profit by this unexpected *tête-à-tête* by seeking out some new aspects of Rodin's personality. So I began: How do you plan out your work, Master?

Rodin: I depend on inspiration.

V.: What time is your brain most active for creative work? Between meals or right after eating?

Rodin: My mind works with the same facility at all times, and except for a little nap . . .

V.: When do you take your nap?

Rodin: After lunch. I follow the advice of my physician in that. One day he pointed to my cat, who had gone to sleep after drinking her bowl of milk, and said: "You ought to emulate the animals."

V.: I do not remember ever having read a description of your bedroom. That is a subject to tempt the pens of our best journalists. What is your bed like? Is it antique or modern?

Rodin: My bed is nothing special. If I were to sleep in an antique or a period bed, I should be afraid of becoming too much attached to it. But I keep a bit of art in my bedroom, for I feel an absolute need for a little beauty upon which to rest my eyes. As a matter of fact, I have one of my *Burghers of Calais* there at present.

V.: When you take your nap, are you dressed or not?

Rodin: Always completely dressed. Even if I should only remove my collar, I would be tempted to take things too easy; an artist lives all too short a life, as it is.

V.: Do you go to sleep easily?

Rodin: Very easily—unless some theme is gestating in my mind.

V.: They say that one can get to sleep readily by fixing one's eyes on some shining object.

Rodin: The Orientals contemplate their navels. But I have a music-box near my bed which was presented to me by one of my lady admirers from New York. When sleep does not come, I just press a button on the cover and in a second I am off like a child.

V.: Do you like music?

Rodin: I adore Wagner. The other day I was discussing music with Saint-Saëns and some friends. I stood up staunchly for Wagner. One must have the courage of one's convictions, you know.

V.: I do not know Saint-Saëns' music, but I have heard that he owes a great deal to Wagner. What brought about his ferocious hatred for his musical progenitor?

Rodin: It is only the truly individual artist who does not turn against the master from whom he received his training. Have you ever heard *me* speak ill of the Greeks?

V.: I have not asked you, Master, what name you would like posterity to know you by.

Rodin (with the modesty characteristic of great men): That is not for me to say. I might tell you, however, that at my last exhibition in Buenos Aires, all the papers there called me the Victor Hugo of Sculpture. Victor Hugo! There was a man surrounded with true friends who were solicitous of their master's glory. "The towers of Notre Dame form the H of his name."[3]

Not one of all the people who make so much over me, would ever conceive of anything like that for me! Think of the glory of having your name linked for eternity with Notre Dame!

The chauffeur had finally come to terms with his motor.

"The Master may start when he wishes," said the footman.

V.: (while Rodin was settling himself in the automobile): One last word, Master. In case you do not leave an epitaph, have you made arrangements for the place where you are to be buried?

Rodin: Just a hole in the garden; I have always been a simple man. But

[3]Vacquerie.

(here with a flattened hand he made the gesture of decapitating something) there are to be no priests. . . . If there were, I would not be a true heir of the Revolution, "a son of the Twentieth Century," as my good friend Frantz Jourdain said. . . .

The car moved forward. The face of the great artist was framed in the window.

"I have no fear of the devil!" he cried.

Chapter Twenty-Five

ARTISTS OF FORMER DAYS

AFTER Rodin's departure, I found Renoir in his studio with an album on his knees.

Renoir: What do you think of my fire-place? There's not too much sham about it, is there? It *is* a bit modern. I found the model for it in this album, which I bought from a dealer in Paris, in Rue Bonaparte. There are all sorts of period motifs in it, from the most complicated ornaments to the most ordinary moulding.

Vollard: You like things of the past, don't you?

R.: There are plenty of people who like the new; I prefer the old. I like old frescoes, ancient pottery, and tapestries that show the patina of time. I use the word advisedly, for the most important thing is that a work of art be able to carry this patina. Only fine things can stand the test. New things weary me, and when I go to the Luxembourg and see that conglomeration of glistening white statues, all of them in strained violent attitudes, I feel like running away for fear of being kicked or punched! When I still had the use of my legs, I found nothing more restful than to walk through the rooms of the Louvre. It was like meeting old friends in whom I was always finding new and charming qualities.

V.: Do you refuse to admit that there has been any progress in the art of painting?

R.: Progress in painting? No, I cannot see any. No progress in ideas, nor any in technique, either. I once tried to change the yellow on my palette; the result was that I floundered about for ten years and then came back to the same one I used before. . . . On the whole, the modern palette is the same as the one used by the artists of Pompeii . . . down to Poussin, Corot and Cézanne; I mean that it has not been enriched. The ancients used earths, ochres, and ivory-black—you can do anything with that palette. Other tones have been added, of course, but we could easily do without them. I have told you, haven't I, about the great discovery people thought had been made by substituting blue and red for black? But it doesn't come anywhere near giving you the richness of ivory-black! With a simple palette the ancients painted as well as the moderns (one must be polite to one's contemporaries) and their work is chemically more permanent.

V.: But if the painter cannot reasonably hope to improve his palette——

R.: What is there left for him to do? He should strengthen and perfect his *métier,* untiringly, but he can only do that with the help of tradition. To-day everybody has genius, that goes without saying; but one thing is certain: nobody knows how to draw a hand any more, and none of us know our craft. The ancients were able to produce that marvellous surface quality and those limpid colours, the secret of which we are still vainly hunting for, because they had a thorough knowledge of their craft. I am very much afraid that modern theories will not discover it for us.

But, although craftsmanship is the foundation of art, it is not everything. There is another aspect of the art of the ancients which makes it beautiful: it is that serenity one never wearies of, that makes us feel that their work is eternal. Serenity was within themselves; it came not only from the nature of their simple and tranquil lives, but from their religious faith. They were conscious of their frailty, and in their triumphs as well as their failures, they associated the spirit of divinity with all that they did. For them, God was always present; man did not count. With the Greeks it was Apollo or Minerva; the painters of Giotto's time had a heavenly protector too. Their works have that aspect of gentle serenity which gives them their profound charm and makes them immortal. But man, in his modern pride, has chosen to reject this partnership, because it belittles himself in his own eyes. He has driven out God, and, in so doing, he has driven out happiness too.

The painters of those enviable days had their faults, of course . . . happily for them. But when you see how the freshness of their work has endured down the centuries, you are blind to anything but their qualities. I love to caress those beautiful marbles, and touch the marvelous impasto of their paintings; I cannot express the joy it gives me.

For several centuries there was keen competition in France in taste and imagination; châteaux rose from the soil, the bronzes, the pottery, the tapestries of that time had a magical beauty; everyone vied with his neighbour in contributing to the richness of France with clay, wood, iron, or marble. In this country of ours everything was beautiful up to the end of the eighteenth century, from the châteaux down to the humblest cottage. You have only to see the albums in the Trocadero Museum to get an idea of the vigour of those artists, of their firmness of design in the smallest detail: even a bolt, or the knob of a door. Those people fortunately were not working for any Salon!

The harm that the Salon does is incredible! Did you hear about the fond mother who said to Bailby: "My son has caught the autumn Salon manner"? Wasn't it you, Vollard, who told me that Matisse had been refused at the Autumn Salon? It's curious how people are positively repelled by real painter qualities in a picture. Rousseau, the Douanier, must make their flesh creep! That *Scene from Prehistoric Times* of his, with the man right in the middle rigged out in a department-store suit and carrying a gun! But all that aside, must a picture have harmonious colours to be enjoyable?

Must it be a subject that you can understand? What a lovely tone there is in that Rousseau! Do you remember the nude woman on the wall opposite the hunter? I am sure Ingres himself would not have disliked that!

V.: How did it happen that the artisans of the past disappeared all at once?

R.: You mean how did the change come so suddenly? A cabinet-maker explained it to me one day without realizing it. "I make the chair legs," he said; "someone else makes the back; another puts them together; but there isn't one of us who knows how to make a complete chair."

There is the whole secret! The worker cannot enjoy the result of his work any more, so he has lost all taste for the job. He used to forge the iron himself, make his own pottery, his own furniture; he knew how to handle wood, stone, and marble. Now he is the poor slave who toils only for his crust of bread, he has no ideals, his head is crammed continually with a mass of ideas foreign to his task. Above all, he has no love for the shop where he works, for nobody sings or laughs there any more. The long and short of it is that the workman has been killed by progress and science.

Is there a power that can check this torrent which is submerging us? It is a universal folly; nothing can stop it; and happiness can only be restored to us through work; but the work that makes for happiness is the slow labour of the hand.[1]

Will we ever see a return to tradition? We must hope for it, but not count on it too much. Since the whirlwind of the Revolution passed and withered everything, we have no more pottery-makers nor joiners nor foundrymen, nor architects, nor sculptors. By the merest chance there are a few painters left: they are like seeds scattered by chance in an abandoned field; they take root in spite of everything.

Open the window, Vollard, and let the sun into the studio. Do you see that clump of roses near the pump? Wouldn't a Maillol look well there? One day Jeanne Baudot took me to Marly to see Maillol. We found him at work on a statue in his garden. He searched out the form without the slightest preparation. It was the first time I had ever seen a sculptor work that way. Other people think they are coming near to the antique by copying it; Maillol, without borrowing anything from the ancients, is so close to them that, as I watched the stone grow under his hands, I began unconsciously to look about for olive-trees; I felt almost as if I had been carried away to Greece.

---

[1]See Appendix I, F.

CHAPTER TWENTY-SIX

THE LAST YEARS

A FEW days after Rodin's visit, my portrait was almost finished.[1] "Another short sitting," said Renoir, "and I shall be through." But he could not give me the sitting until later, because he was even busier at Cagnes than in Paris; in the country, when the weather was good, he liked to work out of doors as much as possible. At Essoyes, where there were almost no automobiles, he went out in his wheel-chair along the road, or by the river's edge. At Cagnes, which is overrun with automobiles, he had himself carried in an arm-chair to various points on his property, to the patch of rose-bushes, the plots full of mandarin and orange-trees, the grape-vines, the Terrain Fayard with its medlar-trees from Japan, the cherry-orchard, and, dominating *Les Collettes,* the olive-trees all in silver.

"I have the right now to idle a little," Renoir liked to say. From his care-free wanderings came many extraordinary landscape sketches; for it goes without saying that the model always followed with the colour-box.

While he was doing the portrait of Madame de Galéa, which required fifty or more sittings and which interested him to such an extent that he kept at it without interruption up to the end, the weather was exceptionally hot, and he remarked one day: "I pay dearly for the pleasure I get from this canvas; but it is so satisfying to give in entirely to the sheer pleasure of painting."

And then when the weather began to grow cold and his goatskin jacket was not a sufficient protection for work out of doors, he had his motor-car to fall back on. Antibes especially had an irresistible attraction for him. When he went round the Corniche, and the neighbouring hills, the sweet penetrating atmosphere gave him an ever-renewing sensation of tranquillity.

"I must stay here at least two months more and paint!" he cried one day when particularly intoxicated by the charm of the landscape. And, quite forgetting that it was necessary for him to live in a special "incubator" house on account of his rheumatism, he ordered the chauffeur to stop every time he saw "Villa to Let."

---

[1]Renoir did still another portrait of me for which I posed in a toreador's costume. (Essoyes, 1917.)

The doctor himself advised Renoir to be out of doors as much as possible. "Nothing is better for cleansing the lungs than plenty of fresh air," he said to his patient. Whenever the doctor ordered something to his liking, Renoir would follow the prescription to the letter.

One day the family had planned to go to Nice to eat a bowl of *bouillabaisse;* it was raining in torrents, but Renoir insisted: "Bah! The doctor said that I breathe better out of doors than in the house. Here I am, past seventy-five years old, and I don't intend being ordered about like a child any more. Now send for the car!"

When Renoir bought *Les Collettes,* he did not at first have a motor-road built to the house. His wife would roll his wheel-chair to the bottom of the hill, and Renoir would be lifted in and out of the car in an arm-chair. "It's a little inconvenient perhaps," he would say, "but the people who like me for myself will take the trouble to come to see me; as for the rest, the fence ought to be high enough to stop them."

But when the Parisian arrives in the Midi, he is soon so bored that he is ready to climb any fence, no matter how high, just to kill time. As soon as Renoir had moved in at *Les Collettes,* the whole swarm of faithful bores from Paris descended upon him, with many new members to boot.

I recall the day I saw Renoir under the big lime-tree in the garden, with a long stick in his hand, dictating volumes to the sculptor who was executing his *Venus Victorious.*[2]

"I'm at my statue at last! With this fine weather, I will be able to work out of doors all afternoon!"

"If you're not interrupted," I suggested.

"So far as that goes, I'd like to see anyone with nerve enough to . . ." He had not finished his sentence, when an automobile drove up, bringing three strange ladies.

"The porter at the Hotel du Palais at Nice," one of them explained, "told us that we could see Renoir's studio at Cagnes——"

Another of the visitors struck in, trying to be agreeable: "But if the Master is busy, we can wait a bit."

Renoir was working away, when other visitors arrived: Monsieur Z., a seed merchant, accompanied by a young woman. By this time Renoir had given up trying to work. One of the three ladies from Nice remarked that she had a literary and artistic circle at Paris. "If the Master would like to come to one of my days," she said, "I could arrange a little talk on painting beforehand."

"Why don't you say something too?" said Monsieur Z.'s companion in his ear, but loud enough for me to overhear.

---

[2]It is not generally known that Renoir produced considerable sculpture in his lifetime. Practically all of it was done after his hands had become crippled, and hence was executed by an assistant, M. Guino, at his dictation. (Trans. Note.)

"I'm trying to think of something . . ." He finally found it, and, turning to Renoir, he said:

"Master, if you did water-colours instead of oils, you'd have everything you need for preparing your colours, with all the rain that's fallen the past week."

As Renoir wagged his head, he continued: "You must be sick of it in this hole!"

Renoir: I have my painting. . . .

Monsieur Z.: Painting! I know what that is; I paint myself. . . .

Everyone had gone, and Renoir's eyes were beginning to close, for a visit tired him more than a model posing. Just then the postman brought a letter.

Renoir was reading it rather indifferently, when all of a sudden he cried: "There's a friend for you! He's interested enough to ask if Jean's dog has been found. . . . His daughters have started knitting a spread for me . . ." Then his face darkened. "It's not me he cares about, it's my painting. He asks me about some pictures that he wants. . . ."

And with a deep sadness in his voice, he went on:

"I have arrived more definitely than any other painter during his lifetime; honours shower upon me from every side; artists pay me compliments on my work; there are many people to whom my position must seem enviable. . . . But I don't seem to have a single real friend!"

Renoir died at Cagnes on the 3rd of December, 1919. The following lines are taken from a letter to Monsieur Durand-Ruel from one of his sons:

My father had been suffering from bronchial pneumonia which lasted two weeks. The last days of last month he seemed better, and had resumed his work, when suddenly, on the first of December, he fell quite ill. The doctor pronounced congestion of the lungs, rather less severe than a similar attack of the previous year. There was no reason to expect any such sudden eventuality. The two last days he kept to his room, but did not stay in bed all the time.

He would say from time to time: "I'm done for," but without conviction, for three years before, he had said the same thing even more often. The constant care annoyed him a little, and he never ceased to make fun of it.

Tuesday he went to bed at seven o'clock after quietly smoking a cigarette. He had wanted to draw a design for a vase, but nobody could find a pencil. At eight o'clock he suddenly went into a light delirium. We were very much surprised at this, and we naturally became very uneasy. The delirium increased. The doctor came. Father was restless until midnight but did not suffer for a moment. He surely did not suspect that he was going to die.

At midnight he became calmer and at two o'clock he breathed his last.

Appendix I

A

(See page 53.) "Renoir paints the caressing suppleness of woman, the disquieting charm of her coy glances, the archness of her smile, her pouting petulant graces, her feline charm. What sly soft eyes, what delicate, pert little noses and gaily smiling lips he paints! With an intuition for these things, Monsieur Renoir gives us eloquent portraits reflecting keen intellect. . . ." (Georges Lecomte, *Impressionist Art,* pages 142–3.)

Camille Mauclair reaches quite a different conclusion about the work of Renoir: "His women do not invite the beholder to look for intelligence; they are happy animals with stupid eyes; they have all the characteristics of the gentle brute. . . ." (*Impressionism,* page 124.)

Monsieur Mauclair seeks an excuse for this lack of mentality—and finds it: "Impressionism has spent one-half of its strength in proving to its adversaries that they were wrong, and the other half in inventing technical processes. It is not astonishing that it lacks intellectual depth." (Page 203.) He deplores no less the fact that they have used "symphonies of magnificent colour for the portrayal of—nothing but boatmen, or a corner of a café. We have come," he continues, "to a degree of complexity in our intellectual life which is no longer satisfied by these rudimentary themes." (Page 207.)

B

(See page 93.) The man who buys a bad picture, on the other hand, buys it for love, not to make money. And his respect for the beloved object is sometimes tremendous. The owner of a bawdy-house has been known to sell all his worldly goods to save his Bouguereaux.

Just the reverse is true abroad. Buying "bad" painting does not engender these noble sentiments; he who collects Bouguereau is an ordinary person, but if he turns to Impressionism, he becomes an accomplished "gentleman." I used to know a man in Munich who was a great collector of Picot, Delaroche, Meissonier, and Bouguereau, and who had all the other artistic vices into the bargain. Recently I found him . . . well, changed in some intangible way . . . more a man of the world—more self-confident. I interrogated his wife discreetly.

"Oh, Fritz buys Cézanne now," she explained.

C

(See page 93.) Coignet was afraid that Bonnat might "turn out badly." Madame de Z. is responsible for the following anecdote about a dinner at which Coignet was among the guests.

"All through dinner Coignet looked as if he had lost his last friend, so that finally his host urged him to unburden his mind.

" 'I had a terrible dream last night, dear friends,' Coignet said. 'In my dream I beheld my favourite pupil, Léon Bonnat, making a drawing on the wall. "My boy," I said to him, "the chimney is not straight. You must observe nature more closely." And he replied: "That isn't a chimney, it's the portrait of an Italian girl." '

"And Coignet turned to Abel de Pujol, whose anxious eyes were fixed on his face:

" 'I tell you, my dear Pujol, modernism is threatening us. You should have seen Léon—and not so very long ago, either—putting pure vermilion on his canvas!' "

D

(See page 98.) When the Triennial Exhibition of 1919 (the year of the painter's death) took place, Renoir said to me: "Vollard, the Triennial is organizing an exhibit for America; they want something of mine. They have elected me their honorary president, you know! Would you attend to sending my statue of Venus for me?"

When I arrived at the Grand Palais, one of the guardians told me that the Jury was in the midst of judging the sculpture.

I entered a room where three persons were seated behind a desk. They were weighing some bronzes on a pair of scales near by.

"Fifty pounds."

"Accepted."

"Seventy pounds."

"Hold over."

"Eighty pounds."

"Rejected."

"How much does the Renoir weigh?" asked the three judges with one voice.

"About three hundred and fifty pounds, I should say," answered the weigher.

"Three hundred and fifty pounds for one statue to be sent all the way to America!" cried one of the examiners. "Then five or six others within the limit of the maximum weight will have to be sacrificed."

As I was stealing out, I heard the president of the Jury say:

"In the case of Monsieur Renoir, we will go as high as a hundred and fifty pounds. I shall take the responsibility upon myself." And, holding up an admonitory finger, he added: "But don't breathe a word of it; we have just refused a 'hundred-and-forty-pounder' by a member of the Institute!"

E

(See page 105.) The reader may be curious to know whether, on my return to Paris, I took advantage of the permission which had been so graciously given me. I did. At Rodin's house I met Madame de Thèbes, Monsieur Camille Flammarion, and Loïe Fuller.

"I've been making you wait for two years for your portrait, Baroness," said Rodin, and, taking up a Phrygian bonnet, he put it on her head. "Some day I shall have to design a tribute to our Republic after you."

In the centre of the studio there was a statue wrapped in cloths. Rodin undid the wrappings and a nude woman in clay emerged. The Master then took up a hammer and chisel; he broke off the arms, the head and the legs. Then he stood in contemplation of the debris that littered the floor around him.

"We must find titles for each piece," he said. "Fortunately I am ingenious." He picked up a piece of the torso. "How beautiful that is! What name shall we give to that?"

"Master," I was bold enough to say, "why not call a head simply 'head,' a hand, 'hand,' a foot, 'foot'? That group of nude women, for instance—how could you call it anything but *Nudes*?"

Rodin: Perhaps; but it vulgarizes things to call them by their names. At first I named the group *Evocation,* and then, on maturer consideration, I chose *Music.*

At this moment a woman entered with a baby in her arms. She threw herself weeping on Rodin's knees. She had come from Siberia on foot to bring greetings to the Master from a group of exiled intellectuals. The child had been born to her *en route.* She held it out to Rodin, saying: "Bless him, Master!"

Rodin put his hand on the child's head.

Just then another visitor arrived, and a truck carrying a bronze group stopped at the door; an *Enlacement* had been brought for the Master to authenticate.

"What an admirable bronze!" Rodin exclaimed.

The Visitor: I knew at once that it was genuine. . . .

Rodin (sharply): No, it's not an original. Anyone who knows anything about the technique can see right away from the finish of the grain that the mould was made from a plaster cast. But I gave them a bronze as a model. A large number of the *Enlacement* were to be cast for America, but plaster has the drawback of becoming soft after a certain number of copies have been made.

Vollard: Then a work is genuine only when the artist has given his authorization, and false when he has not so authorized it? It might happen, then, that an imitation might be more beautiful than the genuine bronze. What is the poor collector to do if he wants a genuine one?

Rodin: He would have to bring it to me. Only once have I made a mistake, and then it was absolutely impossible to tell. Somebody had informed me that he had seen a group of mine called *Chaos* in a dealer's shop. I consulted my list of titles and did not find it. To ease my conscience, I went to examine the statue. I instituted a suit against them, and finally my receipt was found. The trouble was that I had entitled it *l'Envolée!*

One day I heard a sculptor, referring to these statues sold in pieces, call Rodin a dealer in "odds and ends." I related this to an intimate friend of Rodin's. He contended that the production of fragments was, on the contrary, proof of the liveliest artistic conscience. "The hand cannot move as quickly as the mind," he said. "The Master's mind is always ready for creation, and in order not to lose the least of his conceptions, he is obliged to abandon his big projects and express himself in smaller things which are later enlarged. Now it sometimes happens that the different parts of a statuette no longer make a good ensemble after the enlargement, although they have lost nothing of their individual perfection of line and form."

F

(See page 112.) Was not Renoir perhaps under a delusion in thinking that if the workingman could enjoy the result of his labour, he would begin to have a taste for his craft again? One day I met a painter in a printing establishment who was having proofs pulled of some of his etchings for an album.

"I shall put your name in the front," he said to the workman. "You'll have something to show to your friends."

"The hell with that," the printer replied hostilely.

Then, trying another tack, the artist said: "When the blacks come out well in a proof, it surely is a pleasure to the eye. When you are at your press, my friend . . ." He stopped, for the printer had given him an ugly look.

But what happens in the rare cases when a workman has any real taste for his work? I know of an iron foundry where the proprietor made a point of providing his employés with work that "amused" them. One of the booths at a certain exposition in Angers was devoted to wrought-iron work from this foundry. When the committee on awards visited the booth, one of the members remarked what an amusing exhibit it was. Then another juror spoke up: "I'll wager they did those things for the fun of it. It doesn't look like 'regular' work." (It will be recalled that Renoir had always been criticized for painting "for the fun of it.")

The booth proved a success, nevertheless, and the owner of the foundry was encouraged to ask for State support. His standing was investigated, and the first question he was asked was: "Whom do you vote for?"

He made no answer.

"Then you must vote for the wrong party. And what union do you belong to? . . .

"No answer? Well, that's that; you vote wrong and you don't belong to any union. And I'll wager that your wife goes to church. That's a good thing to know! So you mean to tell us that with that kind of a record you expect the State to subsidize you?"

The foundry-owner pointed out that all that had nothing to do with wrought-iron.

"Nothing to do with it! You'll see how much it has to do with it when the union comes around to raid your house some day!"

Appendix II*

LIST OF IMPORTANT WORKS

In this list the translators have tried to present a small number of Renoir's important works with the correct dates and the museums or collections in which they are to be found. The difficulties of the task will readily be seen when it is realized that his works in oil alone probably number over four thousand, and that comparatively few of them are dated. The artist himself was unable to give within five years the proper dates of some of his pictures, and there is a still wider discrepancy in the existing books on Renoir.

A similar difficulty arises in giving accurately the collections to which these pictures belong: they are constantly changing hands, and many of them are in the possession of dealers. Neither Renoir's closest friends nor his family are able to give precise information, even on some of his important works.

It is hoped, however, that this brief list may serve to give an idea of the wide distribution of Renoir's work, and show the importance of his activity over a long period of years.

It will be noticed that there are fewer pictures listed in the last twenty years of his life than in the period before 1900. This must not be taken as indicating that the volume of his work fell off during this period. On the contrary, he painted uninterruptedly until a few days before his death. But from 1900 on, the difficulty of placing the works becomes practically insurmountable. A large percentage of his late pictures are still in the hands of dealers, and many of them are in the possession of his sons, and not as yet to be seen. Furthermore, the repetition of similar subjects and slight variations on a chosen theme become so frequent that a list of names would mean nothing without the aid of an elaborate catalogue of illustrations. Such a catalogue has been in preparation for some time, but it has not appeared at this date.

The years 1900–1919 inclusive have therefore been divided into four five-year periods.

*This appendix is reprinted without change in this 1990 edition, except for the correction of typographical errors.

1861

SLEEPING WOMAN. (G. Rivière Collection, Paris.)

1863

ESMERALDA. First Salon work. (Not extant.)

1865

MOTHER ANTHONY'S "CABARET." (Hébrard Collection, Paris.)

1866

HUNTRESS NYMPH. (Bernheim-Jeune Collection, Paris.)

1867

"LISA." *Exhibited at the Salon of 1867.* (Folkwang Museum, Hagen, Westphalia.)
BOATING, CHATOU. (Ed. Esmond, Paris.)

1868

THE SISLEY FAMILY. (Walraff-Richartz Museum, Cologne.)
BOY WITH A CAT. (Edouard Arnhold Collection, Berlin.)
PORTRAIT OF THE PAINTER BAZILLE (1869?). (Owned by the French State and destined for the Luxembourg Museum.)

1869

BOIS DE BOULOGNE, WINTER.
PORTRAIT OF THE PAINTER'S FATHER. (Pierre Renoir Collection, Paris.)
"LISA." *Small full-length picture of the same model as the "Lisa" painted in 1867.* (Josef Stransky Collection, New York.)

1870

ALGERIAN WOMAN. *Exhibited in the Salon of 1870.* (R. J. Edwards Collection, Boston, Mass.)
THE PROMENADE. (Kochler Collection, Berlin.)

1871

PORTRAIT OF MME. MAITRE.
THE INFANTRY CAPTAIN. (Dresden State Museum.)
WOMAN IN BLACK. (Josef Stransky Collection, New York.)
BREAKFAST. (Barnes Foundation, Merion, Pa.)
PORTRAIT OF MLLE. LEGRAND. (Durand-Ruel Collection.)

1872

THE HAREM. (Matsukata Collection.)
PONT NEUF, PARIS. *Figured at the Hazard sale, 1919.* (Ralph Coe Collection, Cleveland.)

1873

MONET PAINTING DAHLIAS. (Durand-Ruel Collection.)
THE SEINE AT ARGENTEUIL. (Durand-Ruel Collection.)
THE RIDE IN THE BOIS DE BOULOGNE. (Hamburg Museum.)

1874

PORTRAIT OF SISLEY. (Chicago Art Institute.)
THE HENRIOT FAMILY.
THE DANCING-GIRL. (Joseph E. Widener Collection, Philadelphia.)
THE OPERA BOX ("La Loge"). (Courtauld Collection, London.)
THE PARISIENNE. (Formerly Theodore Duret Collection.)

1874–1877

L'INGÉNUE. (Alphonse Kann Collection, Paris.)
MONET AND HIS FAMILY. (Claude Monet Collection, Giverny.)

1875

WOMEN SEATED. (Barnes Foundation, Merion, Pa.)
PORTRAIT OF CLAUDE MONET. (Monet Collection, Giverny.)
YOUNG GIRL JUGGLERS, CIRQUE FERNANDO. (Palmer Collection, Art Institute of Chicago.)
WOMAN IN NÉGLIGÉE. (Barnes Foundation, Merion, Pa.)
WOMAN WITH A SHEPHERD'S STAFF. (Barnes Foundation, Merion, Pa.)
GIRL WITH SKIPPING-ROPE. (Barnes Foundation, Merion, Pa.)
"LE MOULIN DE LA GALETTE." (Caillebotte Bequest, Luxembourg Museum, Paris. *A sketch is in the Coburn Collection, Chicago.*)
THE SWING. (Caillebotte Bequest, Luxembourg Museum, Paris.) *Comprises portraits of Monet and G. Rivière.*
PORTRAIT OF CHOCQUET. (Oscar Reinhardt, Winterthur, Switzerland.)
IN THE STUDIO.
PORTRAIT OF MLLE. DURAND-RUEL AS A CHILD. (André F. Aude, Paris.)
THE SPRING. (Formerly in the collection of the Prince of Wagram, Paris.)

1877

AFTER THE CONCERT ("La Sortie du Conservatoire"). *Originally purchased by Emmanuel Chabrier.*

NUDE WOMAN SURROUNDED BY CLOTHING. (Stchoukine Collection, Moscow.) *A famous model called Nana posed for this picture. It was purchased from Renoir by the composer Emmanuel Chabrier; his family, however, did not consider it proper for the salon, and it was relegated to a small and little-frequented room.*

THE FIRST STEPS: MOTHER AND CHILD. (Pellerin Collection, Paris.)

PORTRAIT OF MLLE. SAMARY: *bust.* (Foyer des Artistes, Théâtre National Français, Paris.)

1878

MME. CHARPENTIER AND HER CHILDREN. *Exhibited at the Salon of 1879.* (Metropolitan Museum, New York.)

PORTRAIT OF MLLE. SAMARY: *full length. Salon of 1879.* (Morosoff Collection, Moscow.)

LANDSCAPE, POURVILLE. (Barnes Foundation, Merion, Pa.)

1879

MME. HENRIOT IN THE COSTUME OF A PAGE. (Stephen C. Clark, New York.)

GARDEN, ALGERIA. (Durand-Ruel Collection, Paris.)

ARAB RIDING A CAMEL. (Durand-Ruel Collection, Paris.)

ARABS AND DONKEYS. (Vollard Collection, Paris.)

AFTER THE LUNCHEON. (Staedelsches Institut, Frankfurt-am-Main.)

FISHER-WOMEN AT BERNEVAL. (Durand-Ruel Collection, Paris.)

CANOEISTS AT CHATOU. (Adolph Lewisohn Collection, New York.)

THE WAVE. (Palmer Collection, Art Institute of Chicago.)

1880

PORTRAIT OF FOURNAISE. (Durand-Ruel Collection, New York.)

PORTRAIT OF MME. PAPILLON. (Durand-Ruel Collection, Paris.)

ALGERIAN WOMEN. *Exhibited at the Salon of 1880.*

AT THE CONCERT. (Private Collection, Paris.)

THE SEINE AT CHATOU. (Museum of Fine Arts, Boston, Mass.)

GIRL WITH A CAT. (Private Collection, Paris.)

PORTRAIT OF CÉZANNE. *Pastel.* (Chicago Art Institute.)

WOMAN WITH A CUP OF CHOCOLATE. *Exhibited at the Salon of 1881.* (Durand-Ruel Collection.)

1881

ON THE TERRACE. (Chicago Art Institute.)
PORTRAIT OF WAGNER. (Alfred Cortot.)
MME. RENOIR AND SON. (Barnes Foundation, Merion, Pa.)
LUNCHEON OF THE BOATMEN AT BOUGIVAL. (Phillips Memorial Gallery, Washington, D.C.)
THE RAILROAD BRIDGE AT CHATOU. (Louvre Museum, Paris.)
STAIRWAY, ALGERIA. (Pierre Renoir Collection, Paris.)

1880–1881

NUDE BATHERS: GUERNSEY.
GRAND CANAL: VENICE. (Museum of Fine Arts, Boston, Mass.)
GARDEN AT SORRENTO WITH VESUVIUS IN THE DISTANCE. (Claude Renoir Collection, Paris.)
FRUIT OF THE MIDI. (Chicago Art Institute.)

1882

PORTRAIT OF MLLE. DURAND-RUEL SEWING. (André F. Aude Collection, Paris.)
MLLES. DURAND-RUEL IN THE GARDEN. (André F. Aude Collection, Paris.)
OLD ARAB WOMAN.
THE GREEN JARDINIERE. (Toledo Museum of Art.)

1883

PORTRAIT OF MME. CLAPISSON. (Chicago Art Institute.)
DANCE PANELS: THE DANCE IN THE COUNTRY; THE DANCE IN THE CITY. (Durand-Ruel Collection, Paris.)
MLLE. MANET WITH A CAT. (Ernest Rouart Collection, Paris.)
UMBRELLAS. (National Gallery, London.)
CHILD IN WHITE. (Chicago Art Institute.)
WOMAN WITH A FAN. (Chicago Art Institute.)
ALGERIAN GIRL: *head.* (Chicago Art Institute.)
APPLES. (Chicago Art Institute.)
YOUNG GIRL WITH A PARASOL. (Barnes Foundation, Merion, Pa.)
BOY IN SAILOR SUIT. (Barnes Foundation, Merion, Pa.)
TWO PANELS: FISHER-GIRL; FRUIT-VENDER. (Barnes Foundation, Merion, Pa.)

1884

THE BÉRARD CHILDREN. (National Gallery, Berlin.)
PORTRAIT OF MLLE. BÉRARD. (Formerly in the Gangnat Collection, Paris.)

WOMAN'S HEAD: *profile.*
MME. RENOIR AT THE GATE. (Ralph Booth, Detroit.)

1885

WOMEN BATHING. (1883–1885.) (Carroll Tyson, Philadelphia.)
BATHER SEATED. (Durand-Ruel Collection.)
PORTRAIT OF MME. RENOIR. (Pierre Renoir Collection, Paris.)
IN THE GARDEN. (Bernheim-Jeune Collection, Paris.)

1886

MOTHER NURSING HER CHILD: MME. RENOIR AND PIERRE. (Formerly in the collection of the Prince of Wagram, Paris.) *There are two replicas of this picture, one done at the same period, in the collection of Claude Renoir, and a second, much smaller, in the collection of Pierre Renoir, done in 1917.*
YOUNG GIRL WITH A ROSE.

1888

MOTHER AND CHILD. (Barnes Foundation, Merion, Pa.) *This curious canvas is an anomaly. It is entirely different in handling from all the rest of the painter's work.*
GIRL BATHING. (Rodin Museum, Paris.)
DAUGHTERS OF CATULLE MENDÈS. (Collection of the Prince of Wagram, Paris.)
BOY DRAWING, PIERRE RENOIR. (Stephen C. Clark, New York.)
LANDSCAPE WITH HARVESTER. (Barnes Foundation, Merion, Pa.)
THE RED BOAT: ARGENTEUIL. (Barnes Foundation, Merion, Pa.)

1889

PORTRAIT OF MME. DE BONNIÈRES. (Formerly in the Vollard Collection, Paris.)
LA TOILETTE. *Pastel.* (Durand-Ruel Collection, Paris.)
BATTLEDORE AND SHUTTLECOCK. (Minneapolis Institute of Arts.)
MONT SAINT-VICTOIRE. (Barnes Foundation, Merion, Pa.)
THE APPLE-VENDER. (Barnes Foundation, Merion, Pa.)
THE BEACH AT PORNIC.
WOMAN, COW, AND SHEEP. (Bernheim-Jeune Collection, Paris.)

1891

WOMAN BATHING.
PORTRAIT OF MME. MORISOT AND DAUGHTER. (Lapauze Collection, Paris.)
THE PIANO LESSON. *Pastel.* (Adolph Lewisohn Collection, New York.)

1892

THE PIANO LESSON. *There are three versions of this picture, one in the Luxembourg Museum, one in the Durand-Ruel Collection, and one in the Paul Guillaume Collection.*
BATHER SLEEPING BY THE SEA.
THE YOUNG BATHER. (Barnes Foundation, Merion, Pa.)
LANDSCAPE: ANTIBES. (Barnes Foundation, Merion, Pa.)

1893–1894

CHILDREN PLAYING BALL. *Pastel.*
STILL-LIFE WITH MELON. (Durand-Ruel Collection.)
THE SEA AT TRÉBOUL.
LA TOILETTE. (Bernheim-Jeune Collection, Paris.)

1895

PORTRAIT OF THE CHILDREN OF M. CAILLEBOTTE.
YOUNG GIRLS PUTTING FLOWERS IN THEIR HATS. (Chicago Art Institute.)
VIEW OF ESSOYES. (Durand-Ruel Collection, Paris.)

1896

THE RENOIR FAMILY. (Claude Renoir Collection, Paris.)
PORTRAIT GROUP: JEAN RENOIR, GABRIELLE, AND LITTLE GIRL. (Barnes Foundation, Merion, Pa.)
GUITAR-PLAYER. (Durand-Ruel Collection.)
BATHER ARRANGING HER HAIR.
GIRL CARRYING A BASKET OF FLOWERS. (A. Barton Hepburn Collection, New York.)

1897

AFTER THE BATH.
GUITAR-PLAYER.
BATHER SLEEPING. (Formerly Dieterle Collection, Paris.)
LA SOURCE. (Gallimard Collection, Paris.)

1898–1899

SPANISH GIRL WITH A GUITAR.
AFTER THE BATH. (Bernheim-Jeune Collection, Paris.)
JEAN RENOIR SEWING. (Pierre Renoir Collection, Paris.)
YVONNE AND JEAN. (Durand-Ruel Collection, Paris.)
GRAPE-GATHERERS. (Adolph Lewisohn Collection, New York.)

1900–1904

VASE OF ROSES.
BATHER AND MAID. (Bernheim-Jeune Collection, Paris.)
WOMEN EMBROIDERING. (Barnes Foundation, Merion, Pa.)
VIEW OF CANNET. (Formerly in the Gangnat Collection, Paris.)
JEANNE.
THE RHÔNE AND THE SAÔNE. *Allegorical composition.*
WOMAN FEEDING BABY: CLAUDE RENOIR. (Barnes Foundation, Merion, Pa.)
WOMAN SLEEPING. (Formerly in the Gangnat Collection, Paris.)
BATHER DRYING HERSELF. (Vollard Collection, Paris.)
RECLINING WOMAN WITH A ROSE. (Pierre Renoir Collection, Paris.) *There is a variant of this done at the same period.*
THE PALM-TREE: CANNES.
NURSE WITH CHILD IN HER ARMS: CLAUDE RENOIR. 1903. (Jean Renoir Collection, Marlotte.)
BOY WRITING: JEAN RENOIR. (Jean Renoir Collection, Marlotte.)

1905–1909

THE WRITING-LESSON. (Barnes Foundation, Merion, Pa.)
PORTRAIT OF MME. EDWARDS. (Sert Collection, Paris.)
FEMALE TORSO. (Formerly in the Collection of the Prince of Wagram, Paris.)
CLAUDE AND THE TWO SERVANTS. (Formerly in the Gangnat Collection, Paris.)
SELF-PORTRAIT; *head.* (Jean Renoir Collection, Paris.)
WOMAN BATHING. (Bernheim-Jeune Collection, Paris.)
PORTRAIT OF VOLLARD. (Formerly in the Vollard Collection, Paris.)
PORTRAIT OF EDMOND RENOIR. (Owned by Edmond Renoir.)
WOUNDED BATHER. (Formerly in the Gangnat Collection, Paris.)
LA TOILETTE: BATHER. (Pierre Renoir Collection, Paris.)
IN THE MEADOW. 1906. (Adolph Lewisohn Collection, New York.)
THE RED CLOWN: CLAUDE RENOIR. 1907. (Pierre Renoir Collection, Paris.)
BATHER DRYING HERSELF. 1908. (Barnes Foundation, Merion, Pa.)
GABRIELLE ARISING. 1909. (Barnes Foundation, Merion, Pa.)
HALF-LENGTH NUDE WITH HANDS CROSSED. 1909. (Barnes Foundation, Merion, Pa.)

1909–1914

AFTER THE BATH. 1910.
PSYCHE. 1911. (Barnes Foundation, Merion, Pa.)
BATHER IN LANDSCAPE. 1910. (Barnes Foundation, Merion, Pa.)
PORTRAIT OF MME. DE GALÉA. (Vollard Collection, Paris.)

RECLINING NUDE. 1911. (Barnes Foundation, Merion, Pa.)
ALGERIAN GIRL. 1910. (Barnes Foundation, Merion, Pa.)
PORTRAIT OF MME. THURNEYSSEN AND HER DAUGHTER. (Thurneyssen Collection, Munich.)
YOUNG SHEPHERD RESTING. (Thurneyssen Collection, Munich.)
PORTRAIT OF HENRI BERNSTEIN. (Vollard Collection, Paris.)
GABRIELLE AT THE MIRROR. 1910. (Bernheim-Jeune Collection, Paris.)
JEAN RENOIR IN HUNTING-COSTUME. 1910. (Jean Renoir Collection, Marlotte.)
PORTRAIT OF PAUL DURAND-RUEL. 1911. (Durand-Ruel Collection, Paris.)
OLIVE-GROVE WITH FIGURES. 1912. (Barnes Foundation, Merion, Pa.)
PORTRAIT OF MME. J. DURAND-RUEL. (Durand-Ruel Collection, Paris.)
PORTRAIT OF MME. COLLONNA ROMANO. 1913. (Luxembourg Museum, Paris.)
THE JUDGMENT OF PARIS. (Jean Renoir Collection, Marlotte.)
MME. RENOIR WITH A DOG. 1913. (Pierre Renoir Collection, Paris.)
WOMAN DRESSING. (Vollard Collection, Paris.)
THE CUP OF CHOCOLATE. 1912. (Barnes Foundation, Merion, Pa.)
GARDEN AT CAGNES. 1912. (Formerly in the Gangnat Collection, Paris.)
ODALISQUE. 1914. (Formerly in the Gangnat Collection, Paris.)

1915–1919

PORTRAIT OF VOLLARD. (Vollard Collection, Paris.)
YOUNG WOMAN READING. 1916. (Formerly in the Gangnat Collection, Paris.)
YOUNG WOMAN READING. 1916. (Formerly in the Gangnat Collection, Paris.)
GIRL IN A RED CORSAGE.
NUDE RECLINING ON A DIVAN.
TOREADOR WITH A ROSE: PORTRAIT OF VOLLARD. (Formerly in the Vollard Collection, Paris.)
THE PREGNANT WOMAN. 1917.
WOMAN IN A MOUSSELINE DRESS. 1917.
WOMAN ARRANGING FLOWERS. 1917. (Formerly in the Gangnat Collection, Paris.)
PORTRAIT OF MME. HENRIOT. 1916.
TWO NUDES RECLINING. *Presented to the State at the wish of the painter by the Renoir family.* (Luxembourg Museum, Paris.)
COMPOSITION OF NUDES. (Jean Renoir Collection, Marlotte.)
BATHING GROUP. 1916. (Barnes Foundation, Merion, Pa.)

LAUNDRY-WOMEN BY THE RIVER. (Jean Renoir Collection, Marlotte.)

PORTRAIT OF MME. JEAN RENOIR. 1918. (Barnes Foundation, Merion, Pa.)

A CATALOG OF SELECTED DOVER BOOKS IN ALL FIELDS OF INTEREST

CONCERNING THE SPIRITUAL IN ART, Wassily Kandinsky. Pioneering work by father of abstract art. Thoughts on color theory, nature of art. Analysis of earlier masters. 12 illustrations. 80pp. of text. 5⅜ x 8½. 23411-8 Pa. $3.95

ANIMALS: 1,419 Copyright-Free Illustrations of Mammals, Birds, Fish, Insects, etc., Jim Harter (ed.). Clear wood engravings present, in extremely lifelike poses, over 1,000 species of animals. One of the most extensive pictorial sourcebooks of its kind. Captions. Index. 284pp. 9 x 12. 23766-4 Pa. $12.95

CELTIC ART: The Methods of Construction, George Bain. Simple geometric techniques for making Celtic interlacements, spirals, Kells-type initials, animals, humans, etc. Over 500 illustrations. 160pp. 9 x 12. (USO) 22923-8 Pa. $9.95

AN ATLAS OF ANATOMY FOR ARTISTS, Fritz Schider. Most thorough reference work on art anatomy in the world. Hundreds of illustrations, including selections from works by Vesalius, Leonardo, Goya, Ingres, Michelangelo, others. 593 illustrations. 192pp. 7⅛ x 10¼. 20241-0 Pa. $9 95

CELTIC HAND STROKE-BY-STROKE (Irish Half-Uncial from "The Book of Kells"): An Arthur Baker Calligraphy Manual, Arthur Baker. Complete guide to creating each letter of the alphabet in distinctive Celtic manner. Covers hand position, strokes, pens, inks, paper, more. Illustrated. 48pp. 8¼ x 11. 24336-2 Pa. $3.95

EASY ORIGAMI, John Montroll. Charming collection of 32 projects (hat, cup, pelican, piano, swan, many more) specially designed for the novice origami hobbyist. Clearly illustrated easy-to-follow instructions insure that even beginning papercrafters will achieve successful results. 48pp. 8¼ x 11. 27298-2 Pa. $2.95

THE COMPLETE BOOK OF BIRDHOUSE CONSTRUCTION FOR WOODWORKERS, Scott D. Campbell. Detailed instructions, illustrations, tables. Also data on bird habitat and instinct patterns. Bibliography. 3 tables. 63 illustrations in 15 figures. 48pp. 5¼ x 8½. 24407-5 Pa. $2.50

BLOOMINGDALE'S ILLUSTRATED 1886 CATALOG: Fashions, Dry Goods and Housewares, Bloomingdale Brothers. Famed merchants' extremely rare catalog depicting about 1,700 products: clothing, housewares, firearms, dry goods, jewelry, more. Invaluable for dating, identifying vintage items. Also, copyright-free graphics for artists, designers. Co-published with Henry Ford Museum & Greenfield Village. 160pp. 8¼ x 11. 25780-0 Pa. $9.95

HISTORIC COSTUME IN PICTURES, Braun & Schneider. Over 1,450 costumed figures in clearly detailed engravings–from dawn of civilization to end of 19th century. Captions. Many folk costumes. 256pp. 8⅜ x 11¾. 23150-X Pa. $12.95

STICKLEY CRAFTSMAN FURNITURE CATALOGS, Gustav Stickley and L. & J. G. Stickley. Beautiful, functional furniture in two authentic catalogs from 1910. 594 illustrations, including 277 photos, show settles, rockers, armchairs, reclining chairs, bookcases, desks, tables. 183pp. 6½ x 9¼. 23838-5 Pa. $9.95

AMERICAN LOCOMOTIVES IN HISTORIC PHOTOGRAPHS: 1858 to 1949, Ron Ziel (ed.). A rare collection of 126 meticulously detailed official photographs, called "builder portraits," of American locomotives that majestically chronicle the rise of steam locomotive power in America. Introduction. Detailed captions. xi + 129pp. 9 x 12. 27393-8 Pa. $12.95

AMERICA'S LIGHTHOUSES: An Illustrated History, Francis Ross Holland, Jr. Delightfully written, profusely illustrated fact-filled survey of over 200 American lighthouses since 1716. History, anecdotes, technological advances, more. 240pp. 8 x 10¾. 25576-X Pa. $12.95

TOWARDS A NEW ARCHITECTURE, Le Corbusier. Pioneering manifesto by founder of "International School." Technical and aesthetic theories, views of industry, economics, relation of form to function, "mass-production split" and much more. Profusely illustrated. 320pp. 6⅛ x 9¼. (USO) 25023-7 Pa. $9.95

HOW THE OTHER HALF LIVES, Jacob Riis. Famous journalistic record, exposing poverty and degradation of New York slums around 1900, by major social reformer. 100 striking and influential photographs. 233pp. 10 x 7⅞. 22012-5 Pa. $10.95

FRUIT KEY AND TWIG KEY TO TREES AND SHRUBS, William M. Harlow. One of the handiest and most widely used identification aids. Fruit key covers 120 deciduous and evergreen species; twig key 160 deciduous species. Easily used. Over 300 photographs. 126pp. 5⅜ x 8½. 20511-8 Pa. $3.95

COMMON BIRD SONGS, Dr. Donald J. Borror. Songs of 60 most common U.S. birds: robins, sparrows, cardinals, bluejays, finches, more–arranged in order of increasing complexity. Up to 9 variations of songs of each species. Cassette and manual 99911-4 $8.95

ORCHIDS AS HOUSE PLANTS, Rebecca Tyson Northen. Grow cattleyas and many other kinds of orchids–in a window, in a case, or under artificial light. 63 illustrations. 148pp. 5⅜ x 8½. 23261-1 Pa. $4.95

MONSTER MAZES, Dave Phillips. Masterful mazes at four levels of difficulty. Avoid deadly perils and evil creatures to find magical treasures. Solutions for all 32 exciting illustrated puzzles. 48pp. 8¼ x 11. 26005-4 Pa. $2.95

MOZART'S DON GIOVANNI (DOVER OPERA LIBRETTO SERIES), Wolfgang Amadeus Mozart. Introduced and translated by Ellen H. Bleiler. Standard Italian libretto, with complete English translation. Convenient and thoroughly portable–an ideal companion for reading along with a recording or the performance itself. Introduction. List of characters. Plot summary. 121pp. 5¼ x 8½. 24944-1 Pa. $2.95

TECHNICAL MANUAL AND DICTIONARY OF CLASSICAL BALLET, Gail Grant. Defines, explains, comments on steps, movements, poses and concepts. 15-page pictorial section. Basic book for student, viewer. 127pp. 5⅜ x 8½. 21843-0 Pa. $4.95

BRASS INSTRUMENTS: Their History and Development, Anthony Baines. Authoritative, updated survey of the evolution of trumpets, trombones, bugles, cornets, French horns, tubas and other brass wind instruments. Over 140 illustrations and 48 music examples. Corrected and updated by author. New preface. Bibliography. 320pp. 5⅜ x 8½. 27574-4 Pa. $9.95

HOLLYWOOD GLAMOR PORTRAITS, John Kobal (ed.). 145 photos from 1926-49. Harlow, Gable, Bogart, Bacall; 94 stars in all. Full background on photographers, technical aspects. 160pp. 8⅜ x 11¼. 23352-9 Pa. $11.95

MAX AND MORITZ, Wilhelm Busch. Great humor classic in both German and English. Also 10 other works: "Cat and Mouse," "Plisch and Plumm," etc. 216pp. 5⅜ x 8½. 20181-3 Pa. $6.95

THE RAVEN AND OTHER FAVORITE POEMS, Edgar Allan Poe. Over 40 of the author's most memorable poems: "The Bells," "Ulalume," "Israfel," "To Helen," "The Conqueror Worm," "Eldorado," "Annabel Lee," many more. Alphabetic lists of titles and first lines. 64pp. 5$\frac{3}{16}$ x 8¼. 26685-0 Pa. $1.00

PERSONAL MEMOIRS OF U. S. GRANT, Ulysses Simpson Grant. Intelligent, deeply moving firsthand account of Civil War campaigns, considered by many the finest military memoirs ever written. Includes letters, historic photographs, maps and more. 528pp. 6⅛ x 9¼. 28587-1 Pa. $11.95

AMULETS AND SUPERSTITIONS, E. A. Wallis Budge. Comprehensive discourse on origin, powers of amulets in many ancient cultures: Arab, Persian Babylonian, Assyrian, Egyptian, Gnostic, Hebrew, Phoenician, Syriac, etc. Covers cross, swastika, crucifix, seals, rings, stones, etc. 584pp. 5⅜ x 8½. 23573-4 Pa. $12.95

RUSSIAN STORIES/PYCCKNE PACCKA3bl: A Dual-Language Book, edited by Gleb Struve. Twelve tales by such masters as Chekhov, Tolstoy, Dostoevsky, Pushkin, others. Excellent word-for-word English translations on facing pages, plus teaching and study aids, Russian/English vocabulary, biographical/critical introductions, more. 416pp. 5⅜ x 8½. 26244-8 Pa. $8.95

PHILADELPHIA THEN AND NOW: 60 Sites Photographed in the Past and Present, Kenneth Finkel and Susan Oyama. Rare photographs of City Hall, Logan Square, Independence Hall, Betsy Ross House, other landmarks juxtaposed with contemporary views. Captures changing face of historic city. Introduction. Captions. 128pp. 8¼ x 11. 25790-8 Pa. $9.95

AIA ARCHITECTURAL GUIDE TO NASSAU AND SUFFOLK COUNTIES, LONG ISLAND, The American Institute of Architects, Long Island Chapter, and the Society for the Preservation of Long Island Antiquities. Comprehensive, well-researched and generously illustrated volume brings to life over three centuries of Long Island's great architectural heritage. More than 240 photographs with authoritative, extensively detailed captions. 176pp. 8¼ x 11. 26946-9 Pa. $14.95

NORTH AMERICAN INDIAN LIFE: Customs and Traditions of 23 Tribes, Elsie Clews Parsons (ed.). 27 fictionalized essays by noted anthropologists examine religion, customs, government, additional facets of life among the Winnebago, Crow, Zuni, Eskimo, other tribes. 480pp. 6⅛ x 9¼. 27377-6 Pa. $10.95

FRANK LLOYD WRIGHT'S HOLLYHOCK HOUSE, Donald Hoffmann. Lavishly illustrated, carefully documented study of one of Wright's most controversial residential designs. Over 120 photographs, floor plans, elevations, etc. Detailed perceptive text by noted Wright scholar. Index. 128pp. 9¼ x 10¾. 27133-1 Pa. $11.95

THE MALE AND FEMALE FIGURE IN MOTION: 60 Classic Photographic Sequences, Eadweard Muybridge. 60 true-action photographs of men and women walking, running, climbing, bending, turning, etc., reproduced from rare 19th-century masterpiece. vi + 121pp. 9 x 12. 24745-7 Pa. $10.95

1001 QUESTIONS ANSWERED ABOUT THE SEASHORE, N. J. Berrill and Jacquelyn Berrill. Queries answered about dolphins, sea snails, sponges, starfish, fishes, shore birds, many others. Covers appearance, breeding, growth, feeding, much more. 305pp. 5¼ x 8¼. 23366-9 Pa. $8.95

GUIDE TO OWL WATCHING IN NORTH AMERICA, Donald S. Heintzelman. Superb guide offers complete data and descriptions of 19 species: barn owl, screech owl, snowy owl, many more. Expert coverage of owl-watching equipment, conservation, migrations and invasions, etc. Guide to observing sites. 84 illustrations. xiii + 193pp. 5⅜ x 8½. 27344-X Pa. $8.95

MEDICINAL AND OTHER USES OF NORTH AMERICAN PLANTS: A Historical Survey with Special Reference to the Eastern Indian Tribes, Charlotte Erichsen-Brown. Chronological historical citations document 500 years of usage of plants, trees, shrubs native to eastern Canada, northeastern U.S. Also complete identifying information. 343 illustrations. 544pp. 6½ x 9¼. 25951-X Pa. $12.95

STORYBOOK MAZES, Dave Phillips. 23 stories and mazes on two-page spreads: Wizard of Oz, Treasure Island, Robin Hood, etc. Solutions. 64pp. 8¼ x 11. 23628-5 Pa. $2.95

NEGRO FOLK MUSIC, U.S.A., Harold Courlander. Noted folklorist's scholarly yet readable analysis of rich and varied musical tradition. Includes authentic versions of over 40 folk songs. Valuable bibliography and discography. xi + 324pp. 5⅜ x 8½. 27350-4 Pa. $7.95

MOVIE-STAR PORTRAITS OF THE FORTIES, John Kobal (ed.). 163 glamor, studio photos of 106 stars of the 1940s: Rita Hayworth, Ava Gardner, Marlon Brando, Clark Gable, many more. 176pp. 8⅜ x 11¼. 23546-7 Pa. $12.95

BENCHLEY LOST AND FOUND, Robert Benchley. Finest humor from early 30s, about pet peeves, child psychologists, post office and others. Mostly unavailable elsewhere. 73 illustrations by Peter Arno and others. 183pp. 5⅜ x 8½. 22410-4 Pa. $6.95

YEKL and THE IMPORTED BRIDEGROOM AND OTHER STORIES OF YIDDISH NEW YORK, Abraham Cahan. Film Hester Street based on Yekl (1896). Novel, other stories among first about Jewish immigrants on N.Y.'s East Side. 240pp. 5⅜ x 8½. 22427-9 Pa. $6.95

SELECTED POEMS, Walt Whitman. Generous sampling from *Leaves of Grass*. Twenty-four poems include "I Hear America Singing," "Song of the Open Road," "I Sing the Body Electric," "When Lilacs Last in the Dooryard Bloom'd," "O Captain! My Captain!"–all reprinted from an authoritative edition. Lists of titles and first lines. 128pp. 5$\frac{5}{16}$ x 8¼. 26878-0 Pa. $1.00

THE BEST TALES OF HOFFMANN, E. T. A. Hoffmann. 10 of Hoffmann's most important stories: "Nutcracker and the King of Mice," "The Golden Flowerpot," etc. 458pp. 5⅜ x 8½. 21793-0 Pa. $9.95

FROM FETISH TO GOD IN ANCIENT EGYPT, E. A. Wallis Budge. Rich detailed survey of Egyptian conception of "God" and gods, magic, cult of animals, Osiris, more. Also, superb English translations of hymns and legends. 240 illustrations. 545pp. 5⅜ x 8½. 25803-3 Pa. $11.95

FRENCH STORIES/CONTES FRANÇAIS: A Dual-Language Book, Wallace Fowlie. Ten stories by French masters, Voltaire to Camus: "Micromegas" by Voltaire; "The Atheist's Mass" by Balzac; "Minuet" by de Maupassant; "The Guest" by Camus, six more. Excellent English translations on facing pages. Also French-English vocabulary list, exercises, more. 352pp. 5⅜ x 8½. 26443-2 Pa. $8.95

CHICAGO AT THE TURN OF THE CENTURY IN PHOTOGRAPHS: 122 Historic Views from the Collections of the Chicago Historical Society, Larry A. Viskochil. Rare large-format prints offer detailed views of City Hall, State Street, the Loop, Hull House, Union Station, many other landmarks, circa 1904-1913. Introduction. Captions. Maps. 144pp. 9⅜ x 12¼. 24656-6 Pa. $12.95

OLD BROOKLYN IN EARLY PHOTOGRAPHS, 1865-1929, William Lee Younger. Luna Park, Gravesend race track, construction of Grand Army Plaza, moving of Hotel Brighton, etc. 157 previously unpublished photographs. 165pp. 8⅞ x 11¾. 23587-4 Pa. $13.95

THE MYTHS OF THE NORTH AMERICAN INDIANS, Lewis Spence. Rich anthology of the myths and legends of the Algonquins, Iroquois, Pawnees and Sioux, prefaced by an extensive historical and ethnological commentary. 36 illustrations. 480pp. 5⅜ x 8½. 25967-6 Pa. $8.95

AN ENCYCLOPEDIA OF BATTLES: Accounts of Over 1,560 Battles from 1479 B.C. to the Present, David Eggenberger. Essential details of every major battle in recorded history from the first battle of Megiddo in 1479 B.C. to Grenada in 1984. List of Battle Maps. New Appendix covering the years 1967-1984. Index. 99 illustrations. 544pp. 6½ x 9¼. 24913-1 Pa. $14.95

SAILING ALONE AROUND THE WORLD, Captain Joshua Slocum. First man to sail around the world, alone, in small boat. One of great feats of seamanship told in delightful manner. 67 illustrations. 294pp. 5⅜ x 8½. 20326-3 Pa. $5.95

ANARCHISM AND OTHER ESSAYS, Emma Goldman. Powerful, penetrating, prophetic essays on direct action, role of minorities, prison reform, puritan hypocrisy, violence, etc. 271pp. 5⅜ x 8½. 22484-8 Pa. $6.95

MYTHS OF THE HINDUS AND BUDDHISTS, Ananda K. Coomaraswamy and Sister Nivedita. Great stories of the epics; deeds of Krishna, Shiva, taken from puranas, Vedas, folk tales; etc. 32 illustrations. 400pp. 5⅜ x 8½. 21759-0 Pa. $10.95

BEYOND PSYCHOLOGY, Otto Rank. Fear of death, desire of immortality, nature of sexuality, social organization, creativity, according to Rankian system. 291pp. 5⅜ x 8½. 20485-5 Pa. $8.95

A THEOLOGICO-POLITICAL TREATISE, Benedict Spinoza. Also contains unfinished Political Treatise. Great classic on religious liberty, theory of government on common consent. R. Elwes translation. Total of 421pp. 5⅜ x 8½. 20249-6 Pa. $9.95

MY BONDAGE AND MY FREEDOM, Frederick Douglass. Born a slave, Douglass became outspoken force in antislavery movement. The best of Douglass' autobiographies. Graphic description of slave life. 464pp. 5⅜ x 8½. 22457-0 Pa. $8.95

FOLLOWING THE EQUATOR: A Journey Around the World, Mark Twain. Fascinating humorous account of 1897 voyage to Hawaii, Australia, India, New Zealand, etc. Ironic, bemused reports on peoples, customs, climate, flora and fauna, politics, much more. 197 illustrations. 720pp. 5⅜ x 8½. 26113-1 Pa. $15.95

THE PEOPLE CALLED SHAKERS, Edward D. Andrews. Definitive study of Shakers: origins, beliefs, practices, dances, social organization, furniture and crafts, etc. 33 illustrations. 351pp. 5⅜ x 8½. 21081-2 Pa. $8.95

THE MYTHS OF GREECE AND ROME, H. A. Guerber. A classic of mythology, generously illustrated, long prized for its simple, graphic, accurate retelling of the principal myths of Greece and Rome, and for its commentary on their origins and significance. With 64 illustrations by Michelangelo, Raphael, Titian, Rubens, Canova, Bernini and others. 480pp. 5⅜ x 8½. 27584-1 Pa. $9.95

PSYCHOLOGY OF MUSIC, Carl E. Seashore. Classic work discusses music as a medium from psychological viewpoint. Clear treatment of physical acoustics, auditory apparatus, sound perception, development of musical skills, nature of musical feeling, host of other topics. 88 figures. 408pp. 5⅜ x 8½. 21851-1 Pa. $10.95

THE PHILOSOPHY OF HISTORY, Georg W. Hegel. Great classic of Western thought develops concept that history is not chance but rational process, the evolution of freedom. 457pp. 5⅜ x 8½. 20112-0 Pa. $9.95

THE BOOK OF TEA, Kakuzo Okakura. Minor classic of the Orient: entertaining, charming explanation, interpretation of traditional Japanese culture in terms of tea ceremony. 94pp. 5⅜ x 8½. 20070-1 Pa. $3.95

LIFE IN ANCIENT EGYPT, Adolf Erman. Fullest, most thorough, detailed older account with much not in more recent books, domestic life, religion, magic, medicine, commerce, much more. Many illustrations reproduce tomb paintings, carvings, hieroglyphs, etc. 597pp. 5⅜ x 8½. 22632-8 Pa. $11.95

SUNDIALS, Their Theory and Construction, Albert Waugh. Far and away the best, most thorough coverage of ideas, mathematics concerned, types, construction, adjusting anywhere. Simple, nontechnical treatment allows even children to build several of these dials. Over 100 illustrations. 230pp. 5⅜ x 8½. 22947-5 Pa. $7.95

DYNAMICS OF FLUIDS IN POROUS MEDIA, Jacob Bear. For advanced students of ground water hydrology, soil mechanics and physics, drainage and irrigation engineering, and more. 335 illustrations. Exercises, with answers. 784pp. 6⅛ x 9¼. 65675-6 Pa. $19.95

SONGS OF EXPERIENCE: Facsimile Reproduction with 26 Plates in Full Color, William Blake. 26 full-color plates from a rare 1826 edition. Includes "The Tyger," "London," "Holy Thursday," and other poems. Printed text of poems. 48pp. 5¼ x 7. 24636-1 Pa. $4.95

OLD-TIME VIGNETTES IN FULL COLOR, Carol Belanger Grafton (ed.). Over 390 charming, often sentimental illustrations, selected from archives of Victorian graphics–pretty women posing, children playing, food, flowers, kittens and puppies, smiling cherubs, birds and butterflies, much more. All copyright-free. 48pp. 9¼ x 12¼. 27269-9 Pa. $5.95

PERSPECTIVE FOR ARTISTS, Rex Vicat Cole. Depth, perspective of sky and sea, shadows, much more, not usually covered. 391 diagrams, 81 reproductions of drawings and paintings. 279pp. 5⅜ x 8½. 22487-2 Pa. $6.95

DRAWING THE LIVING FIGURE, Joseph Sheppard. Innovative approach to artistic anatomy focuses on specifics of surface anatomy, rather than muscles and bones. Over 170 drawings of live models in front, back and side views, and in widely varying poses. Accompanying diagrams. 177 illustrations. Introduction. Index. 144pp. 8⅜ x11¼. 26723-7 Pa. $8.95

GOTHIC AND OLD ENGLISH ALPHABETS: 100 Complete Fonts, Dan X. Solo. Add power, elegance to posters, signs, other graphics with 100 stunning copyright-free alphabets: Blackstone, Dolbey, Germania, 97 more–including many lower-case, numerals, punctuation marks. 104pp. 8⅛ x 11. 24695-7 Pa. $8.95

HOW TO DO BEADWORK, Mary White. Fundamental book on craft from simple projects to five-bead chains and woven works. 106 illustrations. 142pp. 5⅜ x 8. 20697-1 Pa. $4.95

THE BOOK OF WOOD CARVING, Charles Marshall Sayers. Finest book for beginners discusses fundamentals and offers 34 designs. "Absolutely first rate . . . well thought out and well executed."–E. J. Tangerman. 118pp. 7¾ x 10⅝. 23654-4 Pa. $6.95

ILLUSTRATED CATALOG OF CIVIL WAR MILITARY GOODS: Union Army Weapons, Insignia, Uniform Accessories, and Other Equipment, Schuyler, Hartley, and Graham. Rare, profusely illustrated 1846 catalog includes Union Army uniform and dress regulations, arms and ammunition, coats, insignia, flags, swords, rifles, etc. 226 illustrations. 160pp. 9 x 12. 24939-5 Pa. $10.95

WOMEN'S FASHIONS OF THE EARLY 1900s: An Unabridged Republication of "New York Fashions, 1909," National Cloak & Suit Co. Rare catalog of mail-order fashions documents women's and children's clothing styles shortly after the turn of the century. Captions offer full descriptions, prices. Invaluable resource for fashion, costume historians. Approximately 725 illustrations. 128pp. 8⅜ x 11¼. 27276-1 Pa. $11.95

THE 1912 AND 1915 GUSTAV STICKLEY FURNITURE CATALOGS, Gustav Stickley. With over 200 detailed illustrations and descriptions, these two catalogs are essential reading and reference materials and identification guides for Stickley furniture. Captions cite materials, dimensions and prices. 112pp. 6½ x 9¼. 26676-1 Pa. $9.95

EARLY AMERICAN LOCOMOTIVES, John H. White, Jr. Finest locomotive engravings from early 19th century: historical (1804–74), main-line (after 1870), special, foreign, etc. 147 plates. 142pp. 11⅜ x 8¼. 22772-3 Pa. $10.95

THE TALL SHIPS OF TODAY IN PHOTOGRAPHS, Frank O. Braynard. Lavishly illustrated tribute to nearly 100 majestic contemporary sailing vessels: Amerigo Vespucci, Clearwater, Constitution, Eagle, Mayflower, Sea Cloud, Victory, many more. Authoritative captions provide statistics, background on each ship. 190 black-and-white photographs and illustrations. Introduction. 128pp. 8⅞ x 11¾. 27163-3 Pa. $13.95

EARLY NINETEENTH-CENTURY CRAFTS AND TRADES, Peter Stockham (ed.). Extremely rare 1807 volume describes to youngsters the crafts and trades of the day: brickmaker, weaver, dressmaker, bookbinder, ropemaker, saddler, many more. Quaint prose, charming illustrations for each craft. 20 black-and-white line illustrations. 192pp. 4⅝ x 6. 27293-1 Pa. $4.95

VICTORIAN FASHIONS AND COSTUMES FROM HARPER'S BAZAR, 1867–1898, Stella Blum (ed.). Day costumes, evening wear, sports clothes, shoes, hats, other accessories in over 1,000 detailed engravings. 320pp. 9⅜ x 12¼. 22990-4 Pa. $14.95

GUSTAV STICKLEY, THE CRAFTSMAN, Mary Ann Smith. Superb study surveys broad scope of Stickley's achievement, especially in architecture. Design philosophy, rise and fall of the Craftsman empire, descriptions and floor plans for many Craftsman houses, more. 86 black-and-white halftones. 31 line illustrations. Introduction 208pp. 6½ x 9¼. 27210-9 Pa. $9.95

THE LONG ISLAND RAIL ROAD IN EARLY PHOTOGRAPHS, Ron Ziel. Over 220 rare photos, informative text document origin (1844) and development of rail service on Long Island. Vintage views of early trains, locomotives, stations, passengers, crews, much more. Captions. 8⅞ x 11¾. 26301-0 Pa. $13.95

THE BOOK OF OLD SHIPS: From Egyptian Galleys to Clipper Ships, Henry B. Culver. Superb, authoritative history of sailing vessels, with 80 magnificent line illustrations. Galley, bark, caravel, longship, whaler, many more. Detailed, informative text on each vessel by noted naval historian. Introduction. 256pp. 5⅜ x 8½. 27332-6 Pa. $7.95

TEN BOOKS ON ARCHITECTURE, Vitruvius. The most important book ever written on architecture. Early Roman aesthetics, technology, classical orders, site selection, all other aspects. Morgan translation. 331pp. 5⅜ x 8½. 20645-9 Pa. $8.95

THE HUMAN FIGURE IN MOTION, Eadweard Muybridge. More than 4,500 stopped-action photos, in action series, showing undraped men, women, children jumping, lying down, throwing, sitting, wrestling, carrying, etc. 390pp. 7⅞ x 10⅝. 20204-6 Clothbd. $25.95

TREES OF THE EASTERN AND CENTRAL UNITED STATES AND CANADA, William M. Harlow. Best one-volume guide to 140 trees. Full descriptions, woodlore, range, etc. Over 600 illustrations. Handy size. 288pp. 4½ x 6⅜. 20395-6 Pa. $5.95

SONGS OF WESTERN BIRDS, Dr. Donald J. Borror. Complete song and call repertoire of 60 western species, including flycatchers, juncoes, cactus wrens, many more–includes fully illustrated booklet. Cassette and manual 99913-0 $8.95

GROWING AND USING HERBS AND SPICES, Milo Miloradovich. Versatile handbook provides all the information needed for cultivation and use of all the herbs and spices available in North America. 4 illustrations. Index. Glossary. 236pp. 5⅜ x 8½. 25058-X Pa. $6.95

BIG BOOK OF MAZES AND LABYRINTHS, Walter Shepherd. 50 mazes and labyrinths in all–classical, solid, ripple, and more–in one great volume. Perfect inexpensive puzzler for clever youngsters. Full solutions. 112pp. 8⅛ x 11. 22951-3 Pa. $4.95

PIANO TUNING, J. Cree Fischer. Clearest, best book for beginner, amateur. Simple repairs, raising dropped notes, tuning by easy method of flattened fifths. No previous skills needed. 4 illustrations. 201pp. 5⅜ x 8½. 23267-0 Pa. $6.95

A SOURCE BOOK IN THEATRICAL HISTORY, A. M. Nagler. Contemporary observers on acting, directing, make-up, costuming, stage props, machinery, scene design, from Ancient Greece to Chekhov. 611pp. 5⅜ x 8½. 20515-0 Pa. $12.95

THE COMPLETE NONSENSE OF EDWARD LEAR, Edward Lear. All nonsense limericks, zany alphabets, Owl and Pussycat, songs, nonsense botany, etc., illustrated by Lear. Total of 320pp. 5⅜ x 8½. (USO) 20167-8 Pa. $6.95

VICTORIAN PARLOUR POETRY: An Annotated Anthology, Michael R. Turner. 117 gems by Longfellow, Tennyson, Browning, many lesser-known poets. "The Village Blacksmith," "Curfew Must Not Ring Tonight," "Only a Baby Small," dozens more, often difficult to find elsewhere. Index of poets, titles, first lines. xxiii + 325pp. 5⅝ x 8¼. 27044-0 Pa. $8.95

DUBLINERS, James Joyce. Fifteen stories offer vivid, tightly focused observations of the lives of Dublin's poorer classes. At least one, "The Dead," is considered a masterpiece. Reprinted complete and unabridged from standard edition. 160pp. $5\frac{3}{16}$ x 8¼. 26870-5 Pa. $1.00

THE HAUNTED MONASTERY and THE CHINESE MAZE MURDERS, Robert van Gulik. Two full novels by van Gulik, set in 7th-century China, continue adventures of Judge Dee and his companions. An evil Taoist monastery, seemingly supernatural events; overgrown topiary maze hides strange crimes. 27 illustrations. 328pp. 5⅜ x 8½. 23502-5 Pa. $8.95

THE BOOK OF THE SACRED MAGIC OF ABRAMELIN THE MAGE, translated by S. MacGregor Mathers. Medieval manuscript of ceremonial magic. Basic document in Aleister Crowley, Golden Dawn groups. 268pp. 5⅜ x 8½. 23211-5 Pa. $8.95

NEW RUSSIAN-ENGLISH AND ENGLISH-RUSSIAN DICTIONARY, M. A. O'Brien. This is a remarkably handy Russian dictionary, containing a surprising amount of information, including over 70,000 entries. 366pp. 4½ x 6⅛. 20208-9 Pa. $9.95

HISTORIC HOMES OF THE AMERICAN PRESIDENTS, Second, Revised Edition, Irvin Haas. A traveler's guide to American Presidential homes, most open to the public, depicting and describing homes occupied by every American President from George Washington to George Bush. With visiting hours, admission charges, travel routes. 175 photographs. Index. 160pp. 8¼ x 11. 26751-2 Pa. $11.95

NEW YORK IN THE FORTIES, Andreas Feininger. 162 brilliant photographs by the well-known photographer, formerly with *Life* magazine. Commuters, shoppers, Times Square at night, much else from city at its peak. Captions by John von Hartz. 181pp. 9¼ x 10¾. 23585-8 Pa. $12.95

INDIAN SIGN LANGUAGE, William Tomkins. Over 525 signs developed by Sioux and other tribes. Written instructions and diagrams. Also 290 pictographs. 111pp. 6⅛ x 9¼. 22029-X Pa. $3.95

ANATOMY: A Complete Guide for Artists, Joseph Sheppard. A master of figure drawing shows artists how to render human anatomy convincingly. Over 460 illustrations. 224pp. 8⅜ x 11¼. 27279-6 Pa. $10.95

MEDIEVAL CALLIGRAPHY: Its History and Technique, Marc Drogin. Spirited history, comprehensive instruction manual covers 13 styles (ca. 4th century thru 15th). Excellent photographs; directions for duplicating medieval techniques with modern tools. 224pp. 8⅜ x 11¼. 26142-5 Pa. $11.95

DRIED FLOWERS: How to Prepare Them, Sarah Whitlock and Martha Rankin. Complete instructions on how to use silica gel, meal and borax, perlite aggregate, sand and borax, glycerine and water to create attractive permanent flower arrangements. 12 illustrations. 32pp. 5⅜ x 8½. 21802-3 Pa. $1.00

EASY-TO-MAKE BIRD FEEDERS FOR WOODWORKERS, Scott D. Campbell. Detailed, simple-to-use guide for designing, constructing, caring for and using feeders. Text, illustrations for 12 classic and contemporary designs. 96pp. 5⅜ x 8½. 25847-5 Pa. $2.95

SCOTTISH WONDER TALES FROM MYTH AND LEGEND, Donald A. Mackenzie. 16 lively tales tell of giants rumbling down mountainsides, of a magic wand that turns stone pillars into warriors, of gods and goddesses, evil hags, powerful forces and more. 240pp. 5⅜ x 8½. 29677-6 Pa. $6.95

THE HISTORY OF UNDERCLOTHES, C. Willett Cunnington and Phyllis Cunnington. Fascinating, well-documented survey covering six centuries of English undergarments, enhanced with over 100 illustrations: 12th-century laced-up bodice, footed long drawers (1795), 19th-century bustles, 19th-century corsets for men, Victorian "bust improvers," much more. 272pp. 5⅜ x 8¼. 27124-2 Pa. $9.95

ARTS AND CRAFTS FURNITURE: The Complete Brooks Catalog of 1912, Brooks Manufacturing Co. Photos and detailed descriptions of more than 150 now very collectible furniture designs from the Arts and Crafts movement depict davenports, settees, buffets, desks, tables, chairs, bedsteads, dressers and more, all built of solid, quarter-sawed oak. Invaluable for students and enthusiasts of antiques, Americana and the decorative arts. 80pp. 6½ x 9¼. 27471-3 Pa. $7.95

HOW WE INVENTED THE AIRPLANE: An Illustrated History, Orville Wright. Fascinating firsthand account covers early experiments, construction of planes and motors, first flights, much more. Introduction and commentary by Fred C. Kelly. 76 photographs. 96pp. 8¼ x 11. 25662-6 Pa. $8.95

THE ARTS OF THE SAILOR: Knotting, Splicing and Ropework, Hervey Garrett Smith. Indispensable shipboard reference covers tools, basic knots and useful hitches; handsewing and canvas work, more. Over 100 illustrations. Delightful reading for sea lovers. 256pp. 5⅜ x 8½. 26440-8 Pa. $7.95

FRANK LLOYD WRIGHT'S FALLINGWATER: The House and Its History, Second, Revised Edition, Donald Hoffmann. A total revision–both in text and illustrations–of the standard document on Fallingwater, the boldest, most personal architectural statement of Wright's mature years, updated with valuable new material from the recently opened Frank Lloyd Wright Archives. "Fascinating"–*The New York Times.* 116 illustrations. 128pp. 9¼ x 10¾. 27430-6 Pa. $11.95

AUTOBIOGRAPHY: The Story of My Experiments with Truth, Mohandas K. Gandhi. Boyhood, legal studies, purification, the growth of the Satyagraha (nonviolent protest) movement. Critical, inspiring work of the man responsible for the freedom of India. 480pp. 5⅜ x 8½. (USO) 24593-4 Pa. $8.95

CELTIC MYTHS AND LEGENDS, T. W. Rolleston. Masterful retelling of Irish and Welsh stories and tales. Cuchulain, King Arthur, Deirdre, the Grail, many more. First paperback edition. 58 full-page illustrations. 512pp. 5⅜ x 8½. 26507-2 Pa. $9.95

THE PRINCIPLES OF PSYCHOLOGY, William James. Famous long course complete, unabridged. Stream of thought, time perception, memory, experimental methods; great work decades ahead of its time. 94 figures. 1,391pp. 5⅜ x 8½. 2-vol. set.
Vol. I: 20381-6 Pa. $12.95
Vol. II: 20382-4 Pa. $12.95

THE WORLD AS WILL AND REPRESENTATION, Arthur Schopenhauer. Definitive English translation of Schopenhauer's life work, correcting more than 1,000 errors, omissions in earlier translations. Translated by E. F. J. Payne. Total of 1,269pp. 5⅜ x 8½. 2-vol. set. Vol. 1: 21761-2 Pa. $11.95
Vol. 2: 21762-0 Pa. $11.95

MAGIC AND MYSTERY IN TIBET, Madame Alexandra David-Neel. Experiences among lamas, magicians, sages, sorcerers, Bonpa wizards. A true psychic discovery. 32 illustrations. 321pp. 5⅜ x 8½. (USO) 22682-4 Pa. $8.95

THE EGYPTIAN BOOK OF THE DEAD, E. A. Wallis Budge. Complete reproduction of Ani's papyrus, finest ever found. Full hieroglyphic text, interlinear transliteration, word-for-word translation, smooth translation. 533pp. 6½ x 9¼.
21866-X Pa. $10.95

MATHEMATICS FOR THE NONMATHEMATICIAN, Morris Kline. Detailed, college-level treatment of mathematics in cultural and historical context, with numerous exercises. Recommended Reading Lists. Tables. Numerous figures. 641pp. 5⅜ x 8½.
24823-2 Pa. $11.95

THEORY OF WING SECTIONS: Including a Summary of Airfoil Data, Ira H. Abbott and A. E. von Doenhoff. Concise compilation of subsonic aerodynamic characteristics of NACA wing sections, plus description of theory. 350pp. of tables. 693pp. 5⅜ x 8½. 60586-8 Pa. $14.95

THE RIME OF THE ANCIENT MARINER, Gustave Doré, S. T. Coleridge. Doré's finest work; 34 plates capture moods, subtleties of poem. Flawless full-size reproductions printed on facing pages with authoritative text of poem. "Beautiful. Simply beautiful."–*Publisher's Weekly*. 77pp. 9¼ x 12. 22305-1 Pa. $6.95

NORTH AMERICAN INDIAN DESIGNS FOR ARTISTS AND CRAFTSPEOPLE, Eva Wilson. Over 360 authentic copyright-free designs adapted from Navajo blankets, Hopi pottery, Sioux buffalo hides, more. Geometrics, symbolic figures, plant and animal motifs, etc. 128pp. 8⅜ x 11. (EUK) 25341-4 Pa. $8.95

SCULPTURE: Principles and Practice, Louis Slobodkin. Step-by-step approach to clay, plaster, metals, stone; classical and modern. 253 drawings, photos. 255pp. 8⅛ x 11.
22960-2 Pa. $10.95

PHOTOGRAPHIC SKETCHBOOK OF THE CIVIL WAR, Alexander Gardner. 100 photos taken on field during the Civil War. Famous shots of Manassas Harper's Ferry, Lincoln, Richmond, slave pens, etc. 244pp. 10⅝ x 8¼. 22731-6 Pa. $9.95

FIVE ACRES AND INDEPENDENCE, Maurice G. Kains. Great back-to-the-land classic explains basics of self-sufficient farming. The one book to get. 95 illustrations. 397pp. 5⅜ x 8½. 20974-1 Pa. $7.95

SONGS OF EASTERN BIRDS, Dr. Donald J. Borror. Songs and calls of 60 species most common to eastern U.S.: warblers, woodpeckers, flycatchers, thrushes, larks, many more in high-quality recording. Cassette and manual 99912-2 $8.95

A MODERN HERBAL, Margaret Grieve. Much the fullest, most exact, most useful compilation of herbal material. Gigantic alphabetical encyclopedia, from aconite to zedoary, gives botanical information, medical properties, folklore, economic uses, much else. Indispensable to serious reader. 161 illustrations. 888pp. 6½ x 9¼. 2-vol. set. (USO) Vol. I: 22798-7 Pa. $9.95
Vol. II: 22799-5 Pa. $9.95

HIDDEN TREASURE MAZE BOOK, Dave Phillips. Solve 34 challenging mazes accompanied by heroic tales of adventure. Evil dragons, people-eating plants, blood-thirsty giants, many more dangerous adversaries lurk at every twist and turn. 34 mazes, stories, solutions. 48pp. 8¼ x 11. 24566-7 Pa. $2.95

LETTERS OF W. A. MOZART, Wolfgang A. Mozart. Remarkable letters show bawdy wit, humor, imagination, musical insights, contemporary musical world; includes some letters from Leopold Mozart. 276pp. 5⅜ x 8½. 22859-2 Pa. $7.95

BASIC PRINCIPLES OF CLASSICAL BALLET, Agrippina Vaganova. Great Russian theoretician, teacher explains methods for teaching classical ballet. 118 illustrations. 175pp. 5⅜ x 8½. 22036-2 Pa. $5.95

THE JUMPING FROG, Mark Twain. Revenge edition. The original story of The Celebrated Jumping Frog of Calaveras County, a hapless French translation, and Twain's hilarious "retranslation" from the French. 12 illustrations. 66pp. 5⅜ x 8½. 22686-7 Pa. $3.95

BEST REMEMBERED POEMS, Martin Gardner (ed.). The 126 poems in this superb collection of 19th- and 20th-century British and American verse range from Shelley's "To a Skylark" to the impassioned "Renascence" of Edna St. Vincent Millay and to Edward Lear's whimsical "The Owl and the Pussycat." 224pp. 5⅜ x 8½. 27165-X Pa. $4.95

COMPLETE SONNETS, William Shakespeare. Over 150 exquisite poems deal with love, friendship, the tyranny of time, beauty's evanescence, death and other themes in language of remarkable power, precision and beauty. Glossary of archaic terms. 80pp. 5$\frac{3}{16}$ x 8¼. 26686-9 Pa. $1.00

BODIES IN A BOOKSHOP, R. T. Campbell. Challenging mystery of blackmail and murder with ingenious plot and superbly drawn characters. In the best tradition of British suspense fiction. 192pp. 5⅜ x 8½. 24720-1 Pa. $6.95

THE WIT AND HUMOR OF OSCAR WILDE, Alvin Redman (ed.). More than 1,000 ripostes, paradoxes, wisecracks: Work is the curse of the drinking classes; I can resist everything except temptation; etc. 258pp. 5⅜ x 8½. 20602-5 Pa. $5.95

SHAKESPEARE LEXICON AND QUOTATION DICTIONARY, Alexander Schmidt. Full definitions, locations, shades of meaning in every word in plays and poems. More than 50,000 exact quotations. 1,485pp. 6½ x 9¼. 2-vol. set.
Vol. 1: 22726-X Pa. $16.95
Vol. 2: 22727-8 Pa. $16.95

SELECTED POEMS, Emily Dickinson. Over 100 best-known, best-loved poems by one of America's foremost poets, reprinted from authoritative early editions. No comparable edition at this price. Index of first lines. 64pp. 5$\frac{3}{16}$ x 8¼.
26466-1 Pa. $1.00

CELEBRATED CASES OF JUDGE DEE (DEE GOONG AN), translated by Robert van Gulik. Authentic 18th-century Chinese detective novel; Dee and associates solve three interlocked cases. Led to van Gulik's own stories with same characters. Extensive introduction. 9 illustrations. 237pp. 5⅜ x 8½. 23337-5 Pa. $6.95

THE MALLEUS MALEFICARUM OF KRAMER AND SPRENGER, translated by Montague Summers. Full text of most important witchhunter's "bible," used by both Catholics and Protestants. 278pp. 6⅝ x 10. 22802-9 Pa. $12.95

SPANISH STORIES/CUENTOS ESPAÑOLES: A Dual-Language Book, Angel Flores (ed.). Unique format offers 13 great stories in Spanish by Cervantes, Borges, others. Faithful English translations on facing pages. 352pp. 5⅜ x 8½.
25399-6 Pa. $8.95

THE CHICAGO WORLD'S FAIR OF 1893: A Photographic Record, Stanley Appelbaum (ed.). 128 rare photos show 200 buildings, Beaux-Arts architecture, Midway, original Ferris Wheel, Edison's kinetoscope, more. Architectural emphasis; full text. 116pp. 8¼ x 11. 23990-X Pa. $9.95

OLD QUEENS, N.Y., IN EARLY PHOTOGRAPHS, Vincent F. Seyfried and William Asadorian. Over 160 rare photographs of Maspeth, Jamaica, Jackson Heights, and other areas. Vintage views of DeWitt Clinton mansion, 1939 World's Fair and more. Captions. 192pp. 8⅞ x 11. 26358-4 Pa. $12.95

CAPTURED BY THE INDIANS: 15 Firsthand Accounts, 1750-1870, Frederick Drimmer. Astounding true historical accounts of grisly torture, bloody conflicts, relentless pursuits, miraculous escapes and more, by people who lived to tell the tale. 384pp. 5⅜ x 8½. 24901-8 Pa. $8.95

THE WORLD'S GREAT SPEECHES, Lewis Copeland and Lawrence W. Lamm (eds.). Vast collection of 278 speeches of Greeks to 1970. Powerful and effective models; unique look at history. 842pp. 5⅜ x 8½. 20468-5 Pa. $14.95

THE BOOK OF THE SWORD, Sir Richard F. Burton. Great Victorian scholar/adventurer's eloquent, erudite history of the "queen of weapons"–from prehistory to early Roman Empire. Evolution and development of early swords, variations (sabre, broadsword, cutlass, scimitar, etc.), much more. 336pp. 6⅛ x 9¼.
25434-8 Pa. $9.95

THE INFLUENCE OF SEA POWER UPON HISTORY, 1660–1783, A. T. Mahan. Influential classic of naval history and tactics still used as text in war colleges. First paperback edition. 4 maps. 24 battle plans. 640pp. 5⅜ x 8½. 25509-3 Pa. $12.95

THE STORY OF THE TITANIC AS TOLD BY ITS SURVIVORS, Jack Winocour (ed.). What it was really like. Panic, despair, shocking inefficiency, and a little heroism. More thrilling than any fictional account. 26 illustrations. 320pp. 5⅜ x 8½. 20610-6 Pa. $8.95

FAIRY AND FOLK TALES OF THE IRISH PEASANTRY, William Butler Yeats (ed.). Treasury of 64 tales from the twilight world of Celtic myth and legend: "The Soul Cages," "The Kildare Pooka," "King O'Toole and his Goose," many more. Introduction and Notes by W. B. Yeats. 352pp. 5⅜ x 8½. 26941-8 Pa. $8.95

BUDDHIST MAHAYANA TEXTS, E. B. Cowell and Others (eds.). Superb, accurate translations of basic documents in Mahayana Buddhism, highly important in history of religions. The Buddha-karita of Asvaghosha, Larger Sukhavativyuha, more. 448pp. 5⅜ x 8½. 25552-2 Pa. $9.95

ONE TWO THREE . . . INFINITY: Facts and Speculations of Science, George Gamow. Great physicist's fascinating, readable overview of contemporary science: number theory, relativity, fourth dimension, entropy, genes, atomic structure, much more. 128 illustrations. Index. 352pp. 5⅜ x 8½. 25664-2 Pa. $8.95

ENGINEERING IN HISTORY, Richard Shelton Kirby, et al. Broad, nontechnical survey of history's major technological advances: birth of Greek science, industrial revolution, electricity and applied science, 20th-century automation, much more. 181 illustrations. ". . . excellent . . ."–*Isis*. Bibliography. vii + 530pp. 5⅜ x 8¼. 26412-2 Pa. $14.95

DALÍ ON MODERN ART: The Cuckolds of Antiquated Modern Art, Salvador Dalí. Influential painter skewers modern art and its practitioners. Outrageous evaluations of Picasso, Cézanne, Turner, more. 15 renderings of paintings discussed. 44 calligraphic decorations by Dalí. 96pp. 5⅜ x 8½. (USO) 29220-7 Pa. $4.95

ANTIQUE PLAYING CARDS: A Pictorial History, Henry René D'Allemagne. Over 900 elaborate, decorative images from rare playing cards (14th–20th centuries): Bacchus, death, dancing dogs, hunting scenes, royal coats of arms, players cheating, much more. 96pp. 9¼ x 12¼. 29265-7 Pa. $11.95

MAKING FURNITURE MASTERPIECES: 30 Projects with Measured Drawings, Franklin H. Gottshall. Step-by-step instructions, illustrations for constructing handsome, useful pieces, among them a Sheraton desk, Chippendale chair, Spanish desk, Queen Anne table and a William and Mary dressing mirror. 224pp. 8⅛ x 11¼. 29338-6 Pa. $13.95

THE FOSSIL BOOK: A Record of Prehistoric Life, Patricia V. Rich et al. Profusely illustrated definitive guide covers everything from single-celled organisms and dinosaurs to birds and mammals and the interplay between climate and man. Over 1,500 illustrations. 760pp. 7½ x 10⅛. 29371-8 Pa. $29.95

Prices subject to change without notice.

Available at your book dealer or write for free catalog to Dept. GI, Dover Publications, Inc., 31 East 2nd St., Mineola, N.Y. 11501. Dover publishes more than 500 books each year on science, elementary and advanced mathematics, biology, music, art, literary history, social sciences and other areas.